Queer Globalizations

SEXUAL CULTURES: New Directions from the Center for
Lesbian and Gay Studies
General Editors: José Esteban Muñoz and Ann Pellegrini

Queer Globalizations

Citizenship and the Afterlife of Colonialism

Edited by
**ARNALDO CRUZ-MALAVÉ AND
MARTIN F. MANALANSAN IV**

NEW YORK UNIVERSITY PRESS
New York and London

NEW YORK UNIVERSITY PRESS
New York and London

© 2002 by New York University
All rights reserved

Library of Congress Cataloging-in-Publication Data
Queer globalizations : citizenship and the afterlife of colonialism /
edited by Arnaldo Cruz-Malavé and Martin F. Manalansan.
p. cm.
Includes bibliographical references and index.
ISBN 0-8147-1624-5 (pbk. : alk. paper)
ISBN 0-8147-1623-7 (cloth : alk. paper)
1. Homosexuality. 2. Globalization. 3. Human rights.
I. Cruz, Arnaldo. II. Manalansan, Martin F., 1960–
HQ75.15 .Q45 2002
306.76'6—dc21   2002004611

New York University Press books are printed on acid-free paper,
and their binding materials are chosen for strength and durability.

Manufactured in the United States of America

10 9 8 7 6 5 4 3

Contents

Acknowledgments

To edit an anthology is to open yourself up to the words and worlds of experience of others, all the more so if the anthology is about the possibilities of queer collaboration and cross-cultural engagement globally. As cochairs of the "Queer Globalization, Local Homosexualities: Citizenship, Sexuality, and the Afterlife of Colonialism" conference, sponsored by the Center for Lesbian and Gay Studies of the City University of New York's Graduate Center in the spring of 1998, in which many of the essays in this volume were originally presented, we had the good fortune of collaborating with some of the most creative and incisive scholars writing today in the field of queer studies, the conference's planning committee: Gayatri Gopinath, Miranda Joseph, Oscar Montero, José Esteban Muñoz, Geeta Patel, Ann Pellegrini, Chandan Reddy, and Alan Yang. We were also fortunate to count on the dedication, resourcefulness, and intelligence of Heidi Coleman and Jay Plum, the conference's coordinators, and Jill Dolan, CLAGS's executive director at the time. As executive director, Jill ushered in for CLAGS a period of growth in community involvement and exciting scholarly projects, such as the series of Rockefeller-sponsored national events on the theme of "Citizenship and Sexualities: Transcultural Constructions," which our conference inaugurated. She was in many ways our guiding spirit, and she remains an inspiration for us of the kind of engaged intellectualism that CLAGS represents.

We would like to acknowledge the generous support of the Rockefeller Foundation, which was the primary sponsor of the conference, as well as the Michael C. P. Ryan estate, whose additional support made the conference possible.

We wish to thank the CLAGS series editors, José Esteban Muñoz and Ann Pellegrini, and our NYU Press editor, Eric Zinner, and his assistant, Emily Park, for their commitment and belief in the project.

Finally, we would also like to thank the people without whose love and friendship this project would not have been completed. For Martin: *Dacal a salamat* to my comrades: Deb Amory, Rick Bonus, Javid Syed, Jack Guza, Gerry Cuachon for their support during this period. And to my family, who still wonders about the "books" that I am writing and why I am still not rich and famous. Despite their bafflement, I know there is unconditional love. For Arnaldo: *besos y abrazos siempre* to my partner and lover Greg de Silva, for the diasporic routes of affection that have brought us, and kept us, together.

Queer Globalizations

Introduction

Dissident Sexualities/Alternative Globalisms

Arnaldo Cruz-Malavé and Martin F. Manalansan IV

Queerness is now global. Whether in advertising, film, performance art, the Internet, or the political discourses of human rights in emerging democracies, images of queer sexualities and cultures now circulate around the globe. Representations of queer lives and desires in such mainstream Hollywood films as *Philadelphia*, *To Wong Foo*, and *Go Fish*, and in the more arty international productions, the British *The Crying Game*, the Cuban *Strawberry and Chocolate*, and the Indian *Fire*, it is true, sell increasingly well as global commodities to "general audiences." And gay and lesbian lifestyle products, from pink triangles to rainbow flags to the Carlos and Billy dolls and gay.com cruises, are more frequently bought as identity markers by queers around the globe. In a world where what used to be considered the "private" is ever more commodified and marketed, queerness has become both an object of consumption, an object in which nonqueers invest their passions and purchasing power, and an object through which queers constitute their identities in our contemporary consumer-oriented globalized world.

But the increased global visibility of queer sexualities and cultures in the marketplace has also generated multiple opportunities for queer political intervention through an equally globalized coalition politics. Interestingly, as the "private" is ever more commodified and the body is more and more targeted as a site of global

1

consumption, queer sexualities and cultures have come to occupy center stage in some of the most urgently disputed issues of our times. As the essays collected in this volume and scholarship in the growing fields of queer and globalization studies attest, queer sexualities and cultures have often been deployed negatively to allay anxieties about "authentic" national belonging in our massively migratory contemporary world (see, for example, Gayatri Gopinath's lucid analysis of the transnational circulation of the Indian queer film *Fire,* in this volume) and positively by nation-states in order to project an image of global modernness consistent with capitalist market exchange (see Cindy Patton's illuminating discussion of Taiwan's adoption of a human rights policy inclusive of gay men, also in this volume). And yet this position occupied by queer sexualities and cultures in our globalized world as a mediating figure between the nation and diaspora, home and the state, the local and the global, as argued most cogently here by Janet Jakobsen and Miranda Joseph, has not only been a site of dispossession, it has also been a creative site for queer agency and empowerment. It has also provided diasporic queers, for example, the opportunity to connect with other queers and sexuality and gender activists at "home" in order to interrogate the limits both of nationalist discourses and of modern Euro-American lesbian and gay narratives of identity. It has compelled queer activists, feminists, and legal scholars to come together cross-nationally in order to confront the violations of the human rights of queers around the globe in organizations such as ILGA (International Lesbian and Gay Association) and IGLHRC (International Gay and Lesbian Human Rights Commission). And it has made absolutely indispensable the formation of global coalitions in order to address policies whose presuppositions about sexuality and gender only expand and unequally promote the devastation of the AIDS pandemic around the world.

Globalization, then—despite its tendency to reduce the social and political significance of queer sexualities and cultures to a commodity exchangeable in the marketplace—has also provided the struggle for queer rights with an expanded terrain for intervention. In recognition of the promise—and perils—afforded by this new terrain, the Center for Lesbian and Gay Studies (CLAGS) of the Graduate Center of the City University of New York (CUNY) sponsored in the spring of 1998 a conference titled "Queer Globalization, Local Homosexualities: Citizenship, Sexuality, and the Afterlife of Colonialism," from which most of the essays in the present volume have been culled.

CLAGS's conference on queer globalizations drew a wide array of queer activists and scholars specializing in Latin America, Africa, Asia, Europe, the United States,

Canada, and queer diasporas. To a record-breaking audience, the speakers discussed the economic and cultural transformations brought on by global capital around the world and attempted to identify both opportunities and perils inherent in these transformations and their implication for queer cultures and lives. Yet nowhere were the perils of our present global condition more clearly signified than in a rather pregnant moment during the closing plenary of the conference. In the question and answer period, a well-meaning U.S. queer scholar of note stood up and narrated a vignette, a cautionary tale of sorts that urgently demanded a reply. He and a colleague had been strolling through the recently cleaned-up and renovated Bryant Park, across the street from what was then home to CUNY's Graduate Center, the site of the conference, when they were accosted by an ostensibly Latino man distributing literature about the liberating powers of Jesus Christ. Self-possessed, the white scholar answered the Latino man that he and his friend were in fact gay and had no need for this literature. To the bafflement of the scholar, the Latino man replied that he had also been gay once until he had found the Lord. Now turning pointedly to the plenary speakers, the scholar demanded in earnest, How should I have spoken to this Latino man? How could I have made myself understood by him? How could "we" at this conference, well-meaning queer scholars like him, he seemed to imply, communicate effectively with this Latino (formerly gay) man?

At this point the three-day conference, which had progressed smoothly, came to a screeching halt. Our speakers had finally been stumped by one of the opportunities and perils of our present global condition: the complexity of contemporary cross-cultural interactions in our globalized world. They had finally been silenced by the white scholar's attempt to regain his sense of self-possession by wielding, in a destabilized, fluctuating world, what he thought of as a stable identificatory term (gay)—an attempt that faltered because the ostensibly Latino man (no longer the mythical "other" before the shining glass beads of European culture) could wield the same term (gay) with equal authority and impunity.

In order to break the silence, the speakers could have redirected at this point the white scholar's question, forcing him (as Silviano Santiago, the Brazilian novelist, recommends queer scholars to do in his brief and incisive essay in the present volume) to engage with his own presuppositions. In a room full of queers of color, we could have asked him not to presume that we were included in his well-meaning "we." We could have reminded him, that is, that the "other" was already in the room, and that the tendency to figure racial or ethnic difference as impermeable alterity was not so much a symptom of the other's radical difference as of its unsettling proximity.

This anthology on queer globalizations is our insistent attempt *not* to answer the white scholar's query, deflecting thus his colonizing gaze. It is our ethical refusal to provide a grammar that could make the complexity and density of the cross-cultural interactions generated by our present global condition immediately transparent and universally legible. It is our refusal to fix the term "gay," and the powerful legacies of the lesbian, gay, bisexual, and transgender movements, as a prerequisite for global interaction and coalition. For it is in the permutations of this term and its legacies, as they circulate around the globe, in queer organizations and gatherings, from Mexico City's Semana Cultural Lésbico-Gay to New Delhi's Campaign for Lesbian Rights and Beijing's International Women's Conference, from Buenos Aires's Marcha de Orgullo Gay to the diasporic South Asian and Latino Lesbian and Gay Pride Parade in Queens, New York, that the future of the human and civil rights of queers also lies.

Instead of providing a term or a grammar that would dispel the complexity of these cross-cultural interactions, making them universally legible, the contributors to this anthology would rather open them up, and interrupt and interrogate the hegemonic logics and moves that would prematurely solve them, reducing their meaning and their political potential. They would rather develop a situated knowledge of the ways global capital has routed queer cultures and lives, in the hope that these queer itineraries may also yield counterhegemonic routes that can redeploy and redirect global capital's mass dispersions, and pain, toward global cross-cultural engagements and coalitions that are more respectful of queer cultures and lives.[1]

The essays in this collection bring together scholars of globalization and queer studies in order to examine from multiple perspectives the narratives that have sought to define globalization. In examining the tales that have been spun about globalization, these scholars have tried not only to assess the validity of the claims made for globalization, they have also attempted to identify the tactics and rhetorical strategies through which these claims and through which global circulation are constructed and operate. On the one hand, as the essays in this collection show, narratives about globalization argue for "a transformation in the organization of capitalism, from [Fordist] mass production, which required and produced conformity, to . . . 'flexible specialization,'" which promotes niche markets and local and regional interests, in sum, heterogeneity and diversity.[2] On the other hand, this newly liberated heterogeneity is directed, indeed managed and normalized, through multiple rhetorical operations, which the essays in this collection track.

Building on Gayatri Spivak's insights on the question of "value" in Marxist theory,[3] Miranda Joseph and Janet Jakobsen identify analogy as the dominant trope of post-Fordist globalization discourses. Analogy, argues Joseph, works in opposite fashion to the logic of abjection, which had been predominant in nation-building discourses. While the logic of abjection constitutes a proper sense of community and self through the repudiation or foreclosure of an improper, monstrous other, analogy renders an inchoate, emergent alterity into a known, internally continuous, and seemly other. It excludes, as Spivak has forcefully argued, those relationships between the objects analogized, between the known and the unknown that is, that make them heterogeneous and discontinuous with each other, as well as those relationships that are based on their mutual implication and interconnectedness. Analogy in this reading constructs multiple and discrete alterities, disabling in the process a politics that would focus on the interdependence of these alterities across categories and sites.

Another trope of globalization discourses is perhaps potentially more sinister: the appropriation and deployment of queer subjectivities, cultures, and political agendas for the legitimation of hegemonic institutions presently in discursive crisis, institutions such as the nation-state or U.S. imperial hegemony. In a case that is paradigmatic for many emerging democracies around the globe, Cindy Patton documents how, in an effort to demonstrate its global modernness, Taiwan came to adopt a 1993 human rights policy change that allowed gays to serve in its military. This policy, "while seeming to promote human rights locally and adduct toward [Taiwan's] space the global blanket of free self-expression, . . . actually [had the effect of] preempt[ing] identity-based liberation politics." In another example, Joseba Gabilondo shows how the 1990s international craze in queer subjects and cultures in film deploys desiring gay subjects in order to legitimize a new global hegemonic heteronormativity. In yet another example, Lawrence La Fountain-Stokes questions the deployment of the U.S. Puerto Rican or Nuyorican diasporic experience in the Island's "postmodern" critiques of Puerto Rican anticolonial nationalist discourses.

A recurrent trope in discourses of globalization is that of teleological development. While globalization is seen to liberate and promote local sexual differences, the emergence, visibility, and legibility of these differences are often predicated in globalizing discourses on a developmental narrative in which a premodern, pre-political, non–Euro-American queerness must consciously assume the burdens of

5

representing itself to itself and others as "gay" in order to attain political consciousness, subjectivity, and global modernity. Silviano Santiago, Gayatri
Gopinath, Roberto Strongman, and William Leap offer strong critiques of this
trope from the vantage point of different localities: contemporary Brazilian lesbian and gay culture and cultural studies, Indian diasporic film, Afro-American religious practices, and South African gay male life histories, respectively.[4] Arguing
against the teleologically necessary assumption of a modern North American
"gay" identity by Brazilian queers, Santiago contends that the dissemination of
the North American "coming-out" story in Brazil has had the effect of fixing a
bourgeois public/private divide that has reinforced hegemonic class and sexual interests. Tracking the complex transnational trajectories of reception of the Indian
Canadian film *Fire*, Gopinath shows how this diasporic product both adheres to
and challenges "the notion that the proper location of lesbianism is within a politics of visibility in the public sphere." Similarly critiquing and displacing the narrative of teleological development of gay consciousness, Strongman identifies in
Afro-American religious practices, such as Santería, Candomblé and Vodou, alternative sites for the performance of gender categories and queer desires that are not
predicated on the assumption of a "gay" identity. And in a fascinating analysis of
contemporary South African gay male life histories, Leap warns of the dangers of
deploying a teleological developmental trope in reconstructing the gay past.
Framing their life histories as "post-apartheid" narratives, South African gay males
risk, Leap argues, minimizing or glossing over the enduring legacies of racial and
sexual inequities still prevalent in contemporary South African society.

A concomitant figure of the narrative of teleological development is translation. While globalization is presumed to offer multiple avenues of intercultural
contact, these contacts are often constructed in globalizing discourses as following a unidirectional path in which the West, Western cultures, and the English
language stand in as the "origin" of cultural exchanges and non-Western societies
occupy the discursive position of "targets" of such exchanges. In an examination
of the multiple circulations of the identity category "lesbian," Katie King invites
us to reconsider the power relations in intercultural exchanges around ostensively
universal terms such as "lesbian" and to see in its local "mistranslations" the "paradoxical . . . common ground" of an international lesbian and gay movement.

One could argue that the above figures of normalization, substitution, and containment are not inherent in globalization but belong instead to the category of
panicky political reactions to global capital's expansion. And certainly scholars of
globalization have contended that the resurgence of nationalisms and religious

and ethnic activism and intolerance in our times is an attempt to stabilize the dislocations in discursive regimes and in everyday life occasioned by the globalization of capital.[5] But it is one of the particular contributions of the essays in this collection to point instead in a different direction: following once more Spivak's lead, these essays seek to foreground the complicity, rather than the contradiction, between the ethical values of domination embedded in the structures of home, nationalism, and religious belonging and the putatively value-free values of global economic expansion. If positing a binary opposition between the familial space of national, religious, and ethnic belonging and the public, secular, and rational (or rationalized) sphere of the market demands from queer activism that it embrace the latter, the postulation of the mutual complicity of the terms of this binary could offer queer activism enough reflexive distance not to have to fix its allegiances with either side of the binary but to consider instead the possibilities and limitations of both. In this reading, as Janet Jakobsen cogently argues, the domestic, the national and religious belonging, that is, the spheres associated with ethics, would not necessarily have to be dismissed as politically reactionary but neither would the opportunities occasioned by the market have to be disregarded, as Ann Pellegrini cautions. Instead, queer activism might then function as a local yet global, mobile third term that could transform the opposition without transcending it, or as an oblique third position that would cut across fixed binaries, as has been suggested by Eve Kosofsky Sedgwick.[6] Perhaps this oblique or third-term queer activism is best exemplified here by the interventions of the New York–based South Asian Lesbian and Gay Association (SALGA), incisively analyzed by Gayatri Gopinath. Rather than privileging one side of the binary nation/diaspora in Indian national discourses, Gopinath focuses instead on their mutual complicity and demonstrates how "essentialized concepts of national and diasporic identity are most fruitfully contested from a 'queer diasporic' positionality" such as SALGA's.

How should queer critical studies and activism intervene, then, in the multiple rhetorical operations through which globalization discourses manage the local differences they promote? How should queer critical studies redeploy these differences toward global engagements and coalitions that are more respectful of queer cultures and lives, toward alternative globalisms? In their introduction to a recent special issue of *GLQ*, titled "Thinking Sexuality Transnationally," Elizabeth A. Povinelli and George Chauncey, its editors, lament the tendency in literature on globalization "to read social life off external social forms—flows, circuits, circulations of people, capital, and culture—without any model of subjective mediation":

In other words, globalization studies often proceed as if tracking and mapping the facticity of economic, population, and population flows, circuits, and linkages were sufficient to account for current cultural forms and subjective interiorities, or as if an accurate map of the space and time of post-Fordist accumulation could provide an accurate map of the subject and her embodiment and desires.[7]

It is in this area of subjective mediation and agency where, we believe, the essays in this collection can also make a contribution. For these essays do not only aim to track the figures through which globalization would both promote and manage otherness, they also propose to identify and redeploy counterhegemonic rhetorical strategies, like those recently identified by Doris Sommer in Latin American and North American subaltern texts, that resist globalization's managing operations.[8] It is in the deployment of these counterhegemonic moves where the queer subject's agency, we believe, might become legible in mapping the circuits and flows of globalization.

Some of the counterhegemonic rhetorical strategies deployed by the queer critics in this collection have already been glimpsed. Against the normalization of difference through analogy, Janet Jakobsen and Miranda Joseph mark the complicity and interconnectedness of categories and sites of cultural domination and economic exploitation. Challenging the appropriation and substitution of queer cultures by universalizing discourses, Cindy Patton, Joseba Gabilondo, Lawrence La Fountain-Stokes, and Katie King identify resistant queer particularist or minoritizing strategies. Patton shows how, faced with a rhetoric of human rights that is complicit with a masculinist nation-building project and with Euro-American global expansion, Taiwanese queer activism has opted to frame its human rights agenda from a feminist minoritarian perspective. Gabilondo counters the articulation of a global hegemonic heteronormativity in 1990s films through the discourse of the border and queer sexualities by situating the intersections of border and queer discourses in local U.S. Latino texts. La Fountain-Stokes questions Puerto Rican "postmodern" critics' deployment of the experience of the Puerto Rican diaspora as merely a figure for a critique of nationalist discourses by examining how New York Puerto Rican queer performance artists engage with and transculturate their New York Puerto Rican localities. And Katie King interrupts the absorbing logic of globalizing discourses by advocating for local "mistranslations" and gay studies. Contesting the unidirectionality of most transformational narratives of globalization, Gayatri Gopinath, Silviano Santiago, Roberto Strongman, Bill Maurer, and Ann Pellegrini offer alternative genealogies of modernity and of its relationship to the emergence of queer subjectivities and activism. Gopinath demonstrates how the home and local indigenous practices can also be a site for the emergence of lesbian subjectivities. Santiago considers Brazilian cultural practices prior to the dissemination of the North American "coming-out" story in Brazil in the 1960s and advocates a "wily" form of exhibitionism that is centered on the body, on conduct, on the "ambiguity of behavior," rather than on the expression of a marginal identity. Strongman displaces lesbian and gay narratives of identity toward the performance of gender and sexual categories in Afro-American religious practices. Bill Maurer uncovers an aesthetic, experimental, and cosmopolitan model of modernity in the political economy of Keynes, the theorist most often credited with the promulgation of Fordist nation-based systems of mass production and consumption. And Ann Pellegrini identifies uneven development at the heart of metropolitan lesbian and gay culture by proposing that we consider present-day Euro-American lesbian and gay subjectivity not the result of a transformation from a modern disciplinary "identity" à la Foucault to a postmodern consumerist "lifestyle," but the productive tension between both of these. Finally, Chela Sandoval aims to counter the global circuits that link postmodern citizensubjects through the exchange of capital by inciting us to re-member and perform oppositional third world feminist practices and theories of the 1970s in order to constitute an effective coalitional politics of love across differences.

This collection of essays grew out of a conference on the intersections of globalization and queer sexualities sponsored by the City University of New York's Center for Lesbian and Gay Studies in April 1998. Organized on the centenary of the Spanish-American War of 1898, which resulted in the U.S. colonial occupation of Puerto Rico, Cuba, Guam, and the Philippines and inaugurated a violent process of global modernity, this conference sought to examine and interrogate a different—but no less violent—contemporary process of economic and cultural globalization. Ironically, no single essay in this collection addresses the topic that initially motivated us to organize a conference and edit this volume: the intersections of colonialism, queer sexualities, and globalization that are inscribed in the date 1898. Yet as Filipino and Puerto Rican diasporic queers, we feel that it is that articulate absence that has sustained us through the editing and that has compelled us to connect across categories and sites with the diverse positionalities and strategies set forth by the queer critics in this volume.

Notes

1. Instead of enforcing uniformity, globalization brings about contradictory spaces and situations. Here, we note the works of J. K. Gibson-Graham, *The End of Capitalism (As We Knew It): A Feminist Critique of Political Economy* (Cambridge: Blackwell, 1996); and Saskia Sassen, *Globalization and Its Discontents* (New York: New Press, 1998).

2. See, for example, Miranda Joseph's description of the transformation of capital as formulated in discourses of globalization, which draws from Michael Piore, "Economic Identity/Sexual Identity," in *A Queer World*, ed. Martin Duberman (New York: NYU Press, 1997).

3. "Scattered Speculations on the Question of Value," in *In Other Worlds: Essays in Cultural Politics* (New York: Routledge, 1988), 154–75.

4. For other readings that either critique or nuance this teleological narrative by focusing on the local, national, or postcolonial historical context that conditions the emergence of lesbian and gay subjectivities around the world, see Martin F. Manalansan IV, "In the Shadows of Stonewall: Examining Gay Transnational Politics and the Diasporic Dilemma," *GLQ* 2 (1995): 425–38; Dennis Altman, "Global Gaze/Global Gays," *GLQ: A Journal of Lesbian and Gay Studies* 3 (1997): 417–36; and Barry D. Adam, Jan Willem Duyvendak, and André Krouwel, eds., *The Global Emergence of Gay and Lesbian Politics* (Philadelphia: Temple University Press, 1999).

5. See, for example, David Harvey, *The Condition of Postmodernity* (Cambridge: Blackwell, 1990), 171.

6. *Tendencies* (Durham: Duke University Press, 1993).

7. *GLQ: A Journal of Lesbian and Gay Studies* 5, no. 4 (1999): 445.

8. *Proceed with Caution, When Engaged by Minority Writing in the Americas: A Rhetoric of Particularism* (Cambridge: Harvard University Press, 1999).

Part 1

GLOBALIZATION AND DISSIDENT SEXUALITIES

1 The Wily Homosexual

(First—and Necessarily Hasty—Notes)

Silviano Santiago

It is a commonplace that when Brazilian intellectuals travel to metropolitan sites, they are asked, How has Brazilian cultural production contributed to this or that critical theory, or how might Brazilian cultural production contribute to it? The question implicitly underscores not only the peripheral character of Brazilian culture (and thus of the intellectual who represents it) but also the subaltern condition of the Brazilian experience—even the ignorance of the *historic specificity* of Brazilian culture in the West. "Peripheral," "subaltern," and "particular" correspond semantically to the referent of the cosmopolitan question on the *value* of Brazilian culture, and these terms are respectively opposed to "metropolitan," "superior," and "universal," features associated with the place of utterance.

I have a vigorous response for the curious metropolitan, and a polite one as well. In accepting the metropolitan's dialogue I am not seeking a clumsy *inversion* of the hierarchy of values implicit in the metropolitan question; I am, rather, looking for a strategy to supplement such a question. My participation in the dialogue would attempt, then, to raise the inquirer's awareness with respect to his or her utterance—an utterance charged with politically hegemonic values. I answer my interlocutor that I prefer to redirect the question to texts produced in the metropolis. I submit to him or her any and every text and author representative of the West and charge him or her with the task that has been assigned to me. I am indirectly reminding him or her that there is a *moment of mediation* in dialogue, and that that moment should be allowed to speak, for it is that moment that legitimates the values that inform the question initially asked of me.

Here is a contemporary example of the redirection of questions I am addressing. Within the corpus of Susan Sontag's essays, how has Brazil contributed to the theories that she has expounded with such originality? I extract two answers and I *sense* a contribution. In *Against Interpretation*, Sontag credits Brazil, through Carmen Miranda, for contributing to her theory on *camp*; more recently, in the pages of the *New Yorker*, she proposes that the nineteenth-century Brazilian author Machado de Assis might have contributed, with his fiction, to the theory of the Western novel. Who will next be *named* in her texts?

Much more than those produced at great pains by *Brazilianists*, Sontag's texts end up defining the *meaning* of Brazilian culture in a cosmopolitan setting such as the United States.[1] The academic research of the specialist in Brazilian culture, even that which is written in English, the universal idiom, becomes increasingly less significant in our globalized times, for it tends to resituate the peripheral, subaltern, and particular in a sort of cultural ghetto—from which it had ironically attempted to remove it. The many contemporary nationalist regionalisms—fragmented manifestations of political resistance in neoliberal times—are best summed up now by that other regionalism that in the metropolises goes by the name of "Little Brazil."

Here are other classic and modern examples of the attempt to redirect the metropolitan question, this time the European question. The notion of *cannibalism* applied to Brazil, presented with unusual clairvoyance by a thinker of the magnitude of Montaigne in his similarly titled essay, has dominated the general meaning of Brazilian culture from the Renaissance to modern times. Clarice Lispector, promoted with great sympathy in France by Hélène Cixous (*Vive l'orange*), gave universal preeminence to Brazilian women's literature and artistic production. On the rebound, Carmen Miranda, Machado de Assis, Clarice Lispector, and, of course, anthropophagy are overvalued *internally* in Brazil. The vicious circle that constitutes the specificity of national culture is complete.

As Pierre Bourdieu and Loïc Wacquant contend in "On the Wiliness of Imperialist Reason," "cultural imperialism lays the foundation for the power to universalize particularities tied to a single historic tradition, causing them to no longer be known as such." According to these authors, universal conceits thus established are "true *commonplaces* in the Aristotelian sense of notions or theses *with which* one argues, but *over which* one does not argue."[2] Astuteness versus astuteness and a half. Truth versus truth and a half.

The customary metropolitan question with which I began has been more insidiously construed in recent years—from the vantage point of theories about globalization—in various international seminars and conferences. It would not be right for me, though, in my position as a guest of this international conference, to simply redirect the question that you have posed to me. I could redirect your question to me by asking all of you, who have a greater knowledge of the critical texts produced in the metropolis, to tell me how Brazil has contributed to lesbian and gay studies. Tell me the *meaning* and I will tell you the direction. It would not be right, however, not to fulfill half of my obligation by putting the ball back in your court. I will venture, then, a response, knowing full well that I am falling into the trap of partiality (also known as particularity). I hardly hope to be beating out a new path; on the contrary, you will surely speak with greater knowledge than I.

To arrive where I would like to arrive, I will attempt first to refigure, albeit in a simplified manner, the core of the questions that homosexual activism has raised in Brazil. In the 1960s and 1970s a verb acquired enormous significance in the Brazilian gay universe: *assumir* (that is, "to come out" or "to assume" a homosexual identity or lifestyle) and its related terms: *desmunhecar, dar bandeira*, and so forth. From that moment on, it was understood that homosexuals, in whatever social or professional context, would call themselves *bicha* or *sapatona* and exhibit a different behavior in the public sphere and a particular sexual preference. They would come out publicly as marginal to the "norm." It fell upon the homosexual in public life to bear a burden that the heterosexual has never carried.

The verb *assumir* exalted several different things. In the first place, it gave visibility to the private/public dichotomy in individual lives, making it a predominant aspect of research. Second, it showed how, within the area of the private itself, there was camouflaged, in the behavior of family members, another more complex dichotomy: family life/secret (closeted) life. On a subtle level, *assumir* implied a different conception of traditional family life. And finally, it declared the channels between heterosexuality and homosexuality incommunicable—it found, that is, the truth of the bisexual to be suspect.

It is from this time that a broader theoretical interest in the public/private dichotomy may be traced among us—something truly new in discussions about Brazilian society. Traditionally this barrier did not exist in our sociopolitical and economic practices; there was scarcely any widespread confusion on the border because of a lack of critical customs checks. Let me give two simple examples.

Public servants had a private view of the business of the state. Businesspeople got around the financial difficulties of private enterprise with public subsidies. The verb *assumir*, originally pertaining only to homosexual customs and behavior, precipitated a critical shift in the analyses of most social, political, and economic issues.

Without a doubt, there exists in Brazil today an entire theoretical, critical, and cultural production whose weight can be attributed to the question originally raised by the verb *assumir* and its related terms. Its bibliography would be impossible to list in a few pages. Let me continue by making explicit that this production is directly related to the world of American ideas and concepts. One might praise it insofar as it has given us, on the rebound and on a grand scale, a new view of the Brazilian state vis-à-vis its "citizens." One might criticize it, and many have been doing just that, by alerting us to the fact that once again a peripheral culture has adopted processes of modernization by copying the problems raised, debated, and theorized in societies whose historical past—or more precisely, whose ethical-religious past—is not similar to ours.

I will criticize it in this and other ways, showing how the public/private dichotomy ends up nowadays representing a certain social backwardness on a small scale, that is, in the area of gay and lesbian practices and behavior. First, I will try to show how privacy, introduced into Brazilian social practice, is a class conceit. As we shall see, popular classes in Brazil have found more spontaneous ways of transparent social relations that are not based on the clash of marginality and norm. Second, in becoming more widespread, the conceit of privacy made patently visible how gay and lesbian marginality did not exist among the lower classes, since lesbians and gays were there accepted as they were by their social peers.[3] In this sense, as we see in Aluisio Azevedo's novel *O cortiço* (1888), homosexuals are presented as marginal, and therefore as downtrodden, only upon crossing the borders of their lower-class community to enter into contact with the middle classes.

In the novel *O cortiço*, it is impossible for anyone to have privacy. The solidarity of the poor and the privacy of the rich have their own respective spaces: the tenement and the two-story house. In the latter, a woman is caught by her husband with the cashiers of the store of which he is the owner. The husband is prevented, however, from rejecting his wife because the store is his only because of her dowry. He is then obliged to compensate for her betrayal by betraying her with the household servants. Despite his hatred of his wife, the husband makes love to her one night, acting as if nothing had happened. The second time they make love, the woman does not pretend anymore and bursts out laughing. The narrator states, "She enjoyed the dishonesty of the act that debased each in the eyes of the other." And continues, "Between them there was established a habit of mutual sexual satisfaction, as complete as either had ever enjoyed, despite the fact that deep down in each of them there persisted the same moral repugnance against the other, which in no way had weakened." In the novel, heterosexual marriage appears as a faulty institution that gains meaning only in the perturbing privacy of the bedroom, and the nuclear family is meaningful and solid only to the extent that money backs up its private behavior, laying the foundations of its plenitude in the debasement of the married couple and in moral corruption.

In the tenement, doors are opened, lives are open, and everyone participates in a daily ritual in which everything is public and private at the same time. A Portuguese immigrant, dissatisfied with his wife, abandons her and goes to live with a Brazilian neighbor. The discussion of their separation and their new union is private and public. Day-to-day life in the tenement begins thus: "From some rooms, women emerge to hang outside, apparently, the cages of the parrot and parakeets, and with the birds' resembling their masters, they complemented each other boisterously." The morning cleaning is done collectively, the washerwomen taking turns at the water to fill their tubs. Among the washerwomen, one stood out, Albino, a homosexual. The narrator states, "He was a washerman who always lived among the women, with whom he was so familiar that they treated him like a person of the same sex; in his presence, they spoke of things that they never mentioned in the presence of other men."

As a favor to his fellow washerwomen, Albino leaves the tenement and goes all over the city to collect laundry fees for them. He does this until one day when on his way to a student boarding house, they give him (nobody knew why) a dozen cakes, and the poor devil swears, between tears and sobs, that he will never again take up collecting fees. The text adds, "from then on . . . [Albino] would no longer go out of the building, except during carnival, when he would dress as a dancing girl and spend the afternoon out in the streets." In the tenement, Albino is who he is; in the city, he dresses up as a dancing girl during carnival.

The male homosexuality of Albino, openly known in the tenement and dressed up in drag during carnival, is complemented in the novel by a case of female homosexuality. It is the case of Pombinha. An eighteen-year-old girl who is engaged to be married, Pombinha has not yet had her period. The novel reads, "There, in the tenement, everyone knew about this story; it was not kept *secret* [my emphasis] from anyone." Leonie, a high-class prostitute, who often visits her former neighbors in the tenement, has a decided preference for Pombinha. One day, she invites Pombinha and her mother for lunch. The mother gets drunk on wine and falls asleep, and Leonie is left alone with Pombinha. Leonie loses control and devours the young girl with "violent, repeated, hot kisses." And the next day, in the tenement, "the scream of puberty finally emerges from [Pombinha's] viscera in a hot, vermilion wave." In the end, Pombinha leaves her fiancé to follow in her godmother's footsteps.

Couldn't we suggest that the public exhibitionism and protesting demanded of homosexuals by North American activist movements might be balanced by a wily form of exhibitionism, also public, in the style of the Catholic confession, or of the rogue? Working necessarily with the ambiguity of language and behavior, lucidly separating conduct from norm, instead of distinguishing norm and deviancy, refusing to exhibit the appropriate condition, linguistically or through buttons or etiquette, the homosexual rogue would allow the social violence against him or her to be made explicit.

In exhibiting less social violence against themselves, homosexual rogues would better reveal the way the "norm" was and is being constituted socially and politically by heterosexual violence. It is precisely the violence of a heterosexual identity movement that expels from its space both homosexuals (whether out or not) and any and every other citizen who has "traits" that differ from the "norm." The homosexual rogue inhibits, on the one hand, and exhibits, on the other, heterosexual violence by linguistically refusing to adopt appropriate *bicha/sapatona* conduct.

The linguistic violence, responsible for the constitution of a homosexual space as a margin, is, after all, the exclusive work of heterosexuals. It is up to heterosexuals to change their behavior, adopting contractual norms of tolerance. It is not up to homosexuals to assume guilt for "deviant" conduct—to atone for it by punishing themselves and to succeed at it by adopting contractual norms in which they exclude themselves from society as a whole as a way to attain normalization.

In other words, I ask whether the homosexual couldn't and shouldn't be more wily. Whether subtler forms of activism are not more profitable than aggressive ones. Whether subversion through the courageous anonymity of subjectivities in play—a slower process of consciousness-raising, I admit—doesn't provide better conditions for future dialogue between homosexuals and heterosexuals than the open confrontation on the part of a group that marginalizes itself, proposed by North American culture as more rapid and efficient. More rapid and efficient, yes, but certainly less wily.

Notes

The author wishes to thank Italo Moriconi for his comments. Translated by Robert Mckee Irwin and edited by Arnaldo Cruz-Malavé.

1. See, by the way, the excellent book by the young researcher Marcelo Sacron Bessa, *Histórias positivas–a literatura (des)construindo a AIDS.* Rio de Janeiro: Editora Record, 1997.

2. "Sur les ruses de la raison imperialiste," *Actes de la recherche en sciences sociales,* March 1995.

3. A distinction should be made here between the poor community and the lower-class nuclear family. The nuclear family has always reacted violently toward gay or lesbian behavior—in the same way as it reacts violently to interracial marriage. A reading that contrasted two novels with a homosexual theme published in the same year, *O cortiço* and *O Ateneu,* by Raul Pompéia, on the dichotomy private/public would be long and quite rich. This reading could be complemented by an analysis of Adolfo Caminha's *Bom Crioulo,* in which the homosexual couple, two poor sailors, are accepted equally well aboard their ship as in the city.

2 Dissident Globalizations, Emancipatory Methods, Social-Erotics

Chela Sandoval

The erotic is the nurturer . . . of all our deepest knowledges.
—Audre Lorde, 1978

Being the supreme crossers of cultures, homosexuals have strong bonds with the queer white, Black, Asian, Native American, Latino and with the queer in Italy, Australia and the rest of the planet. We come from all colors, all classes, all races, all time periods. Our role is to link people with each other. . . . it is to transfer ideas and information from one culture to another.
—Gloria Anzaldúa, 1987

Four Dissident Globalizations

Since 1969 Native American activist/scholar Bea Medicine has begun her public speeches with the greeting, "All my kinspersons, with a good heart, and strong hands, I welcome you."[1] The aim of this greeting is to interpellate connection-by-affinity: to call up the proximities-of-being that can ally individual citizen-subjects into collectivity. These are coalition politics, and they function on a profoundly different register than those politics that similarly network and link citizen-subjects in the great global exchange of capital.

Like the coalition politics of Bea Medicine, twenty-first-century transnational capitalism is conducted through linking-transactions. But globalizing capital links through a politics of transgression that crosses all bodies (with a hungry desire) while murmuring vanilla reassurances: "Just relax." "Have fun." "This is easy, it's all for the best."[2] There are, of course, the expected resistances: the tightening up, the defensiveness, the denials, the efforts to clamp down roving global energies. Nationalism thus exerts the true vanilla erotics: no transgressions permitted, border crossings monitored and militarized, and within these limits "only our kind allowed," a homogenization that disciplines the passions—puts them under control. But if postmodern globalization is polymorphous, taking on all comers, and if its resistances monitor and control the passions, then it is possible to identify an optional force, another and dissident kind of globalization that eroticizes differently, that tattoos its citizen-subjects with "*amor en Aztlán*," with love drawn from mythical and forbidden territories come-to-life. When Bea Medicine welcomes a diverse community as "kinspersons" to whom she offers "heart," "hands," "goodness," and "strength," it is this community she is calling up, new citizen-warriors of alternative, decolonizing, and dissident global forces.

The afterlife of colonialism shimmers with this new dissident mode of global cosmopolitics. Dissident globalization depends on the activism of an internationalist citizen-warrior who is able to call upon the transformative capacities of consciousness and of the collective body. In this essay, I will schematize the principles on which such a dissident mode of globalization becomes embodied in the social erotic. I begin by summarizing three historically prior modes of dissident globalization (Marxism, third world liberation, and U.S. third world feminism).[3] I conclude by positing the queer, postcolonial, and feminist *method* that is necessary for bringing into being the fourth, emancipatory mode of globalization I have already described as "dissident." This method has been articulated across ethnic, women's, queer, and subaltern interdisciplinary studies since the 1960s. In this essay, its most salient potential for liberatory globalization is emphasized: This method generates the social-erotics necessary for activating the "coalitional" global future of Bea Medicine's imaginary.

Relocating Citations

At the turn of the previous century, an internationalist movement attempted to associate the working classes across nations into an economic, moral, and political union that would dehierarchize and transform the world. But by the 1950s that location of political insurgency and of emancipatory and collective will had relocated away from the site of the working classes, the "proletariat," to that of another social body, which was identified by Sartre, Fanon, and Barthes as being comprised of "non-European" peoples of color. This shift in the location from which an emancipatory global consciousness might arise represented a fundamental challenge to Marxism, and introduced the possibility of a new kind of transnational alliance and revolutionary class formation. "Today," Barthes wrote in 1957, "it is *colonized* peoples who assume to the full the ethical and political condition described by Marx as being that of the proletariat."[4] At that historic moment, Barthes was right.

Nineteenth- and twentieth-century geopolitical struggles for decolonization had generated a new form of global network among peoples of color that culminated during the 1950s in a transnational/transcultural slogan—and demand for "third world liberation." This term signified solidarity among new masses of peoples who were differentiated by nation, ethnicity, language, race, class, culture, sex, and gender demarcations but who were allied nevertheless by virtue of similar sociohistorical, racial, and colonial relations to dominant powers. Third world liberationists of this period imagined a new decolonizing coalition of resistance that would cross national as well as racial and cultural borders—a dissident, internationalist citizenry. This fresh sense of alliance profoundly influenced the transforming identities of U.S. peoples of color, especially the participants of the great social movements of the 1950s, 1960s and 1970s. Activists of color involved in the civil rights, antiwar, Black, Chicano, Asian, Native American, student, women's, and gay liberation movements saw themselves as bonded, despite distinct and sometimes contrary aims and goals, in a coalitional form of "third world" consciousness opposed to dominating powers and oppressive racial and social hierarchies.

During the late 1960s and early 1970s a new feminist U.S. social movement took up these class, third world, and internationalist genealogies, and extended their trajectories to include the imperatives of gender and sex. The name selected for this new radical social movement linked two apparently contradictory world power geographies in the phrase "U.S. third world feminism," as if the "U.S." and the "third world" could together represent a single political locality.[5] In a sense simply voicing this name enacted an untried revolution: a geopolitical upheaval of nation-state and its social imaginaries, and an innovative pulling together again of what leaders and visionaries of the movement hoped would become a trans-national, -gendered, -sexed, -cultured, -raced, and coalitional political site. If the dissident global imaginary that was Marxism became momentarily eclipsed by the radical notion of "third world liberation" during the sixties, then the global imaginary that was third world liberation also waned during the seventies. U.S. third world feminism, however, took up their trajectories and extended them by agitating for a unique politics of inclusion that would stand in direct relief to the predominant politics of exclusion that defined U.S.-based ethnic, race, gender, and sex liberation movements during that period. For the purposes of this conference on "Queer Globalization/Local Homosexualities: Citizenship, Sexuality, and the Afterlife of Colonialism," it is useful to point out that the coalitional utopian imperatives of this globalizing version of "U.S. third world feminism" were in large part formulated and guided through the leadership and vision provided by U.S. activists who were self-identified lesbians of color.

Today, few scholars are unfamiliar with the (often infamous) texts that were produced by this particular cohort of lesbian activists who, by 1975, had organized into a unique U.S. collectivity under the rubric of "radical women of color." Even this highly abbreviated list of names, Barbara Smith, Cherríe Moraga, Paula Gunn Allen, Barbara Noda, Audre Lorde, Merle Woo, Janice Gold, and Gloria Anzaldúa, recalls the political and aesthetic influence of their activism. Whether examining texts such as *This Bridge Called My Back* (1981), *Homegirls* (1982), *Borderlands* (1987), *Sister Outsider* (1983), the journal *Conditions* (1976), or Third Woman (1979) and Kitchen Table (1982) Presses, one encounters a constantly applied force that was aimed at creating a social movement that would be capable of organizing on behalf of *all* people. The U.S. third world feminist writings of this period invite citizen-subjects who had previously been separated by gender, sex, race, culture, nation, and/or class into a trans-difference coalition, inviting them to become "countrypeople" of an unprecedented psychic terrain. This trans-difference citizenship, it was argued, would come about through a shared and specific form of oppositional consciousness, constructed through what U.S. third world feminists dared to theorize in 1981 as an embodied "politics of love."[6]

The great theorist of history, sex, and power, Michel Foucault, wrote in 1980 that to creatively enter the new millennium we must "refuse what we have been trained to become, that we must promote new forms of subjectivity."[7] The idea is to call up subjectivity with an erotic panache, suggested the lesbian and U.S. third world feminist intellectual Audre Lorde in 1976, to recognize that the "erotic" itself comprises a mode of political power.[8] But simply being "homosexual," they both believed, was not sufficient grounds on which to call up this new, emancipatory mode of oppositional praxis. Rather, a shared social-erotics is necessary, or as Fredric Jameson later pointed out, what is required is a specific *methodology* that can be used as a compass for self-consciously organizing consciousness, praxis, coalition, and resistance under late capitalist cultural conditions.[9] Examination of the feminist texts developed by U.S. third world feminist activists between 1965 and 1990 reveals their combined insistence on a structured theory and method of consciousness-in-opposition to U.S. social hierarchy that is capable, when all actors can agree to its methods, of aligning a variety of oppositional social activists with one another across differing gender, sex, race, culture, class, or national localities. This theoretical and methodological compass was developed, represented, and utilized by U.S. lesbians and feminists of color because, as lesbian Native American theorist Paula Gunn Allen put it in 1981, so much has been taken away that "the place we live now is an idea"—and in this place new forms of identity, theory, practice, erotics, love, and community become imaginable.

In 1981, Chicana lesbian Gloria Anzaldúa described these new terms of exchange in a "collection of writings by radical women of color," where she wrote, "we are the queer groups, the people who don't belong anywhere, not in the dominant world, nor completely in our own respective cultures. We do not have the same ideologies, nor do we derive similar solutions, but these differences do not become opposed to each other."[10] Instead, Audre Lorde explained in 1979, each and every difference, all tactical positions are recognized as "a fund of necessary polarities between which our creativities spark like a dialectic. Only within that interdependency," she insisted, each ideological position "acknowledged and equal, can the power to seek new ways of being in the world generate," along with "the courage and sustenance to act where there are no charters."[11] In 1987 Anzaldúa continued by defining this "queer" consciousness as born of a life lived in the "borderlands" between races, nations, languages, genders, sexualities, and cultures. *La conciencia de la mestiza* is a form of Chicana consciousness, she wrote, but is also a learned subjectivity capable of transformation and relocation, movement that must be guided by a specific methodology she calls *la facultad*, the capacity to read, renovate, and make signs on behalf of the dispossessed. That same year philosopher Maria Lugones maintained that only nomadic "travel" across "worlds of meaning" could create the type of "loving perception" required in the political activism and social-erotics these women named U.S. third world feminism. And in 1984 Gayatri Spivak suggested "shuttling" between meaning systems in order to enact the "strategic essentialism" that would be necessary for intervening in power on behalf of the marginalized. Put together, these different quotes describe a political practice that Alice Walker dared to define in 1983 as "womanism." This was a political hermeneutic, she argued, a social movement theory that would depend on and construct a new social-erotics—"love" in the postmodern world.[12]

These voices were connected in their insistence on the recognition of a specific mode of oppositional consciousness and behavior, a social-erotics, an eccentric theory, method, and politics that had evolved from those who, as Audre Lorde put it in 1977, must "live at the shoreline" between sex, gender, race, language, culture, class, and social locations.[13] This shoreline, or "borderlands," consciousness and politics generated a method for redefining identity, community, and love

("love" understood as a mode of political action—as social-erotics). This method is utilized not only within racialized and feminist forms of so-called minority discourse. It is a methodology capable of mobilizing queer and other oppositional modalities into a coalitional and dissident-global-praxis.[14]

To Re-Member the Method

We can re-member this method by examining 1970s U.S. third world feminist theory and practice. U.S. third world feminism apprehended oppositional forms of consciousness, aesthetics, and politics as organized around five points of resistance to U.S. social hierarchy: (1) the "equal rights" (or "liberal") mode; (2) the "revolutionary" mode; (3) the "supremacist" (or "cultural-nationalist") mode; (4) the "separatist" mode; and (5) the "differential" (or "womanist," "Sister Outsider," "*mestiza*," "strategic essentialist," "third force") mode.[15] It was this last differential mode that enabled U.S. third world feminists during the 1970s to understand and utilize the previous four, not as overriding strategies, but as *tactics* for intervening in and transforming social relations.[16] Under the auspices of the U.S. third world feminist form of social movement *understood as a differential oppositional practice,* the first four modes were *performed* (however seriously) only as forms of "tactical essentialism."[17] The differential praxis of U.S. third world feminism understood, wielded, and poetically deployed each mode of resistant ideology as if it were only another potential *technology of power.* The cruising mobilities required in this effort demanded of the differential practitioner commitment to the process of metamorphosis itself: This is the activity of the trickster who practices subjectivity-as-masquerade, the oppositional agent who accesses differing identity, ideological, aesthetic, and political positions. This nomadic "morphing" was not performed only for survival's sake, as in earlier, modernist times. It was a set of *principled conversions* that require movement through, over, and within any dominant system of resistance, identity, race, gender, sex, class, or national meanings.

This form of differential consciousness recognizes and identifies all technologies of power as consensual illusions. When resistance is organized as integrationist, revolutionary, supremacist, or separatist in function, the differential mode of consciousness reads and interprets these technologies of power as transformable social narratives that are designed to intervene in reality for the sake of social justice. The differential maneuvering required here is a *sleight-of-consciousness* that activates a new space, a *cyberspace,* where the transcultural, transgendered, transnational leaps necessary to the play of effective stratagems of oppositional

25

praxis can begin (a process recently theorized by Judith Butler as "the performative").[18] It was this 1970s U.S. third world form of feminism that advocated for a specific form of politics that was not assimilationist, revolutionary, supremacist, or separatist, but that utilized and activated all these and more in a differential form of politics. This eccentric politics is a powerful paradigm for generating coalition between oppositional groups, for accessing horizontal comradeship, for carrying out effective collaborations between divided constituencies, for making interdisciplinary connections.

As Bea Medicine hopes, this differential consciousness and social movement permit *affinities inside difference* to attract, combine, and relate new constituencies into transnational coalitions-of-resistance. But successful practice of the differential can occur only when it is activated by particular guiding principles. When utilized together, these principles function as a procedure, as a set of techniques I have elsewhere identified as the "methodology of the oppressed," but they are techniques perhaps better described as a "methodology of emancipation."[19] The four principles of this method guide the founding precepts of such intellectual and practical inventions as cyborg feminism, genealogical analysis, subaltern studies, U.S. third world feminism, and radical *mestizaje*, and they have energized the ongoing development of feminist, queer, postcolonial, American, and global studies. Indeed, these principles create and circulate a social-erotics; they cast queer love across the postmodern world.

Queer Love across the PoMo World

At the turn of the twenty-first century the zones are clear: postmodern globalization is a neocolonizing force. Meanwhile, decolonizing alliance forces are mobilizing under eclectic, mobile, and presentist banners that are only too similar in structure and function to postmodern globalization. Such equivalencies, however, remain *de*-colonizing when their substance, values, and degrees of force are guided by what can be recognized across disciplines as a methodology of emancipation. Its function is to develop the kinds of oppositional powers that are *analogous* to but at the same time *homeopathically resistant* to postmodern transnationalization, along with peoples who are skilled enough to wield those powers. Like U.S. third world feminists, practitioners of this methodology act as interventionists, negotiators, assimilationists, radical transformers, separatists, and so on. They can be unified as cadres into a dissident form of cosmopolitics, however, when practitioners enact the following principles:

1. To develop sign-reading skills, reading power everywhere and always.
2. To engage interventionary tactics that are designed to shift the powers that operate inside any sign system: The choices on the level of the sign are (a) to deconstruct, or (b) to meta-ideologize.
3. To willingly inhabit an eccentric consciousness that permits its practitioner to carry out any of these techniques by moving within, between, or through meaning *differentially*.
4. To enact any of these principles with the purpose of equalizing power among interlocutors. This *democratizing aim* directs all other techniques toward the goal of egalitarian redistributions of sexed, gendered, raced, physiological, social, cultural, and/or economic powers.

Each of these principles can be operated independently. But when utilized as a single apparatus they become what a dissident globalization must insist upon–a social-erotics, an interrelated hermeneutics of "love," a methodology *for* the oppressed and *of* emancipation. Commitment to this methodology is what permitted 1970s–1980s lesbians of color to ally across their own racial geographies and to envision a coalition politics that extended beyond their own identity politics and cultural differences. Moreover, this shared methodology can generate other kinds of cross-national coalitions as well. For, like Bea Medicine's greeting, its guerrilla operations call new kinspeople into being: county-women, -men, and -children of the same psychic terrain. Their aim? To carry on irresistible revolutions, to wage love across the postmodern world.

Notes

This essay was delivered as a plenary speech for the conference on "Queer Globalization: Sexuality, Citizenship, and the Afterlife of Colonialsim," held in April 1998 at the Graduate Center of the City University of New York, CLAGS. My thanks to conference organizers Arnaldo Cruz-Malavé and Martin F. Manalansan IV, who asked me to contextualize my previous work around queer and postcolonial studies; to plenary speaker Norma Alarcón for the Broadway *Chicago* experience; and to Lisa Biddle for her incisive comments on an earlier draft of the speech.

1. Bea Medicine, in *Two Spirit Peoples* and as cited in *Haciendo Caras,* ed. Gloria Anzaldúa (San Francisco: Aunt Lute Foundation, 1990) 55.
2. See, Pheng Cheah and Bruce Robbins, eds., *Cosmopolitics: Thinking and Feeling beyond*

the Nation, (Minneapolis: University of Minnesota Press, 1998) and, *The Politics of Culture in the Shadow of Capital* Lisa Lowe and David Lloyd, eds., (Durham: Duke University Press, 1997).

3. The mystery of the academic erasure of U.S. third world feminism as a critical apparatus for decolonizing race, sex, and gender studies is a disappearing trick. Its exemption from academic canon short-circuits knowledge, but secures the acquittal of a "third," feminist "force" (about which Derrida said, "it should not be named"). Not named, he thought, in order that what is performative and mobile never be set into any place: freedom, he believed, could thus reside everywhere. It is out of this mobile terrain that the 1970s social movement named U.S. third world feminism called up countrypeoples of a new territory. For these countrypeople today, who are no longer "U.S. third world feminist," the game begins again. New names (queer theory this time), new rules, new players.

4. Frantz Fanon, *Black Skin, White Masks,* trans. Charles Markmann (New York: Grove, 1967); Roland Barthes, *Mythologies,* trans. Richard Miller (New York: Hill and Wang, 1972), 148.

5. The contemporary social movement called "U.S. third world feminism" arose in recent times, though there are long histories of alliance between women of color in the United States. Examples range from the councils held by Seminole, Yamassee, and African women during times of territorial colonialism and slavery, to the coalitions made among Chinese, Chicana, and African women in protective leagues and labor movement struggles during the 1920s, 1930s and 1940s. The most cited examples of U.S. feminists of color arguing for a specific method called "U.S. third world feminism" can be found in Cherríe Moraga and Gloria Anzaldúa's collection *This Bridge Called My Back: Writings by Radical Women of Color* (New York: Kitchen Table/Women of Color Press, 1981). See also Chandra Talpade Mohanty's renowned collection and her essay "Cartographies of Struggle: Third World Women and the Politics of Feminism," in *Third World Women and the Politics of Feminism,* ed., Chandra Talpade Mohanty, Anne Russo, and Lourdes Torres (Bloomington: Indiana University Press, 1991). Also see Chela Sandoval, "Comment on Susan Krieger's 'Lesbian Identity and Community,'" in *Signs* (spring 1983). For histories of U.S. women of color in struggle, see Antonia Casteñeda's prizewinning essay "Women of Color and the Rewriting of Western History: The Discourse, Politics, and Decolonization of History," *Pacific Historical Review* 61 (1992); Asian Women United of California, ed., *Making Waves: An Anthology of Writings by and about Asian American Women* (Boston: Beacon, 1989); Paula Giddings, *When and Where I Enter: The Impact of Black Women on Race and Sex in America* (New York: W. Morrow, 1984); Ellen DuBois and Vicki Ruiz, eds., *Unequal Sisters: A Multicultural Reader in U.S.*

Women's History (New York: Routledge, 1990); Gretchen Bataille and Kathleen Mullen Sands, eds., *American Indian Women, Telling Their Lives* (Lincoln: University of Nebraska Press, 1984); Rayna Green, ed., *Native American Women* (Bloomington: Indiana University Press, 1983); Paula Gunn Allen, ed., *Spider Woman's Granddaughters*, (Boston: Beacon, 1989); Albert Hurtado, *Indian Survival on the California Frontier* (New Haven: Yale University Press, 1988); Nobuya Tsuchida, ed., *Asian and Pacific American Experiences* (Minneapolis: University of Minnesota Press, 1982); Toni Cade Bambara, preface to Moraga and Anzaldúa, *This Bridge Called My Back*. For excellent work on third space feminism, see Emma Pérez, "Feminism-in-Nationalism: Third Space Feminism at the Yucatan Feminist Congresses of 1916," in *Between Women and Nation: Transnational Feminisms and the State*, ed. Norma Alarcón, Caren Kaplan, and Minoo Moallem (Durham: Duke University Press, forthcoming). The work on *la conciencia de la mestiza*, *la facultad, coatlique*, and *nepantla* is by Gloria Anzaldúa in *Borderlands/La Frontera: The New Mestiza* (San Fransisco: Spinsters Aunt Lute, 1987). See also Pat Mora, *Borders* (Houston: Arte Público Press, 1986) on *nepantla*. For the relationship of the differential and *la conciencia de la mestiza* to "cyberspace," see Chela Sandoval, "Re-Entering Cyberspace: New Sciences of Resistance" in the journal *Dispositio: Sub-altern Studies*, ed. José Rabasa et al. (1996). This definition appears as "U.S. Third World Feminism" in the *Oxford Companion to Women's Writing in the United States*, ed. Cathy Davidson and Linda Wagner-Martin (New York: Oxford University Press, 1995) 880–82. For an excellent discussion and analysis of this definition, see Katie King, *Theory in Its Feminist Travels: Conversations in U.S. Women's Movements* (Bloomington: Indiana University Press, 1994).

6. Merle Woo, "Letter to Ma," and many of the other essays in Moraga and Anzaldúa, This Bridge Called My Back. For an excellent overview of U.S. third world feminist politics, see King, *Theory in Its Feminist Travels*.

7. Michel Foucault, "The Subject and Power," in *Michel Foucault: Beyond Structuralism and Hermeneutics*, ed. Hubert Dreyfus and Paul Rabinow (Chicago: University of Chicago Press, 1983), 212.

8. Audre Lorde, "Uses of the Erotic: The Erotic as Power," in *Sister Outsider* (New York: Crossing Press, 1984).

9. Fredric Jameson, *Postmodernism, or the Cultural Logic of Late Capital* (Durham: Duke University Press, 1991). See especially the sections on "Cognitive Mapping."

10. Gloria Anzaldúa, "La Prieta," in Moraga and Anzaldúa, *This Bridge Called My Back*, 209.

11. Audre Lorde, "Comments at the Personal and the Political Panel" ("Second Sex Conference," New York, September 1979), in *Sister Outsider*.

12. Paula Gunn Allen, "Some Like Indians Endure," in *Living the Spirit* (New York: St.

Martin's, 1987); Anzaldúa, *Borderlands*; Maria Lugones, "Playfulness, 'World'-Traveling, and Loving Perception," *Hypatia* 2 (1987); Patricia Hill Collins, *Black Feminist Thought: Knowledge, Consciousness, and the Politics of Empowerment* (New York: Routledge, 1990); Gayatri Spivak, "Criticism, Feminism and the Institution," *Thesis Eleven* 10–11 (1984–85 and "Explanations of Culture," in *The Post-Colonial Critic* (New York: Routledge, 1990), 156; and Alice Walker, *In Search of Our Mothers' Gardens: Womanist Prose* (New York: Harcourt Brace Jovanovich, 1983).

13. Audre Lorde, *The Black Unicorn* (New York: Norton, 1995).

14. Note here already the implication of another "third space" gender, which today is being theorized as the category of the decolonizing "queer" as conceived by scholars of color. See, for example, the works of Cherríe Moraga, Gloria Anzaldúa, Emma Pérez, Audre Lorde, Kitty Tsui, Makeda Livera, and Paula Gunn Allen. Yvonne Yarboro-Bejerano, *The Last Generation* (Boston: South End, 1995); Emma Pérez, "Sexuality and Discourse: Notes from a Chicana Survivor," in *Chicana Lesbians*, ed. Carla Trujillo (Berkeley: Third Woman, 1991); Lorde, *Sister Outsider*; Kitty Tsui, Nelly Wong, and Barbara Noda, "Coming Out, We Are Here in the Asian Community: A Dialogue with Three Asian Women," *Bridge*, spring 1979; Asian Women United of California, *Making Waves*; Paula Gunn Allen, "Beloved Women: The Lesbian in American Indian Culture," *Conditions* 7 (1981); Makeda Livera, ed., *A Lesbian of Color Anthology: Piece of My Heart* (Ontario: Sister Vision, 1991); Deena Gonzáles, *Chicana Identity Matters* (Oxford: Oxford University Press, 2002); Sandoval, "Comment on Susan Krieger's 'Lesbian Identity.'" Judith Butler's work on the performative develops parallel structures with the forms of U.S. third world feminism and its differential *mestiza* consciousness discussed here.

15. For in-depth descriptions and analyses of the social movement theory of U.S. third world feminism, see "U.S. Third World Feminism: The Theory and Method of Oppositional Consciousness in the Postmodern World," *Genders* 10 (spring 1991). The following schema provides its fundamental premise, which is structured to understand resistance as coalescing around the following five responses to social hierarchy:

1. The Equal Rights Mode. Within the first "equal rights" enactment of consciousness in opposition, members of the subordinated group argue that those differences—for which they have been assigned inferior status—lay only in appearance, not reality. Behind only *exterior* physical differences from the most legitimated form of the human is a content, an essence that is the same as the essence of the human-in-power. These oppositional actors thus argue for civil rights based on the philosophy that all humans are created equal. Aesthetically, this mode of consciousness seeks duplication; politically it seeks integration; psychically it seeks assimilation.

2. The Revolutionary Mode. Whereas the "equal rights" tactic insists on profound similarities between social, cultural, racial, sexual, or gender identities across their (only) external differences, the second ideology-as-tactic identifies, legitimizes, claims, and intensifies its differences—in both form *and* internal content—from the category of the most-human. Practitioners of the "revolutionary" form believe that assimilation of such myriad and acute differences is not possible within the confines of the present social order. Instead, the only way society will be able to affirm, value, and legitimate the differences they represent is if the categories by which society is ordered are fundamentally transformed.

3. The Supremacist Mode. Under "supremacism" not only do the oppressed claim their differences, but they also assert that those differences have lifted them to a higher evolutionary level than those against whom they fight. Whether practitioners understand their superior-differences as originating biologically or as developed through a history of social conditioning is of little practical concern. What matters is their effect: the subordinated group understands itself as functioning at a higher state of psychic and social evolution than do its protagonists.

4. The Separatist Mode. This is the final tactic of resistance of the four most commonly mobilized under previous capitalist modes. As in the previous three forms, practitioners of separatism recognize that their differences are branded as inferior with respect to the category of the most-human. Under this fourth mode of agency, however, the subordinated do not desire an "equal rights" type of integration with the dominant order. Neither do they seek its "revolutionary" transformation, nor its leadership through history. Rather, this form of political resistance is organized to protect and nurture the differences that define its practitioners through their complete separation from the dominant social order.

5. The Differential Mode. See text above.

16. These strategies were understood and utilized as tactics for intervention by U.S. women of color in 1960s–1970s ethnic liberation movements as well as in women's liberation movements. For explication of these usages, see Adaljiza Sosa Riddell, "Chicanas en el Movimiento," *Aztlan* 5 (1974); Moraga and Anzaldúa, *This Bridge Called My Back*; Barbara Smith, "Racism in Women's Studies," in *All the Women Are White, All the Blacks Are Men, but Some of Us Are Brave*, ed. Gloria Hull, Patricia Bell Scott, and Barbara Smith (New York: Feminist Press, 1982); Bonnie Thornton Dill, "Race, Class, and Gender: Perspectives for an All-Inclusive Sisterhood," *Feminist Studies* 9 (1983); Mujeres en Marcha, eds., *Chicanas in the '80s: Unsettled Issues* (Berkeley: Mujeres in Marcha Colectiva, 1983); bell hooks, *Feminist Theory: From Margin to Center* (Boston: Beacon, 1984); Alice Chai, "Toward a Holistic Paradigm for Asian American Women's

Studies: A Synthesis of Feminist Scholarship and Women of Color's Feminist Politics," *Women's Studies International Forum* 8 (1985); Cynthia Orozco, "Sexism in Chicano Studies and the Community," in *Chicana Voices: Intersections of Class, Race, and Gender*, ed. Teresa Cordova, Norma Cantú, Gilberto Cardenas, Juan Garcia, and Christine Sierra (Austin: Center for Mexican American Studies, 1986); Chela Sandoval, "Feminist Agency and U.S. Third World Feminism," in *Provoking Agents: Gender and Agency in Theory and Practice*, ed. Judith Kegan Gardiner (Urbana: University of Illinois Press, 1995), and "U.S. Third World Feminism."

17. See Gayatri Spivak's famous essay on strategic essentialism, "Criticism, Feminism, and the Institution," and "Explanations of Culture."

18. Judith Butler, *Gender Trouble: Feminism and the Subversion of Identity* (New York: Routledge, 1990).

19. Chela Sandoval, *Methodology of the Oppressed* (Minneapolis: University of Minnesota Press, 2000).

3 "There Are No Lesbians Here"

Lesbianisms, Feminisms, and Global Gay Formations

Katie King

"There are no lesbians here." Who might make such a statement and for what in-tellectual and political purposes? What counts as a lesbian? Where is "here"? Struggles with the meanings of this statement and its corollary questions today signal an intersection of feminism, lesbian and gay studies, and globalization processes. Can the term "lesbian" (or can other wordings) be used at this historic moment as a meta-term, a structural category laboriously produced as a new uni-versal, plucked from its local particularisms and strategically deployed as the sign under which divergent local sexualities and specific alternative social arrange-ments can be displayed? Is this possible in an anti-essentialist feminist politics? How would various politics of naming produce responses to the statement "There are no lesbians here"?

Productive Instabilities and Contests for Universals

Some feminists, lesbians, human rights activists, and others have worked hard to produce just such a "global" category, in at least two meanings of the word "global." Activists from a variety of global regions came together in preparation for the UN's Beijing Conference (the Fourth World Conference on Women, 4–15

September 1995, Beijing, China), drafting regional versions of the projected Platform for Action precisely to construct this new global category. With its moral dimensions drawn from the Universal Declaration of Human Rights, a multination response to the genocide and other war crimes of World War II, the document and the project to include lesbianism as a human rights issue are shadowed by Enlightenment humanism and politically mobilized within globalization processes activating individualism in neoliberal economic relationships of power and labor. Evidence of human rights abuses was provided by testimonies gathered by activists; for example, the report *Unspoken Rules: Sexual Orientation and Women's Human Rights* was compiled by the U.S.-based International Gay and Lesbian Human Rights Commission (IGLHRC), in partnership with other groups, such as ABIGALE in South Africa, Chadra Kirana in Indonesia, NVIH COC in the Netherlands, El Closet de Sor Juana in Mexico, and the National Center for Lesbian Rights in the United States. (Rosenbloom 1995). At the eleventh hour (actually 4:30 A.M. on the last day of the conference) the phrase "sexual orientation," the phrase around which all this planning and preparation had finally coalesced, was stricken from the closing version of the Platform for Action (see discussion in Reinfelder 1996, 20ff). Constructing universals, stabilizing contested categories, is labor-intensive political work, sometimes only too ephemeral or situational, other times only too compromised within the materialities both constraining and enabling their construction.

So actually in this particular context it was the phrase "sexual orientation" that was offered as the new universal, not the word "lesbian." What would count as this universal term is differently inflected by the various human rights groups, strategically and in relation to particular constituencies. In its report intended for presentation at Beijing, the IGLHRC uses the term "lesbian" unproblematically, since its concern in *Unspoken Rules* is to focus on abuses, extensively documented for legitimate challenge within a particular legal and moral framework, rather than on the issues of "local variation" among sexual practices and political identities. Elsewhere, the draft Platform for Action for Beijing from the European and North American region used phrases such as "single women" and "women who are not attached to men" as alternative paraphrases, in response to arguments that Eastern European women would not identify themselves as "lesbians" (Reinfelder 1996, 10).

Both "lesbian" and "feminist" have local and global meanings for particular nationalisms and challenges to nationalism by women. Using them as global terms is a political act. Refusing them as global terms is also a political act. No uses are neutral and purely descriptive, although some users intend them to be and long for such possible categories. Contests over metalanguage and object languages here, that is, over the languages talked about (object languages) and the languages used to do that talking about (metalanguages), over etic and emic categories, are material and activist, not only theoretical and abstract. Etic categories are broad, structural, analytic categories, which present themselves as descriptive rather than prescriptive. They facilitate abstract comparison by structure and function, but also produce new subjects and subjectivities within particular epistemic regimes, that is, within institutionalized powers of regulation and control. Emic categories are the ones used by "the people themselves," that is, by local populations under scrutiny by various powers, intellectual, political, religious, economic, and so on. Such emic categories are plucked from their contexts as exemplary, and thus are put to purposes not always intended by their users despite their representation as from "the people themselves." "Etic" is borrowed from "phonetic" and "emic" from "phonemic," thus traveling out of their strictly linguistic uses to other sites of discourse, often anthropological or sociological, and reflecting origins within the foundations of U.S. academic linguistic anthropology and a kind of colonial functionalism. Some emic categories are appropriated for etic purposes: for example, the term "berdache."

Recently, within a set of political contestations, the term "berdache" as an emic term appropriated for use as an etic term was replaced by another emic term, "two-spirit," in recognition that "berdache" was an emic term of the disparaging powers of colonialism when confronted with practices they demonized. Who counts as the "local" population, the colonizer or the colonized, has been renarrativized in this contest. Indeed, which "local" population the term is borrowed from is also renarrativized.

In 1988 an activist gay anthology, *Living the Spirit: A Gay American Indian Anthology,* could give several histories of the term "berdache," critical histories of its colonial uses, and still use it relatively unproblematically as a meta-term, including it as such in its table of contents and in its resources and appendices (Roscoe 1988). By 1998 an academic anthropological text attempting to situate the study of sexualities within the histories of social science investigation comments on its own production over the time in which the term becomes less acceptable and deproblematizes the political contests by putting in a footnote rather simply, "Although the term *berdache* is widely used in the literature under review, it has acquired pejorative connotations. Since the original publication of this essay, *Two-spirit* has replaced *berdache* as the preferred term" (Weston 1998, 223).

In Randy Burns's preface to *Living the Spirit*, a simultaneous history and definition is offered: "French explorers used the word *berdache* to describe male Indians who specialized in the work of women and formed emotional and sexual relationships with other men. Many tribes had female berdaches, too—women who took on men's work and married other women" (Burns 1988, 1). Midnight Sun, in an essay "Sex/Gender Systems in Native North America," offers a different history and definition. (The relationship between these two histories could emphasize their differences, or could synthesize one as a more expanded definition that is the same but with more detail than the other. Synthesizing such differences marks new alliances produced in the course of the contest for terminology. I emphasize the differences at this moment in this essay not to undermine such alliances, but to point out the moments in the labor-intensive processes of producing of such activist allies throughout "theoretical" debates.)

One of the most frequently used terms in the literature is berdache, *derived from a Persian word meaning "kept boy" or "male prostitute" and first applied by French explorers to designate "passive" partners in homosexual relationships between Native American males. This is complicated, however, by the fact that many individuals labeled berdaches also engaged in cross-dressing and cross-gender behavior. . . . I use "cross-dressing" to refer to male or female transvestism; "cross-gender behavior" to the assumption of the role of the other sex; and "homosexual" or "lesbian" to refer to the identity of those engaging in patterned same-sex sexual behavior. This latter definition distinguishes between behavior and identity and also separates male homosexuality from lesbianism.* (Midnight Sun *1988, 34–35*)

How the French explorers come to use a Persian word is not explained, nor is the history of its use by ethnographers, as they move from traders and religious, to explorers and bureaucrats, to anthropologists and social workers. What Midnight Sun emphasizes are the categories that must be separated when analyzed by the methods produced by lesbian and gay studies in the United States, where distinguishing between identity and behavior has become pivotal as political identities and indeed identity politics itself are contested, and where feminism has influenced the political and erotic significance of differences between lesbians and gay men. The term "queer" might be understood today (2002) as a location of opposition to the terms in which these contests are framed within the kinds of distinctions made by Midnight Sun in 1988. "Queer" too, in its productive instabilities, is implicated in the struggles for universals that can mobilize global activism and yet can honor particularisms of meaning and action.

Human rights activists might mobilize such universals in attempts to create a new global citizen, whose claims on human rights are not claims on single nation-states, but rather on such continually-recreated-as-stable ideas of the "universal." Such politics can be understood as "essentialist," but with the caveat that "essentialism" properly marks the moment of stabilization in a contested social construction, a stability that changes momentarily. Such stability is perhaps continually reproduced as "the same" through the institutionalizations of repressive political powers, or perhaps deconstructed and destabilized by oppositional movements, or perhaps struggled for as a liberatory practice, process, or identity, or—most likely—is a complex, always changing mixture of all these contradictions and contestations. Such politics might make global political interventions with strategic use of such universals, for example, asking of nation-states, as a transparently demographic question, "Where are the missing gay people?" With the assumption of a range of human variability within "sexual orientation" and with the weight and authority of new genetic research that works to stabilize sexuality as biologically determined, diadic and mutually exclusive, nation-states might be held accountable for their own insistence that "There are no lesbians here," the corollary being that such absences mark "disappeared" people for whom human rights intervention is necessary. That such "human rights" intervention could be put to repressive as well as liberatory purposes is only too obvious, as is also the ever present possibility that a biologically essentialized "gay" gene is subject to genetic manipulation and attempts at control and genocide.

"There are no lesbians here" may at other times actually be a local anticolonial liberation politics that refuses the narrow social institutionalizations of some particular cultural formation, under the term "lesbian," as inadequate to represent local practices, activisms, sexualities, or identities. The historical and fictive status of colonialism in the production of alternative sexualities or in the recognition or rejection of indigenous sexualities is various. Nevertheless, the insistence that homosexuality or lesbianism, even in its "globalized" versions, is an imposition of colonial rule can itself be repressive, as local lesbians document in *Unspoken Rules*, where they speak against their governments' claims that "There are no lesbians here." Feminism similarly may be refused in local anticolonial liberation politics, as a set of traveling political practices not applicable to some local political concerns, or as a threat to cultural values not easily separated from liberatory politics. Nationalisms may valorize marriage, the family, and traditional sexual regulatory practices, while local women's movements—feminist, nonfeminist, and even antifeminist—need local strategies for giving liberatory meaning to their challenges

37

to or adoptions of such "cultural" concerns. (Some of these so-called local strategies travel globally; for example, feminist refigurations of meaning around "the veil," or rereadings of the Koran and Islamic history.)

Lesbian Feminisms in Globalization Processes

Chandra Mohanty's critiques of feminist scholarship and colonial discourses have emphasized the dangers of a globally traveling U.S. feminism unself-consciously promoting itself as a universal project (Mohanty 1991). The problems and powers of such "global" representations are at stake in the refusal of such universals as "lesbian" and "feminist," however collaboratively produced. Such "global" and appropriative intentions of IGLHRC's *Unspoken Rules*, now reprinted in London in Cassell's series on lesbian and feminist international concerns, are made more explicit in another book in the series, *Amazon to Zami: Towards a Global Lesbian Feminism* (Reinfelder 1996). *Amazon* is a groundbreaking anthology and political project of importance, its difficulties of production heroically met, and necessarily immersed in tentative conceptualizations by a variety of activists in various political and national locations. Such an anthology produces its own fragile and formative alliances and affiliations within the collection of its authors, as individuals and as representatives of countries, activist groups, and coalitions, and exemplifies particular political visions and particular strategies for achieving social change.

The central political meanings established by the editor and displayed in her introduction crystallize around the term "lesbian feminism." Although the term shifts a bit in its ranges of inclusion throughout the various essays in the book, it tends to solidify a particular political formation, not simply lesbians who are feminists (however contested even those terms might be) but a particular political position produced in the tension between feminisms and lesbianisms traveling globally, and local particularisms of place, nation, and political moment. In editor Reinfelder's introduction, this "lesbian feminism" is produced by analogy with other feminisms taxonomized by implicit and explicit theories of the origins of oppression: "Lesbian feminism, unlike other forms of feminism, sees the institutionalization of heterosexuality as one, if not *the*, cornerstone of oppression" (Reinfelder 1996, 4). It acknowledges several theories of the origins and meaning of lesbianism, while locating itself most comfortably in lesbianism as a political choice (a claim made more explicitly in some of the other essays in the book): [in describing the effects on women of human rights abuses of lesbians]:

Some give in to compulsory heterosexuality; but for others a change to heterosexuality is perceived as desirable, but an impossibility. Fortunately, for many of us our lesbianism is a conscious "choice," albeit one that the institution of heterosexuality structures and constrains. But in spite of the extreme difficulties and constraints this "choice" may impose on us, we like and prefer *being lesbians. (Reinfelder 1996, 26)*

(Obviously one hears echoes of debates embedded in terms "sexual orientation" and "sexual preference" here and tentative strategies for inclusion and alliance in a range of parallelisms.)

Throughout the essays in the book, individual authors describe local practices of identity, political meaning (including its apparent absence), and practices—sexual, social, and gender-structured. The terms "butch" and "femme" are used comparatively by most authors, to distinguish and connect practices that depend on gender-specialists very different in their performances and their stratifications in terms of power. Authors simultaneously elaborate the local particularisms of such "butch/femme" relationships, while conflating them with feminist global critiques that theorize butch/femme pairs as modeled in political error upon heterosexuality. The meanings of lesbianism-as-political-choice and the critique of butch/femme pairs come to define the kind of global lesbian feminism embodied in the political project of the anthology.

Which Differences Make a Difference

I teach both *Unspoken Rules* and *Amazon to Zami* in an advanced undergraduate women's studies class I call "Lesbianisms in Multinational Reception." The first time I taught this class I plunged immediately into the international questions of "what counts as a lesbian," offering to students some of the examples of social practices least like contemporary U.S. lesbian performances, identities, and behaviors. I thought beforehand of the dangers of making some social and sexual practices "exotic" but had naively not thought about my students' simple refusal to consider any of these social and sexual forms as having any connection to U.S. lesbianism. I assumed the kind of universal constructed by human rights activists as the metacategory under which local variations would be meaningfully connected under the sign "lesbian" as I labored to demonstrate complexities of variation. I made this assumption despite the very title I had chosen for the course, a title that valued the refusal of the term by women in many locations and politics, the refusal to use it to describe themselves, and that highlighted the neoliberal economics of globalization. The kind of refusal I privileged unself-consciously was that by international women critiquing the neocolonialisms embedded in the term "lesbian." If anything, I assumed my students might find themselves using the term as a kind of colonizing universal.

But my students instead were refusing to use the term to create alliances and meaningful relationships across variation, variations that were more powerfully significant, and less interesting to them than I had anticipated (and not innocent, either, of assumptions of universalisms of many sorts). The social formation that over and over was the site of their refusal to connect was what in *Amazon to Zami* was called globally "butch/femme." Butch/femme relationships were, they felt, not feminist, and therefore not really "lesbian." Until this experience I thought I had understood but really had not fully digested the power of conflations of "feminist" and "lesbian." I had also assumed that my students, especially lesbian students, were not only aware of, but indeed active participants in reconstructed U.S. meanings of butch/femme practices. Instead I discovered that my students were unaware of such contemporary debates in lesbian/feminist/academic/theo-retical/erotic communities. I was clearly only too implicated myself in all these possible formations and assumptions. What struck me most was the sadness that my students demonstrated when they were confronted with a range of "global lesbian" practices in many variations on "butch/femme" gender specializations, as if an old fear had been realized rather than repudiated. (They were somewhat consoled, however, by the reiterated feminist critique of such practices in *Amazon to Zami*.)

Global Gay Formations and Local Homosexualities in Layers of Locals and Globals

As is the case with the Homosexual, the Lesbian is an object within an epistemo-logical history that can be interrogated within a history of sexuality or within an anthropology of sexuality. Thinking through "global gay formations and local ho-mosexualities" emphasizes that diachronic and synchronic investigations are each accountable to and also always metaphors for and about today's sexual pol-itics under the regime of globalized capital. Such investigation requires thinking in layers of locals and globals, emphasizing that they are relative and relational. Thus implicit in a history or an anthropology of sexuality is the question "What counts as a lesbian?"—where the word "lesbian" has multiple uses and meanings, uses and meanings not exhausted by local particularisms, valuable though they are, central though they are to particular projects. What this means is that no localism or particularism is not caught up in the dynamic interactions between globals and locals, be they geographical or across time. This does not, however, assume that all trajectories are toward the dominations of U.S./Euro cultural, political, economic formations, or the dominations of presentist conceptualizations of sexuality and the self, rather than the possibilities of reassertion by multiple "locals" of the general priority and wide travel of local forms. Which locals, and their relative powers under the regime of globalization, their material abilities to "travel" and within what fields of power, from immigration to the Internet to currency as new archival objects, are the present circumstances that create new gay formations.

Within a global gay human rights activism the question "What counts as a lesbian?" is made transparently powerful within "sexual orientation" as an element of the humanist individual self that is emancipated through inalienable rights as a human. Anthropological and historical concerns with particularist cultural forms are subordinated to the difficulties of producing international laws, treaties, and conventions that are answerable to democratic machinery that dates from the end of World War II and draws on Enlightenment notions of liberty. Such productions create a new global citizen, whose claims upon human rights are not claims upon single nation-states, but rather upon continually-recreated-as-stable ideas of the "universal." Such "universals" are in fact quite unstable, produced and reproduced with great difficulty, legally, militarily, economically, scientifically, and through other discourses, representational and materially powerful.

One particular "local" formation, both geopolitically and chronologically local, the U.S. 1970s feminist version of the "Lesbian," may unself-consciously be used as the standard, the unmarked category, by a variety of locals and globals, of the term "lesbian," especially in the phrase, "There are no lesbians here." Local, but also materially powerful under processes of globalization, this formation has traveled widely, back through time in various historical and fictional discourses and today via gay and feminist activisms, tourism, media, commerce, and medical, legal, and psychological discourses. This U.S. 1970s feminist Lesbian's construction can be emblematized by three political claims: "Lesbianism is not a passing phase," "Lesbians don't ape heterosexuals," and "Bisexuals are confused Lesbians." Such claims create disjunctions from other sexual formations, historical or cross-cultural, that at various times have or could have also been displayed under the sign "lesbian."

For example, "Lesbianism is not a passing phase" excludes from naming under the sign "lesbian," sexual and cultural practices that do not construct as mutually exclusive from marriage (especially) or other institutional forms of heterosexuality, sex, sex play, love or affection, or varieties of stimulations between females, ones socially sanctioned, socially prohibited or socially trivial. Especially "Lesbianism is not a passing phase" excludes from naming as this "lesbian," sexual or cultural practices that are restricted to particular periods or to specific situations in a life cycle that prescribes marriage and motherhood. "Lesbians don't ape heterosexuals" excludes institutionalizations of gender-specialists, such as in some cultural-theatrical communities, or so-called butch/femme couplings, the so-called mannish lesbian, and sexual play with objects such as dildos, or sexual practices that figure the clitoris as an organ of penetration. Indeed, it is penetration itself that is especially prohibited with this claim. "Bisexuals are confused lesbians" excludes all practices and identities that are either not accommodated within a mutually exclusive, diadic homo/hetero sexuality, or that insist on identity-priority rather than practice-priority in an epistemology of polymorphous perversity. Bisexuality is figured only as a gateway in the production of Lesbians out of false heterosexuals. What is constructed is a Lesbianism that is lifelong, stable after "coming out," autonomous of heterosexuality, sex-centered, politically feminist, not situational, and exclusive of marriage. That this formation is both powerful and unstable is made clear by the range of contestations in U.S. lesbian feminism over the decades of the 1970s, 1980s, and 1990s, all sorts of debates/struggles from the lesbian continuum to butch/femme couples to gays in the military to sex toys and S/M to lesbian bed-death and lesbian motherhood and lesbian domestic violence to gay marriage. This formation shadows dramatically the question "What counts as a lesbian?" in any investigation of sexualities historically or cross-culturally. The range of contestations incompletely synthesized here could be taken to demonstrate the material power of this "local" (both historically and culturally) version of the Lesbian, or conversely could be taken to show how unstable such domination is, how powerful other local formations are in their reassertion of the priority of their own forms. Within an anthropology of sexuality other forms have come to vie for any such power: such forms as the gender-specialist, the penetrator, and the bisexual.

Bisexuality, rather than the identity the bisexual, may be the formation in greatest global circulation today. As one global gay formation, bisexuality has currency in a globalized economy of niche markets where the most circulated objects are those that can be viewed within the greatest range of divergent local markets as "like-us." This doesn't mean that bisexuality is actually "all things to all people," but rather that a highly commodified version of bisexuality can be exploited as differently important in a local and distinctive reception by a wide range of markets, especially media markets, as are also all local and global forms of "sexuality," especially in their specious "(hetero)sexual" variations. And in any collectivities of activisms that are international, bisexuality must be reprioritized. In such activist locations the term "bisexuality" is useful in at least three contexts: (1) as a liminal category, such as its use as "gateway" from heterosexuality to homosexuality, in a universe of discourse effectively exhausted by hetero/homo sex; (2) as a third identity, modeled on the "sexual orientations" homosexual and heterosexual, thus bisexual, essentialist or anti-essentialist, within identity politics or in a queer anti-identity politics; (3) as an overflow category, in a universe of discourse not exhausted by hetero/homo sex, and thus representing all other possible local sexual practices without distinguishing among them under the sign "bisexual." Thus as overflow category, bisexual can also, like queer, name and valorize as well inchoate noninstitutionalized processes and formations connected with sexuality, possibly (or fictitiously) not "disciplined." This version of bisexual may be interchangeable with queer, and participate in a range of its meanings and productive instabilities as well.

Lesbianisms in Multinational Reception

The phrase "Lesbianisms in Multinational Reception" suggests that the term "Lesbian" is plural and various, that in some global locations it is engaged only as an outside term, not there a local term, that there are many kinds of reception of the term, that such receptions are inextricable from its traveling possibilities. Those travels are interconnected with other globalizing processes in an economy of multinationals in late capitalism, an economy also including representations and media, as well as activisms, art, and cyberspace, and inextricably intertwined too with worldwide movements against colonialism. It includes the possibility that "lesbianism" is a rejected term, as well as the possibility of using it as an inclusive, unmarked, or continually reconstructed "universal," although plural, not singular. Naming lesbian in this context, through this phrase, is a method coming-into-being that arises from acts of translation across fields of power. Often one knows such methods when one sees them only in the midst of misunderstandings and struggles, when previously held assumptions are ruptured by micro and macro movements of power. To pay attention to such methodology coming into focus requires a high tolerance for conflict and for beginning again, tasks with emotional, intellectual, and political costs.

Misunderstandings and mistakes are the paradoxical "common ground" on which such methodology is made, and misunderstandings and mistakes have their own consequences, sometimes separate from the coming into being of such methodology, and not at all necessarily mended by it. In this vision such conflicts as the ones shaped through political generations and differing geopolitics, and even through (inter)interdisciplinarities in the academy, are pivotal in producing "lesbigay" methodology. At this time I consider the most important task to be first the never simple recognition of such methods when we see them. I believe in eclectic methods that emerge in different local politics out of political and institutional struggles, that require always problematic translations, which themselves shape these methods. No generation of political activists can claim mastery or ownership of such methods, nor can any academic disciplines or political theories, nor can any national liberation movements.

Such new methods enable new translations, new visionary reframings of contemporary geopolitical realities. For example, Chela Sandoval translates "hyperoppression" under globalization into another vision, an ironic one that recognizes simultaneously both terror and possibility, calling it "the democratization of oppression," and naming the activities, activisms, and oppressions of a new global citizen brought into being within shifting fields of power in late capitalism. She speaks of an alignment among decolonial theorists who, surviving "conquest, colonization, and slavery," develop methodologies "crucial to the project of identifying citizen-subjects and collectivities able to negotiate the globalizing operations of the next century" and names queers as one set of agents in these negotiations (Sandoval forthcoming). Any new political movements, among them lesbian, gay, and feminist human rights activisms, must be very sophisticated in their understandings of their own commodification within such layered global and local structures, and willing to take risks in their appropriations of pleasures, identities, and political strategies.

References

Burns, Randy. 1988. Preface to *Living the Spirit*, ed. Will Roscoe, 1–5. New York: St. Martin's.

Midnight Sun. 1988. "Sex/Gender Systems in Native North America." In *Living the Spirit*, ed. Will Roscoe, 32–47. New York: St. Martin's.

Mohanty, Chandra Talpade. 1991. "Under Western Eyes." In *Third World Women and the Politics of Feminism*, ed. Chandra Talpade Mohanty, Ann Russo, and Lourdes Torres. 1991. Bloomington: Indiana University Press.

Reinfelder, Monika, ed. 1996. *Amazon to Zami: Towards a Global Lesbian Feminism*. London: Cassell.

Roscoe, Will, coordinating ed. for Gay American Indians. 1988. *Living the Spirit: A Gay American Indian Anthology*. New York: St. Martin's.

Rosenbloom, Rachel, ed. for International Gay and Lesbian Human Rights Commission. 1995. *Unspoken Rules: Sexual Orientation and Women's Human Rights*. San Francisco: IGLHRC.

Sandoval, Chela. Forthcoming. *Oppositional Consciousness and the Methodology of Love in the Postmodern World*. New York: Routledge.

Weston, Kath. 1998. *Long Slow Burn: Sexuality and Social Science*. New York: Routledge.

Part 2

QUEER VALUES IN A GLOBAL ECONOMY

4 Can Homosexuals End Western Civilization As We Know It?

Family Values in a Global Economy

Janet R. Jakobsen

What does it mean when Christian ministers stand up and say, "Homosexuality can end Western civilization as we know it"? Now, perhaps we "homosexuals" have secret powers that I don't know about, but overall it's difficult to say that something called "Western civilization," particularly insofar as we are witnessing the triumph of the "new world order," is coming to an "end." And yet, what would it mean to take this statement seriously rather than simply dismissing it as the hyperbolic claims of a fanatical religiosity that, precisely because religious, is indicative of at best irrationality and at worst insanity: "Of course, they hate us," the story goes, "They're religious." In fact, the story of religious irrationality sets up a, shall we say, "straightforward" counterdiscourse that mirrors some of the claims that the right most wants to make, including the naturalization of religion in relation to values.[1] This logic of reduction is precisely that of the right: "Of course we hate them, we're religious, and to be religious is to have values and to have values is to be conservative." Thus, to impute a natural connection between religion and sexual regulation can reinforce, rather than contest, the claims of the right.[2]

The chain that connects religion, values, conservatism, and sexual regulation is further connected to another chain in a story of Americanness: America must

49

have values and the site of values is religion and to be appropriately religious is to be Christian is to be Protestant (which is why the Christian Coalition pretty much failed in its attempts to form Catholic and Jewish alliances) and finally is to be reformed rather than, for example, those troublesome Anabaptists who won't even take oaths for the state, much less be properly capitalist. The working of this second chain is crucial because it articulates a network of social relations that connect the secular and the Christian and that through "the Protestant ethic and the spirit of capitalism" connect the secular market with Christianity and with "family values." Thus, the right's investment in sexist, racist, or antihomosexual discourse is precisely as a crucial site to construct a whole series of social relations that fundamentally revolve around the relationship between what we might call economic value and those cultural or moral values that in right discourse carry the name "family." Specifically, I will argue that "family values" mediates between the economy and the "American" nation under contemporary market conditions by offering a discourse that can mediate between exploitation and domination. In other words, "family" (rather than the state) mediates between economy and nation, and "values" mediates between exploitation and domination. (Thus, I don't understand the bumper sticker that says, "Hate is not a family value" either, because hate may very well be one.)[3]

The problem, then, that I want to pose for radical politics is that the current "fight the right" stance does not intervene in any effective way in the network that empowers the right. Rather, "we" (which for our purposes here means queer politics) tend to embrace the "secular" as a bulwark against the "religious" right, when, in fact, secularism in America is a complicated thing. The specifically American brand of secularism is itself a specific form of reformed Protestantism that is intertwined with the market and that is, since at least the inauguration of Ronald Reagan as president, part of the network that sustains the right (and "the secular" is not any one thing, but varies across cultures depending in part on the form of "religion" to which it is contrasted). To begin to understand the contemporary power of conservative and specifically antihomosexual politics in the United States, then, we must understand a number of issues about "America," about its place in a global economy, and about this thing called "religion."

On Presidents, Christians, and America

To say that the United States is a Christian-dominated nation is to say something so obvious as to be banal. To say that every president has been Christian and to marvel at the fact that only one of those presidents has even been Catholic is both to remark on the obvious and not to say very much. In fact, the election of John F. Kennedy in 1960 may tell us more about the denominationalization of the Catholic Church in its American incarnation than about some new religious openness, simply indicating that religious freedom in the United States is the freedom to act like Protestants.[4] Kennedy reassured us repeatedly during the election with words to the effect of "I'm an American first and it is the President's job to uphold the Constitution of the United States." This kind of talk reflects precisely the U.S. denominational model of relation between church and state, in which each religious body is a particular (and similar) type of organization within the broader framework of the American "nation."

To understand fully the all too obvious Christianity of American presidents, we need to keep in mind a second and intertwined understanding of things religious in the United States, which is that we are a largely "secular" country—that the effect of the disestablishment of religion has not been so much the right to religious freedom as the right to build a secular nation in which "religion" is nice, but really doesn't matter very much. This story of secularization has been very popular both outside and within religious studies, but of course, it has not produced the expected (happy?) ending, that religion will matter less and less in "public" at least, but instead in 1980 produced the election of Ronald Reagan through a candidacy tied specifically and openly to organizations we might term the "Christian-identified radical right."

The question is "why?" Why after more than two hundred years of U.S. nationalism and, according to the predominant story, a few hundred more years of the process of secularization, does the United States remain a country where the president still has to be Christian and preferably (all but tokenistically) Protestant? And, more urgently, how is it that Ronald Reagan in particular was able to embody the Christian presidency in such a way as to mark the sharp turn (although we had been going around the bend for a while) to the right, toward a massive shift in the purpose of government and the relationship between government and nation? After all, as was often remarked during his presidency, Ronald Reagan never went to church, although the public circulation of this remark had no apparent effect on his Christian credentials. In fact, his not going to church combined with his stated commitment to (re)Christianizing America is precisely what enabled his presidency to be the site of the alliance between fiscal and social conservatives that was the 1980s Republican Party (and that continues in perhaps even more virulent form in the new Bush administration.) Specifically, to be Christian and never to go to church is how Reagan embodied and articulated a "renewed" Christian dominance in the United States, which rearticulates the intertwining of the Christian and the secular, and is the fabric for a network of (contradictory) social relations that became the "Reagan revolution." And here is the provocative part—his articulation of secular = Christian = American means that we cannot comfortably claim a site called the "secular" as necessarily resistant to this configuration.

The power of this secular-Christianity (alliance) can be briefly illustrated through an encounter that I had with the Christian Coalition. In 1995 I was asked to be on a panel at the Society for Biblical Literature. The panel was entitled "Lesbian Theory and Biblical Criticism." Not being a biblical critic myself, I was somewhat at a loss for a topic. I was, however, working on the relationship between the "Contract with America" and the "Contract with the American Family," and so I called the Christian Coalition and asked for its materials on the biblical basis for the "Contract with the American Family."[5] After a series of phone calls in which my requests became repeatedly more general, asking for materials on the biblical basis for "family values," or simply for the work of the Christian Coalition, I was finally informed that they had no literature on the Bible whatsoever. In the face of this apparent "lack," the final response from a relatively high-level public relations manager was, "Let me assure you, ma'am, that this is a very Christian organization. It's in our name, the Christian Coalition." And that statement, "It's in our name, the Christian Coalition," was the final word. What does it mean that the Christian Coalition need be Christian in name only?

Religion and the Secular: Secular-Christianity

The working alliance of secular-Christianity is so powerful (and so dangerous) because it offers a reinvention of the relationship between Christianity and capitalism, between a site of moral values and the morally value-free market. This articulation does not collapse values into the market, but it allows them as separate sites to work together in a particular way.[6] This articulation occurs through a circuit that connects (value-free) exploitation with (value-laden) domination. In order to understand this circuit, we have to be able to read it in both directions, from cultural values to the value-free market and back from market to culture again, just as in an electric circuit the current runs in both directions at once. I accomplish this bidirectional reading of culture and capital through the particular incitements of Gayatri Spivak (1988a), who explicitly raises the question of the relationship between exploitation and domination.[7] I start, however, with a reading of the relationship between market and culture as narrated by David Harvey (1990) in *The Condition of Postmodernity*, which provides important pieces of the puzzle, but which because it depends on the opposition between the secular and the religious cannot fully explicate the network that we face.

Harvey's reading is emblematic of the secularization narrative in both cultural and religious studies. The secularization narrative is most often told as part and parcel of the progress narrative stemming from the Enlightenment, in which reason, later termed rationalization, emancipates humanity from the bonds of dogma, later termed religion. "Religion" and the "secular" are thus invented together (Baird, forthcoming). This move was to accomplish a number of social changes, not least of which was to establish a newly harmonious order to European society in the wake of the "wars of religion" sparked by the Reformation. Here reason replaces the god-term as the guarantor of order and harmony. Secularization configured in this way is "progress"—the more secular, the more rational, the more enlightened/emancipatory/progressive, and religion becomes configured as both irrational and regressive. Thus, if religion "reappears," as it has, for example, in the last two decades in what is sometimes termed the contemporary "resurgence of religion," this is a sign of regression.

Now, there are good reasons to have doubts about this story. Cultural critics, among others, have over the last few decades raised many questions about the progress narrative of the Enlightenment. And yet it has also been extremely difficult to give up, particularly given that both the contemporary university and left (progressive?) social movements are in some sense products of this narrative. Moreover, there has been, at least from left/progressive sites, much less questioning of the secularization narrative, in part, because the secular is seen as a bulwark against the irrational regressive aspects of religion. (When the Christian-identified radical right has identified you as a target, secularism can look pretty good.)

This story of freedom from dogma is also tied specifically to a story of freedom as instituted in the market, where, for example, John Guillory (1993) argues (and he's careful in his choice of language here) that the market provided a site of interaction between producers and consumers that "felt like" freedom from ecclesiastical authority. The invention of the "secular" in relation to the religious is specifically about instituting the market (as freedom). Weber (1930), however, in *The Protestant Ethic and the Spirit of Capitalism*, tells a story that could line up with Guillory's but is different from the common progressive secularization story by reminding us that Reformation preceded Enlightenment, instituting a form of rationalization that was to Weber decidedly irrational and yet extremely effective as what in these post-Foucaultian times we might call a technology of body regulation.[8] This form of regulation, "worldly asceticism," takes place in order to demonstrate freedom in the other world of salvation and it takes place as a discourse of "freedom" from the church. It may "feel" like freedom, and it becomes so naturalized as part of the market that it becomes unnoticed, both as restraint and as specifically "reformed" Protestant. Out of this "irrational" rationalization comes the rationality of the Enlightenment as secular, and the intertwining of the "secular" and the religious is forgotten, but not lost, meaning that it can still be operative. What are lost are the possibilities for embodying other forms of "freedom" that are not dependent on either the irrational rationality diagnosed by Weber or its specific bodily disciplines. Thus, the secular is, even at its moment of institution, not necessarily "free" from the religious, and the market is never as "value-free" as it is supposed to be. In the contemporary moment, "family values" is a reinvention of this connection precisely in order to enact a variety of forms of body regulation. "Family values," then, is in some sense a reworking of the Protestant ethic and the spirit of capitalism. Thus, the reduction of the "religious" to the Protestant reformed tradition is so crucial, because in buying into this reduction we buy into the specifically Protestant version of the secular as well.

What difference does it make how we think about secularization (to anyone except perhaps arcane religious studies scholars)? As we shall see below, by depending on the usual secularization narrative in his story of the shift from modernity to postmodernity, Harvey connects religion to what he calls "stable values." (We should note that this is precisely the connection between religion and stable values that the Christian right wants to make.) Harvey then posits the contemporary flexibility of capital against these values, failing thus to see the way in which values (that both he and the right identify with religion) are themselves mobile and in complicity with a new flexible capitalism.

In rehearsing the story of modernity as precursor to the "condition of postmodernity," Harvey narrates as follows: "Enlightenment thought . . . embraced the idea of progress, and actively sought that break with history and tradition which modernity espouses. It was, *above all*, a secular movement that sought the demystification and desacralization of knowledge and social organization in order to liberate human beings from their chains" (1990, 12–13, emphasis added). Then he describes the return of religion in the shift to postmodern conditions and flexible accumulation:

While the roots of this transition are evidently deep and complicated, their consistency with a transition from Fordism to flexible accumulation is reasonably clear even if the direction (if any) of causality is not. To begin with, the more flexible motion of capital emphasizes the new, the fleeting, the ephemeral, the fugitive, and the contingent in modern life, rather than the more solid values implanted under Fordism. . . . But, as Simmel (1978) long ago suggested, it is also at such times of fragmentation and economic insecurity that the desire for stable values leads to a heightened emphasis upon the authority of basic institutions—the family, religion, the state. And there is abundant evidence of a revival of support for such institutions and the values they represent throughout the Western world since about 1970. (1990, 171)[9]

Harvey's story can tell us some important things about how the shift to a post-Fordist economy with flexible labor markets and an increasing disjunction between U.S. financial markets and U.S. industrial production have influenced the production and circulation of "family values," but because it also in some sense participates in the progressive narrative of secularization, it cannot fully explain what is going on with "family values." It can read in one direction, from market to culture, but ultimately not the other way around.[10] (And when Harvey speaks of the "return" of irrationality, he does seem to invoke some type of nostalgia for Fordism.)

As Harvey tells it, capital has left the Fordist marriage[11] to the nation-state and the state is left to pick up the contradictory pieces of protecting the "national interest" and looking good to "transnational" capital.[12] In the Fordist compromise the role of the state was both to mediate the compromise between corporations and organized labor and to constitute a single nation, which this compromise sustained in part through federal programs. Thus, the nation and the state could be maintained as the single entity "nation-state" that marks the modern period. In the turn to postmodernity, however, if the state is going to continue to work for business, it cannot as easily integrate the nation into the state at the federal level because of the ways business and finance in particular have become transnational. So we might now say that the president does not (as the president once did) work for Lee Iacocca (as signified by that 1965 Mustang that President Clinton was so proud to display as a sign of his "Americanness") but rather that he works for Alan Greenspan.

The shift toward the primacy of transnational finance has also implied a shift toward the mobility of industrial production, which has significantly destabilized U.S. labor markets, even as it has intensified the class and race divisions in the

United States. Once industrial production becomes mobile, any critical discourse in relation to corporations appears to run the danger of prompting a corporation to leave town. Thus, the threats to the livelihood of "middle America" that are effected by the loss of both capital and industrial production overseas have been transposed from corporate America to those "others" who are understood to be "outside" the middle and thus to be part of the external threat. The effectiveness of this transposition has been an apparently paradoxical embrace of corporate America just as it betrays the marriage, so that we can no longer speak of corporations as enacting "special interests," but rather those who would challenge corporate policy or the boundaries of middle America become the transposed site of threat and are now named with the pejorative "special"—special interests, special rights, and so on. The state now needs a new means of mediating between transnational capital and the American nation, and I would suggest that this contradictory project is being managed in part by shifting the site of the nation, away from the state, which can take care of business, and toward the "family," as an appropriate site of nationalism that can be reintegrated at a different level into the transnational economy.

Here is at least part of the work of "family values," which can explain why we are currently facing both smaller government and an extension of certain forms of government control in arenas that can be associated with the "family." The "culture wars" (Hunter 1991) between "queer nation" and "Christian nation," then, are not battles for the "soul" of America, but rather for the existence of the American nation, the continuation of something that can be recognizably called the American nation under conditions of transnational capital. Thus, it is fundamentally social (as well as "cultural"). Here we can also begin to see some of the "sense" of hyperbolic claims about homosexuality. If "America" is dependent on a particular and narrow understanding of family, then homosexuality could, in fact, threaten the nation. Moreover, the conjunction of "family" with "values" provides the link between "civilization" and nation, making America and its embodiment in family values both dependent on and constitutive of civilization, "Western civilization" itself. In this logic, because "America" is the only nation that has the proper values, the loss of American values would mean the loss not only of America as a nation, but of Western civilization itself. "America" is, in this sense, in Madeline Albright's term an "indispensable" nation to both the new world order and Western civilization.

How do we distinguish "Americanness," however? The discourse of family values says that we do so through our values and their "peculiarly" (and I use this word advisedly) American embodiments. To read this work of distinction (Bourdieu 1984) requires a reading of the reverse current from market to culture that can recognize the positive (productive) work of values and religion in contrast to the type of negative relation between religion and economy that Harvey articulates in his language of relation between stability and flexibility. Family values discourse articulates a particularly potent secular-Christianity precisely by providing this type of connection between the (value-free) market and a discourse of values employed in the service of nation building. What Harvey's story can't tell us is why the work of distinguishing "Americanness" takes the form that it does. Why does "family" have to have a narrow definition? Why can't we simply say that "homosexuals" have families too and create a more inclusive sense of "America"? Why wouldn't such a move make everyone happy? Why do "family values" also have to be dominative values?

The Question of Value(s)

In "Scattered Speculations on the Question of Value," Gayatri Spivak (1988a) asks that we consider the relationship between domination and exploitation, as both separate and interrelated sites.[13] Spivak asks us to think about how Value is produced through the work of what she in the mid-1980s calls "textualization." She pursues the question of textuality in order to open and denaturalize the chain that leads from value through money to capital by way of representation and transformation. She argues that the origin of this chain is usually closed by beginning with a naturalized concept of labor rather than with Value as a differential produced through the discontinuous relationships among the terms. Denaturalization of labor leads to the question of embodiment, of how bodies that labor are themselves produced in relation to the differential production of Value. If labor is not so denaturalized we lose sight of the process by which bodies are made into labor power—bodies, in Mary Poovey's terms, "simply disappear into labor power" (1995, 31), thus reenacting the very fetishization that Marx would incite us to critique. If we denaturalize the chain, by recognizing discontinuities at each of its transitions, however, we recognize that bodies themselves may carry a double discourse (inscribed in domination) even before they enter the chain of value. While embodiment is, as Judith Butler (1993) points out, a materialization, because bodies materialize norms, embodiment is always itself a double discourse—the materialization of the immaterial. This double discourse could be articulated in a number of ways, but in domination it is articulated as abjection, as a splitting

57

that abstracts the subject from that which it excludes (the abject) even as it (the abject) is inscribed within the subject. This double discourse through which bodies carry norms opens the possibilities of bodies also carrying value(s), and the particular (in Spivak's terms) "material predication of the subject" through domination opens the door to the (connected, but discontinuous) abstraction of value from labor power. Spivak, thus, rethinks domination and exploitation by reading in both directions, reading domination as both a tool of exploitation and as in some sense preceding exploitation. She rereads the Marxist originary moment of initial capital accumulation as itself a site of domination, of producing bodies that could be exploited. Here we could read her as not disagreeing with Weber about the particular forms of embodied regulation that constituted the Protestant ethic as the precedent to capitalism, while the reinvention of the Protestant ethic in the form of "family values" similarly funds other forms of the regulation of bodies that make for both contemporary domination and exploitation.[14]

Spivak's incitement is to think through the relationship between domination and exploitation as one of complicity rather than analogy (where cultural values are read as analogous to the economic). This complicity is based on a complicity between use-value and exchange-value, so that, in part, she's arguing that you cannot separate out use-value as a site that is good (she has lots of negative references to "utopian socialism"), while the abstraction of exchange-value is the problem. A socialist politics that works simply to restore society to a society of use-value misses the ways use-value, and in particular the use-value of labor power itself, is fully determined by cultural values, and these cultural values may themselves be dominative. This determination occurs through "desire," both the desire for consumption and the desire of the body disciplined in Weberian or Protestant terms to labor, to, in Spivak's terms, "consume the (affect of) work itself." These desires make for "affectively necessary labor," such that the predication of the subject "can no longer be seen as the excess of surplus labor over *socially* necessary labor" (1988a, 162, emphasis in original). Exploitation is never itself "value-free," because it is *both* dependent on *and* structured by the values carried by the normatively inscribed, the dominated, body. Thus, for Spivak, the commonly criticized moment of the abstraction of exchange-value from use-value is a complicitous moment of both abstraction and materialization, presence and absence.

This complicity between economic value and cultural or moral values has wide-ranging implications. Economic and cultural values are not the same, but neither are they wholly distinguishable, as if they are or could be unrelated. Furthermore, their relation is complex. One cannot be established as the original or base to the other. This means that domination must be read as having its own basis in cultural values, rather than simply as a function of exploitation. Dominative values, those values that structure heterosexism among other dominations, may work with and for capitalism, but they also make capitalism work in the way that it does, thus making dominative values co-originary with the imperative to produce value under capitalism. Capitalism could not make sense, it could not be the social organization for accomplishing certain types of material labor, if the disciplining of the body in Protestant terms did not already make sense. In particular, the "freedom" of the market could make sense as "freedom" only if the terms connecting these particular disciplines to freedom already made sense. Spivak argues against a politics that emphasizes use-value, because recognizing the complicity of domination and exploitation and denaturalizing the chain of value imply that the use of any object is not natural, and use-value must itself be read in terms of representation, in terms of the values that use represents. Thus, radical politics has to address the ways use-value is itself constituted by values that may be dominative.

The relationship between domination and exploitation is further complicated by the points of discontinuity to which Spivak refers. At each point along the chain of value the question of values becomes relevant as materiality is formed and transformed through (the material effects of) representation. Thus, value is itself riddled with discontinuities. There is no smooth transition from, for example, money to capital, and the ways money is represented—gold, paper, electronic—have differing material effects. Similarly, there are discontinuities among representations that are nonetheless linked. There is, for example, a discontinuity between the representation of money and the representation of the desire (to work) to acquire it. Each of these discontinuities means that there is no necessary relationship among the links in the chain of value. The lack of such necessity at the beginning of the chain of value and at each of its points of transition implies that it could be otherwise—that at each point one thing was valued (not consciously, but effectively) over another. The denial of these alternative possibilities and the obfuscation of these gaps in the chain are what allow capitalism to perform its magic. Thus, central to the technologies of government through capitalism are the technologies of discontinuity that cover over the gaps in the chain and the various embodied interrelations between values and value, as well as various potential relations, those that could be otherwise.

The complicitous and complex relationship between exploitation and domination has direct implications for organizing. For instance, it explains why it has not been possible simply to appeal to the values of the state over against the corrosive aspects of the value-free market, and why it will be ultimately ineffective to appeal to the market as a value-free site over against dominative values. The market may not care if individuals are gay in the way that lawmakers apparently do, but the appeal to market-niche status as a site of gay liberation seriously underestimates the intertwining of the value-free with values and of the market and the state. Even apparent conflicts may enact the intertwining of the two. For example, if lesbian and gay politics just turns to the market over against the dominative values of the state, such efforts will produce the most limited of "benefits." If family values are simply the site of stability over against flexible capital, then, we would read, for example, the Defense of Marriage Act as a contestation between market and state, with the state articulating values and the market acting in a value-free manner. Fair enough. But what this reading does not include is the intertwining of the two, the ways these values also work for capitalism, the ways even when incorporated into the state as resistances to "diversity" and "transnationalization" in the economic sector, family values can operate to remake the nation as a family that can work in the "new world order."[15] Constructing the family as nation allows the state to be relatively autonomous from the nation in such a way as to work for corporations, and since corporations don't really care whether "gays" who are not of the type eligible for employment can get married or not, the contradiction is not in any way disabling to the management of diversity in both the workforce and the nation. In fact, corporations are aided in this project because diversity is only benefited as it suits the workplace, and thus, corporations don't also have to pay through taxes for gays who might want the benefits of marriage in noncorporate sectors of the economy, while gays can be posited as getting benefits they don't deserve because they're an "overprivileged minority." In other words, corporations can laugh all the way to the proverbial and the actual bank on this one, because both moves—the offering of benefits in the workplace and the restriction of benefits in the nation—are in their interest. Conflicts between the state and the market, thus, need to be understood as structured by complicity.

This analysis means that the political field for addressing the Christian right and its religious and political conservatism, along with the moral and political conservatism of the "American" mainstream, is extremely complicated. On the other hand, it also implies that there are a number of sites for intervention that are often ignored. Each point along the chain, each discontinuity, is a site for potentially effective intervention. Discontinuities also express the limits of representation (both linguistic and political), of whose interests and needs can be articulated. These limits can be challenged but they can never be fully removed; nor would it be in our interests to do so, because the limits are also spaces of possibility, spaces that have not already been completely written over (overwritten) by domination. The difficult task of radical politics is to find ways to challenge these limits while keeping open spaces of possibility.

Ending Western Civilization

To say that homosexuals are a threat to the nation, that they can end the American nation (as we know it), is not irrational or insane, but is rather the rationality of postmodern nationalism. Positing homosexuals as a threat is rational because it works for a structure of exploitation that is intertwined with domination. Specifically, if moral values rather than economic value now locate that which is peculiarly "American," then the supposed loss of values indicated by an increasingly visible "homosexual minority" is indicative of a loss of Americanness itself. Similarly, the regulation of family through "welfare reform" is dedicated to managing the "threat" to the nation posed by "uncontrolled" family form, even as it contributes to smaller government. Middle America needs values because without them all that is left is the market. Americans are simply subject to the invisible hand of the market, which if you'll recall, has jilted America and left town. In the now clearly triangulated relationship between American labor, capital, and the international division of labor, America's hope, as articulated through "family values," is to be the wife rather than the mistress, to keep the nice house and the car by reaping at least some of the benefits of finance, while leaving the truly transitory (and exploitative) relationship to others. Values not only serve as a cultural control on the market, the stable discourse of regulation to be appealed to in times of change, they also serve the socially constructive function of making the crucial distinction between those persons whose lives are inscribed only in economic value and those who have values and so are empowered to be agents in relation to the market and economic value.

Talk of "family values" thus signals a reconstruction of American citizenship that regulates and distinguishes those Americans who deserve the rights and benefits of citizenship from those who do not—whether they are actually U.S. citizens or not—hence, in part, the anxieties about immigration and so-called illegal aliens, who threaten the borders of the United States even as those boundaries are weakened (and penetration is welcomed?) by a queer subversion from within. This makes sense of the ways queers are frequently told to "go back where they came from." (Coming from middle America myself, I'm always baffled by this invocation and think to myself, "Iowa? They would be happier if I lived in Iowa?") It also makes sense of the ways "illegal aliens" are posited as an extremely dangerous economic threat to the United States, when economic studies repeatedly show that they generally do not "take jobs away from Americans" (but rather often work in "underground economies"), nor do they drain state resources in excess of what they contribute, for example, through sales taxes. This construction of citizenship also distinguishes the American nation as the land of values, distinct from those countries that are simply marked by, and thus sources of, economic value. America thus becomes the appropriate site from which to run both transnational capitalism and the new world order.

To say that homosexuals can end Western civilization as we know it is, thus, also rational, but the rationality of the appeal to civilization is the rationality of a domination that is not simply functional for exploitation. In this discourse, domination is not only functional, it is valued. The particular values that structure the market-reformed-Protestant secular are values that make for, that produce, the embodiment of domination. In other words, the rationality of domination extends beyond a functionalist or instrumental rationality to the rationality of ethics itself.[16] The particular rationality of domination provides one of the reasons that movement efforts to explain away irrationality—to say that "Homosexuals *cannot* end Western civilization as we know it"—prove to be ineffective.[17] This has obvious implications for political strategies of mainstreaming, often argued for on the basis of effectiveness. An attempt to explain that homosexuals are "normal" or "nonthreatening" to social structures, that "gay marriage" does not threaten heterosexuality and does not require a "defense of marriage act," will often fail, as it did in the summer of 1996, because it does not dislodge the underlying logic or address the depth of the desire and commitment of the "American" public to maintaining heteronormativity. To give up this commitment is in some sense to give up the values of "Western civilization as we know it." Even when successful, such a strategy will provide only the most narrow range of political gains for those "gays and lesbians" willing and able to participate in the various normative systems that are complicit with heteronormativity. This is not to say that movements shouldn't refuse the logic of domination, shouldn't intervene in the supposedly commonsensical nature of claims about homosexuality, but it is to say that such interventions, to be effective, must also be complex.

Such an analysis is not surprising to a queer politics that often provides a critique of "gay and lesbian" politics for these very reasons. And yet the complicity of domination and exploitation has implications that create complexities for queer politics as well. In particular, queer politics in its dependence on the category of "resistance" as a description of political activity often hopes to avoid the problems invoked by positive commitments to values. The problem of values is not so easy to avoid, however. Like the hope that the "secular" will leave us a space "free" from the religious, when in fact this space is determined by religion, so also "resistance" is not so easily separable from the problematic of "values." Even some of the texts of Michel Foucault, the "father" of resistance, display some ambivalence about this question, which is one of the reasons his work on ethics is currently so popular.[18] What queer movements are facing, then, is the need for a broad engagement with the question of values. We can simply assert neither secularism nor resistance as safe sites that remove us from the problematics of rethinking values. While some forms of secularism may prove crucially useful to queer movements, we need to rethink how such forms are structured in order not to reiterate the market-reformed-Protestant form of secularism that is currently dominant in the United States. Moreover, engagement with the complex questions of various forms of religious practice may be similarly important to the actualization of queer possibilities.

In Harvey's story of modernity, the connections between religion and the secular disappear. As a result, the secular seems to be something wholly separate from religion. In the turn to postmodernity, religion reappears, this time articulated with the values that can function to stabilize the now flexible production of value. Here, what is elided is the complexity of the intertwining of value and values. They are described as separable categories in order to posit a simple relation in which one serves as stable counterpoint to the other. The various ways values enter into the production of value are then lost. Thus, what are lost in this narration are the power and complexity of domination. Also lost, consequently, are various points for intervention in the chain of value and of potential struggle over the "conditions of postmodernity." We cannot see the ways the structure of the secular in the United States is overdetermined in favor of the Protestant. This overdetermination, while crucial to the contemporary success of the right, is not, however, determination.

Secularism itself is obviously complex and contradictory. The secular does offer some possibilities for alternative articulations, but these alternatives can be enlivened only if the complexity of religion and secularism is taken into account. For example, there are, of course, others in the story of modernity—those whose lives and values are not articulated by either the dominant story of America as a

Christian nation or the story of America as a secular (Protestant) nation. In the postmodern moment, these "others" might slip the constraints of the dominant modern configuration, but the means for doing so is undercut when many parts of the political left actively participate in the progress narrative. Thus, the modern articulation of a realm called "secular" does leave some room for public articulations that are not those of the dominant configuration, but simply defending the secular will not necessarily increase the social space for such possibilities, but may rather reinforce the dominations and disciplines of market-reformed-Protestantism. In fact, in so doing, we may simply reinforce the current efforts on the right to reestablish market-reformed-Protestantism as the (singular) expression of "American" values, an effort that funds the crucial and powerful alliance between fiscal and social conservatives in the Republican Party. The effort to make the secular a site that articulates, without naming, market-reformed-Protestant "values" is an effort to erase potential differences. Thus, making market-reformed-Protestant "values" the quintessentially "American" values is to make them the publicly acceptable articulation of all "religions" and of the "secular." Moreover, sites that are predominantly religious but that are religious in a "different" way may also be important sites for developing such alternatives. Thus, the assumptions enacted by much "lesbian and gay" and even "queer" politics that religious sites are always necessarily "homophobic" or at least more homophobic than the dominant culture can lead to a disregard for important connections among various "others" who have traveled through those spaces named by "modernity" or "postmodernity." The challenge of postmodernity, then, is not simply to defend progress against the resurgence of religion. The challenge of specifically queer politics is not to fight a domination that is solely in the service of exploitation. Rather, on both counts we must reengage the question of values in a way that challenges both those who wish to reassert an expressly Christian understanding of America and those for whom progress means the not expressly, but nonetheless effectively, Christian values of a market-reformed-Protestantism.

Notes

I would like to thank my colleagues in the fall 1996 Culture and the Market seminar at the Center for the Humanities at Wesleyan University, particularly the director of the center, Elizabeth Traube, and Christina Crosby, Walter Johnson, and M. Grazia Lolla. I would also like to thank Miranda Joseph for numerous conversations.

1. Throughout this chapter, when referring to "the right," I mean specifically the "Christian-identified radical right."

2. I would suggest, however, that this type of naturalization is extremely common in relation to religion. Two of the major problems in the study of religion are such a naturalization, in which the appeal to religion apparently explains everything, and the opposite move, in which religion is regarded simply as epiphenomenal. In this second case, the reference to religion explains absolutely nothing. It doesn't tell us, for example, why the "religious right" should be so empowered at this particular historical moment as to be able to promote successfully various forms of body regulation legitimated by the discourse of "family values" and materialized through legislation like the Defense of Marriage Act and the welfare "reform" bill. These problems appear within as well as outside those fields that are explicitly dedicated to the study of religion. For example, Henry Abelove's (1990) historical study of John Wesley shows this problem in the study of religion with a critical reading of earlier studies of Wesley that naturalize the attraction of his followers.

3. For more specifically on the question of "hate" in relation to "family values," see Jakobsen (forthcoming).

4. The argument is that in the U.S. context the Catholic Church must subordinate its transnationality to act as another (disestablished, i.e., Protestant) denomination in the United States. Some of this argument on denominationalization can be found in Katie Cannon's (1995) reading in *Katie's Canon: Womanism and the Soul of the Black Community* of the work of mid-twentieth-century social theorist Oliver C. Cox. Certainly the questioning of Kennedy during the election about his Catholicism had precisely this quality when he was asked questions to the effect of, "Would you be loyal to the pope or to America first?"

5. See Jakobsen (1998a).

6. By "reinvention" I mean a new articulation built out of those materials that Jameson, dependent on Catherine Hall, recognizes as articulated, "only provisionally, for a 'historically specific moment,' before entering into new combinations, being systematically worked over into something else, decaying over time in interminable half-life, or being blasted apart by the convulsions of a new social crisis" (Jameson 1995, 269).

7. Obviously, Pierre Bourdieu's reading of "cultural capital" as extended by John Guillory (1993) is important here. I turn to Spivak's text because she raises the question of the relation between exploitation and domination directly.

8. Guillory's story shows some tensions with the Weberian story, some of which turns on how one understands terms like "the church" and "ecclesiastical authority." For

example, in the last chapter of *Cultural Capital*, Guillory states, quoting Pierre Bourdieu's "The Market of Symbolic Goods,"

During the period when the cultural production "progressively freed itself from aristocratic and
ecclesiastical tutelage" it began to be represented as an autonomous field of production ("Mar-
ket," 15). The nature of that autonomy was obviously "relative" . . . [such that the relation-
ship between producers and consumers is now mediated more by the market than by the
church], a mediation that was capable of being experienced as a relative measure of freedom
from direct determination of artistic forms or contents. (1993, 328)

Guillory's point about a relative freedom from direct control of artistic production is an
important one, yet it is also important to note that for Weber the Reformation brought
about a shift in the location of church control, such that one may experience freedom
from "ecclesiastical tutelage," and yet specifically religious authority (in its Protestant
form) is experienced through the market. In other words, Guillory locates religious authority in the church, whereas Weber locates *reformed* religious authority in relation to
the market:

The emancipation from economic traditionalism appears, no doubt, to be a factor which would
greatly strengthen the tendency to doubt the sanctity of the religious tradition, as of all tradi-
tional authorities. But it is necessary to note, what has often been forgotten, that the Refor-
mation meant not the elimination of the Church's control over everyday life, but rather the sub-
stitution of a new form of control for the previous one. It meant the repudiation of a control
which was very lax, at that time scarcely perceptible in practice and hardly more than formal,
in favour of a regulation of the whole conduct which, penetrating to all departments of private
and public life, was infinitely burdensome and earnestly enforced. (1930, 36)

The moment of repudiation—the secular market repudiates ecclesiastical authority—
can simultaneously allow the continuation of much of that which is repudiated, often
under the very name of its repudiation—so religious authority can be continued under
the name of "freedom."

9. There has been extensive debate within religious studies over the relationship between "religious resurgence" or "fundamentalism" and modernity/postmodernity.
Some, like Nancy Ammerman (1987), have argued that fundamentalism is an antimodern reaction, where the premodern roots of religion are used as a base for resistance to modernity. Beverly Harrison (public comments, American Academy of Religion
annual meeting, 1993) has argued that fundamentalism is quintessentially modern and
its current "resurgence" is not the return of the pre- or antimodern, but the intensification of the modern under the conditions of postmodernity. Harrison's explanation

has the advantage of taking into account why the family structure advocated within family values is certainly not premodern, but is, in fact, a recent form. Both explanations, however, position religion as the site of some form of stasis or stability—either premodern or modern—in relation to the movement of time or social structure. I wonder if we too easily accept the discourse of the right that family values are about "going back" to a particular family structure.

10. Harvey's story establishes an essentially negative relationship between economic shifts and the "return" of "stable" values in relation to "basic" institutions (1990, 172), as if either the institutions he names or the values they institutionalize are stable. It is not, however, clear that all these sites and their "authority" have been resurgent in the same way. If anything, in the United States, the "authority" invested in the state has diminished, as antigovernment discourses are on the rise, while the majority of people become disarticulated from even the most basic forms of democratic participation, including the electoral process. Note also how Harvey's story mirrors the secularization story told about religion generally. In the turn to modernity, religion vanishes, then in the turn to postmodernity, religion simply reappears as the site of "stable" values, as if these values were somehow stable and coherent both within themselves and over time. The parallel between these two stories shows that Harvey is not alone in configuring "religion" as an essentially premodern phenomenon that simply returns (as the repressed?) in order to stabilize the essentially unstable move to postmodern flexibility.

11. If the marriage metaphor is in any way indicative, "America" in its newly disempowered relationship to capital is also in an extremely feminized position, of having to look good and manage the home while the husband is away on business (in the hope that he may someday return?), which could account in part for contemporary anxieties, if not phobias, around masculinity, U.S. borders, and penetration.

12. Here is how Harvey describes the transition to post-Fordism with regard to the nation-state:

Arenas of conflict between the nation state and trans-national capital have, however, opened up, undermining the easy accommodation between big capital and big government so typical of the Fordist era. The state is now in a much more problematic position. It is called upon to regulate the activities of corporate capital in the national interest at the same time as it is forced, also in the national interest, to create a "good business climate" to act as an inducement to trans-national and global finance capital, and to deter (by means other than exchange controls) capital flight to greener and more profitable pastures. (1990, 170)

13. We need to consider domination and exploitation as separate, because if we understand them in conflated terms we maintain the "continuist" error in our reading of the chain of value. A politics resistant to domination is concerned with the implications of normative power relations, with the question of how norms (and, in Spivak's example from literary study, how the canon based on those norms) are formed and operate in relation to systems of power frequently called normativity. How, for example, does normativity (and the power relations it inscribes) produce not only a canon, but an abject excluded from, but always also inscribed within, the canon? Spivak points out, however, that in order to understand the production of the subject (whether canon or human being), one must also understand the operation of exploitation and the predication of the subject in relation to value in such a way as to recognize that "if the subject has a 'materialist' predication, the question of value necessarily receives a textualized answer" (1988a, 155).

14. Spivak asks us to think domination and exploitation in relation to the international division of labor in particular, a point that can be connected to Katie Cannon's (1995) reminder via Oliver C. Cox's to think of the relations among church, state, economy, and racism in terms of Christianity as a missionary religion dedicated to expansion.

15. And possibly these families are themselves "flexible" rather than "stable." The imperative of "family values" doesn't seem to be, for white men at least, that you're supposed to get married and stay married. If that were the case, then it would matter that almost all the congressional proponents of "family values" have been married more than once. The imperative to (re)produce that Henry Abelove (Parker et al. 1992) speculates is tied to the shift in industrial production is also, it seems, being reworked through contestation in the contemporary shifts in production. The acceptance of birth control, for example, has become widespread such that even the pope advocates "natural" family planning. The current capitalist imperative is both to monogamy and to what Jeff Nunokawa (1996) in his reading of Oscar Wilde and *The Picture of Dorian Gray* has called "the importance of being bored," of needing to move on.

16. For more on the relationship between domination and ethics, specifically between domination and the "communicative rationality" argued for by Habermas, see Jakobsen (1995).

17. For more on the effectiveness of irrationality in maintaining hegemony, see Jakobsen (1998b).

18. The most obvious point of this ambivalence is the one with which Gayatri Spivak (1988b, 272) begins "Can the Subaltern Speak?" where she criticizes Foucault's concept of "subjugated knowledges" that can "speak for themselves," as articulated in conversation with Gilles Deleuze. This conversation is published as Foucault (1977). Foucault's ethical turn near the end of his life also provides rich material for considering the complexities of resistance and the engagement with values. See the new collection under the rubric of "ethics" in Foucault (1997).

References

Abelove, Henry. 1990. *The Evangelist of Desire: John Wesley and the Methodists*. Stanford: Stanford University Press.

Ammerman, Nancy. 1987. *Bible Believers: Fundamentalists in the Modern World*. New Brunswick: Rutgers University Press.

Baird, Robert. Forthcoming. *Inventing Religion in the Western Imaginary*. Princeton: Princeton University Press.

Bourdieu, Pierre. 1984. *Distinction: A Social Critique of the Judgement of Taste*. Cambridge: Harvard University Press.

Butler, Judith. 1993. *Bodies That Matter: On the Discursive Limits of "Sex."* New York: Routledge.

Cannon, Katie Geneva. 1995. *Katie's Canon: Womanism and the Soul of the Black Community*. New York: Continuum.

Foucault, Michel. 1977. "Intellectuals and Power: A Conversation between Michel Foucault and Gilles Deleuze." In *Language, Counter-Memory, Practice: Selected Essays and Interviews*. Trans. Donald F. Bouchard and Sherry Simon, 205–17. Ithaca: Cornell University Press.

———. 1997. *Ethics: Subjectivity and Truth*. Ed. Paul Rabinow, trans. Robert Hurley. New York: New Press.

Guillory, John. 1993. *Cultural Capital: The Problem of Literary Canon Formation*. Chicago: University of Chicago Press.

Harvey, David. 1990. *The Condition of Postmodernity*. Cambridge, MA: Blackwell.

Hunter, James Davison. 1991. *Culture Wars: The Struggle to Define America*. New York: Basic Books.

Jakobsen, Janet R. 1995. "Deconstructing the Paradox of Modernity: Feminism, Enlightenment, and Cross-Cultural Moral Interactions." *Journal of Religious Ethics* 23.2 (fall): 333–63.

———. 1998a. "Why Sexual Regulation? Family Values and Social Movements." In *Religion and Sex in American Public Life*, ed. Kathleen Sands. Cambridge, MA: Oxford University Press.

———. 1998b. "Queer Is? Queer Does? Normativity and Resistance." *GLQ: A Journal of Lesbian and Gay Studies* 4.4.

———. Forthcoming. "Family Values and Working Alliances: The Production of Hate as Public Policy." In *Troubling the Welfare Waters: Some Feminist Perspectives on Welfare Policy*, ed. Elizabeth Bounds, Pamela Brubaker, and Mary Hobgood. New York: Pilgrim Press.

Jameson, Fredric. 1995. "On Cultural Studies." In *The Identity in Question*, ed. John Rajchman, 251–95. Routledge: New York.

Nunokawa, Jeff. 1996. "The Importance of Being Bored: The Dividends of Ennui in *The Picture of Dorian Gray*." *Studies in the Novel* 28.3 (fall): 357–72.

Parker, Andrew, et al. 1992. *Nationalisms and Sexualities*. New York: Routledge.

Poovey, Mary. 1995. *Making a Social Body: British Cultural Formation, 1830–1864*. Chicago: University of Chicago Press.

Spivak, Gayatri. 1988a. "Scattered Speculations on the Question of Value." In *In Other Worlds: Essays in Cultural Politics*, 154–75. New York: Methuen.

———. 1988b. "Can the Subaltern Speak?" In *Marxism and the Interpretation of Culture*, ed. Cary Nelson and Lawrence Grossberg. Urbana: University of Illinois Press.

Weber, Max. 1930. *The Protestant Ethic and the Spirit of Capitalism*. Trans. Talcott Parsons. New York: Scribners.

The Discourse of Global/Localization

Miranda Joseph

In a talk presented at the CLAGS conference on Homo Economics and now published in *A Queer World,* Michael Piore argues that since the 1970s capitalism has become much more tolerant of diversity. He notes that there are more and more businesses catering to the gay market and he claims that "we are developing an entrepreneurial class, a capitalist class of our own." He says that "It is hardly in the interest of these businesses to assimilate to the dominant culture," and that "our" capitalist class "has an interest in preserving a distinctive gay culture and niche markets" (505). Piore attributes this increased tolerance to a transformation in the organization of capitalism, from mass production, which required and produced conformity, to what he elsewhere calls "flexible specialization," which can cater profitably to niche markets.

His account of a transformation in capitalism is just one version of a story we hear relentlessly these days. The transformation is narrated in popular and business media as the emergence of "globalization" and "flexibility."[1] In the academy, it is recounted as a transition to post-Fordism or flexible specialization or flexible accumulation or disorganized capital.[2] The popular media cast globalization as inevitable progress, as the post-Soviet world triumph of capitalism; Merrill Lynch advertisements, for instance, claim, "the world is 10 years old," thus dating the birth of the world to the fall of the Berlin Wall. The academic story, only somewhat less triumphalist, is that at some point in the late 1960s/early 1970s the world economy based on Keynesian strategies of national economic management and Fordist modes of mass production and consumption went into crisis. In response to this crisis, the story goes, capitalism has had to innovate by undoing the rigidities of national economic regulation and mass production. Globalization is one response, while a reemergence of local or regional economic development and governmentality is the other. (The terms "local" and "regional" sometimes have to do with *place*, the particular town or "industrial district," but often metamorphose into connoting social *spaces* that do not correlate with place—kinship, ethnicity, culture, or community.) The general implication is that capital is and should be aligning itself with a more organic or authentic set of social formations—formations posited in opposition to the nation, the site of the old Fordist organization of production. Whether or not we like capitalism, the notion that it now addresses us in our diversity and particularity is quite seductive.

For popular promoters of capitalism, who are concerned not with the emancipation of oppressed groups but rather simply with the health of capitalism, this global/local rescaling is a movement toward a more thoroughly free market. In Kenichi Ohmae's formulation, "regionalism" rationalizes the global flow of capital, liberating it from national constraints—which consist of protectionism and other irrational economic behaviors provoked by the conflictual diversity within nations—allowing it instead to accommodate (and take advantage of) the variety of local circumstances.[3] In the new "borderless" world, the unequal economic participation of diverse (internally harmonious) regions and localities will be guided by a global invisible hand that will lift the boat for all. Meanwhile globalization is seen as freeing individuals from the constraints of local culture to pursue the best jobs and commodities (Ohmae; Stanley).

The global/local rescaling is valued as well, however, by those whose claimed interest is the emancipation of oppressed groups. While noting class-based limitations on its liberatory reach, Piore claims that capitalism is now directly emancipatory of "diverse cultures." (And as Avery Gordon's discussion of the business school and consulting literature on diversity management reveals, this view is enthusiastically proclaimed within corporate culture itself.) Alain Lipietz and Margit Mayer, in articles in *Post-Fordism: A Reader*, suggest that localized economic development implies an increase in local power and autonomy and that this is good because the local is a more democratic space than larger social units.[4]

72

Left cultural studies scholars tend to offer a more dialectical account; Lowe and Lloyd, for instance, state, "Our interest is not in identifying what lies 'outside' of capitalism, but in what arises historically, in contestation, and 'in difference' to it" (2). But they also claim that this new version of capital produces an excess, enabling an elaboration of diverse cultures of resistance to or difference from capitalism. Lowe and Lloyd contend

that transnational or neo-colonial *capitalism, like colonialist capitalism before it, continues to produce sites of contradiction that are effects of its always uneven expansion but that cannot be subsumed by the logic of commodification. We suggest that "culture" obtains a "political" force when culture comes into contradiction with economic or political logics that try to refunction it for exploitation or domination. (1)*

While they might seem here to suggest a greater continuity between contemporary globalized capitalism and previous forms of capitalism than the other scholars I have cited, their claim that relatively autonomous sites of contradiction "have the potential to rework the conception of politics in the era of transnational capital" (2) depends on "a recognition of the heterogeneity of the contemporary capitalist mode of production" (2–3). The strategy of resistance through cultural heterogeneity is portrayed as an improvement in the mode of resistance, surpassing an impossible and homogenizing class-based opposition to capital (2).[5]

In all these cases, the moment of political optimism depends on and affirms some version of the narrative of a transformation in the nature of capital. And it is on this point that I want to offer a caution. While I don't doubt that capital's penetration and saturation of the globe are both more extensive and intensive, or that corporations use innovative as well as tried and true strategies to promote that extension and intensification, the crucial change as I see it is in the story capitalism is telling about itself, or rather in capital as a story, a discourse. And so I want to explore the implications of this narrative of transformation. What social formations are being promoted, legitimated, naturalized through this story? Is this a story the left should really want to promote? To what extent does our elaboration of optimistic implications leave in place or even reaffirm a set of very troubling implications? While the power of the texts I address to produce the social structures they name varies dramatically, I think they are all symptomatic of a pervasive discourse, its saturation demonstrated not only by the almost daily *New York Times* articles that describe the various features of the new world economy but also by the fact that progressive cultural studies critics often simply take the narrative to be true and work from there.

My critique of this discourse has been substantially inspired and informed by recent articles by J. K. Gibson-Graham and David Harvey that have called for critical analyses of the discourse of globalization. Gibson-Graham argues that the universal acceptance of a narrative of "globalization" as a new, rapid, and inevitable transformation toward a telos of the total global penetration of capital operates as a "regulatory fiction" (2). Harvey rightly points out that capital has always operated globally: "In my more cynical moments I find myself thinking that it was the financial press that conned us all (myself included) into believing in 'globalization' as something new when it was nothing more than a promotional gimmick to make the best of a necessary adjustment in the system of international finance" ("Globalization," 8). He argues that we have to view the advent of the term "globalization" as having particular political purposes and effects, especially that of deterring local and national working-class and political movements ("Globalization," 1).

Harvey and Gibson-Graham attempt to disrupt the proclaimed totality and inevitability of globalization by disrupting the narrative. They propose to analytically break apart the capitalist monolith, with its supposedly homogenizing effects, thereby opening the space in which to imagine and thus potentially enact various resistances. Harvey suggests a shift in terminology from globalization to "a process of production of uneven temporal and geographic development" ("Globalization," 8).[6] And certainly there is much ground for contesting the accuracy of a narrative of a totalizing and homogenizing global capital. In the economic and geographic literature there is great debate over the extent to which Fordist mass production was ever hegemonic and the extent to which it has actually broken down now; many argue that Fordist productive regimes have simply been displaced from more to less developed economic locations. It would be more appropriate to talk about capitalisms than capitalism. But the recognition of the global diversity of capitalism is not, I think, quite as optimistic a discovery as Harvey and Gibson-Graham would seem to suggest. If, as Brenner and Dirlik (who both draw on Lefebvre's work) argue, globalization and localization (fragmentation) are corollary symptoms of the same process of capitalist evolution, then this local heterogeneity does not necessarily imply resistance to globalization, at least not based on externality to globalization either in the form of authentic original otherness or excess.[7]

While Harvey and Gibson-Graham usefully contest the notion that globalization is actually totalizing and homogenizing, as Lowe and Lloyd point out, many critiques do assume that globalization implies a production of equivalence and homogeneity, the McDonaldization of the globe (1). Such critics reiterate a Romantic critique of capitalism, which would find resistance and emancipation in the communal.[8] And many resort to a romanticized view of the liberal nation-state, as though in the face of globalization out-of-control, the nation could act as the preserver simultaneously of communal history and of democratic agency.[9] In contrast, the global/localization discourse is striking because at first glance it seems to acknowledge the crucial role of particular communities for capitalism. In fact, the focus in these narratives on the interdependence of capital and culture (or community or kinship) at first seemed to me a congenial insight. Making this interdependence of culture and capital explicit has also been a central project of left cultural studies and of my own work.

However, the particular role of the local and communal in the discourse of economic transformation is not unproblematic. Even among many of those who recognize that globalization actually depends on localization, or in Storper's terms, that deterritorialization is paired with territorialization, localization is seen as the silver lining of the current transformation. Part of the seductiveness of the global/localization story (by contrast with the globalization as totalizing story) is that it seems such a precise answer to the yearning for community produced in the Romantic narrative. But it is too perfect an answer; it reiterates the very terms of the Romantic discourse of community. In a blatant disavowal of the transformation process it describes, most popular iterations constitute community as autonomous from capitalism and modernity.

The narrated discovery of the local and communal by capitalism serves, I will argue, to legitimate hierarchies within and among cultures, localities, and communities. The discursive technology of this legitimation, this naturalizing articulation of hierarchical social formations, is an ongoing interplay of binary narratives of exclusion and analogic narratives of inclusion. The current economic transformation involves a particular emphasis on analogy. To contest this analogic strategy, we need not narratives of heterogeneity, but rather ones of supplementarity; difference is already accounted for by capitalism; it is the complicity, the relationships, among localities and between local and global that we must articulate if we are to work the points of weakness, of contradiction and crisis, within capital.

Michael Piore is primarily known not for his contributions to lesbian/gay studies but as the author, with Charles Sabel, of *The Second Industrial Divide*, one of the most influential accounts of the current economic transformation. In that text,

Piore does not articulate flexible specialization as opening spaces for diverse sub-cultural niche markets associated with progressive social change as he did in his CLAGS talk. Rather, the spaces within which prosperity might be created are (actual or fictive) kinship-based communities. This text has been roundly criticized on a number of fronts—for its technological determinism, for its reductive characterization and differentiation of historical periods, for lumping together very different regional economic formations, and for its overly optimistic assessment of industrial districts as a means for local or regional economic development.[10] I take it up not to reiterate these criticisms per se, but rather because it is elaborately symptomatic of the discourse of community that structures much of the optimistic literature on post-Fordism and globalization across the political spectrum.

Piore and Sabel make two moves in this book. The first is to claim that at this historical moment, due to a crisis in capital, there is an opportunity for a form of production they call flexible specialization to supersede mass production, which they claim has been dominant since the nineteenth century, when it superseded an earlier version of flexible specialization. Their second claim is that flexible specialization is politically and socially preferable to mass production precisely because it depends on and facilitates communal, local, regional economic development.

In flexible specialization, workers with flexible craft skills use general-purpose machines to produce small batches of diverse products; this is contrasted with mass production, in which deskilled workers deploy specialized machines to produce long runs of one commodity. Flexible specialization and the production of diverse short runs of products require not only skilled workers but a high degree of cooperation among firms, between suppliers and producers and distributors. Further, the success of such firms often requires what Piore and Sabel call self-exploitation. They argue that the extra-economic communal ties that they presume can be found in the regional specificities of kinship, ethnicity, culture, and history will promote the necessary skill sharing, cooperation among firms, and voluntary contributions to the common project of economic growth. While other narrators of the post-crisis transformation of capital offer alternative causal accounts, the notion that capitalism is now more dependent on extra-economic cultural values and relationships is quite typical. Nigel Thrift, for instance, attributes this increased dependence on personal relationships to the increased quantity and anonymity of information flowing across the globe, information that must be sorted and interpreted.

Francis Fukuyama—author of *The End of History and the Last Man*—likewise, in a new book, *Trust*, argues that kinship ideology, as the key to trust, is crucial to the success or failure of various nations and regions within globalizing capital:

If the ["modern"] institutions of democracy and capitalism are to work properly, they must coexist with certain premodern cultural habits that ensure their proper functioning. Law, contract, and economic rationality must . . . be leavened with reciprocity, moral obligation, duty toward community, and trust, which are based in habit[s, customs, and ethics] rather than calculation. (11, [5])

Liberal political and economic institutions depend on a healthy and dynamic civil society for their vitality. "Civil society" . . . builds, in turn, on the family, the primary instrument by which people are socialized (4–5).

Fukuyama distinguishes between low trust societies (China, France, Italy, South Korea), in which he suggests that literal kinship is overvalued and thus it is difficult for people to engage in trusting business relations on a global scale, and high trust societies (Japan and Germany), in which the family instills values that allow trust beyond the literal family and thus allow easier participation in global capital. (The United States is a problem case for him—not categorizable as either high or low—because of a failure of family to socialize people at all.) It is notable that he describes nation-states as "societies," to which he then attributes the features of "culture," that is to say a common set of values, practices, history. This reimagination of the nation as a culture rather than as a political-economic administrative entity is the opening move of Robert B. Reich's book *The Work of Nations* as well.

The notion that the intimate relationship between community (or kinship or culture) and capital is or should be *new* implies that there is some prior autonomy of those spheres. The Romantic story relied on a historical discontinuity between the era of community and the era of society to establish the autonomy of community; the narrative of a reconciliation between community and society presupposes this autonomy and reproduces it. In the articulation of a historical break between Fordism and post-Fordism, the cultural communities and localities with which capital interacts are hypostatized—our production of our social formations through our participation in production and consumption is erased; both capitalism and social formations appear inevitable. Appadurai calls this phenomenon "production fetishism," "an illusion created by contemporary transnational production loci, which masks translocal capital, transnational earning-flows, global management and often faraway workers . . . in the idiom and spectacle of local (sometimes even worker) control, national productivity and territorial sovereignty" (16).

The first contact between capitalism and culture implied by the suggestion that global/localization is new elides the effects of the first contact narratives articulated in the anthropology of colonialism, even as it builds on those effects and redeploys its discursive techniques. That anthropology treated its objects of study—"primitive" cultures—as timeless, as outside the progressive history of the West, but also suggested that they could/must join history through a process of modernization, through the salutary, if simultaneously destructive, effects of colonization. As Johannes Fabian argues, "it promoted a scheme in terms of which not only past cultures but all living societies were irrevocably placed on a temporal slope, a stream of Time—some upstream, others downstream" (17). Each "primitive culture" contacted by the more civilized West would begin its own history, moving independently across a common trajectory of development. Each culture would be at a different stage of the process but its course would be analogous to that of others.

Likewise, global/localization discourse builds upon and elides, while reiterating, postwar development discourse. As Neil Smith argues, "the language of globalization that has captured the public imagination since the late 1980s heralds some important shifts in world political economy, but . . . also represents a trenchant continuity with previous processes and patterns of uneven development" (170).

The development discourse aimed at the Third World between the 1940s and the 1970s found the causes of underdevelopment in the Third World nations themselves, rather than in their wider political, economic, and cultural relations with the rest of the world. Specifically, the lack of development in Third World countries was variously attributed to inadequate technology, cultural backwardness, and inappropriate and inefficient political and economic institutions. The solution, the road to development, was to be found in modernization. . . . Modernization theory . . . argued that all modern industrial societies had undergone an established sequence of stages. . . . the development of Third World economies means learning lessons from the advanced industrial economies and following their lead. (170–72)

Kenichi Ohmae, for instance, argues in *The End of the Nation State* that regions, defined as units that are internally coherent and analogous with each other based on per capita GNP, will follow "a fairly predictable trajectory along which priorities shift as economic areas move through successive phases of development" (21). "This notional GNP ladder does apply across dividing lines defined by culture, to all developing economies. . . . The pull of the global economy, coupled with a growing ability to use that connection to move up along the ladder's various stages, is universal—and universally attractive" (24). The ladder applies across cultures, but culture does seem to correlate with the stage of a particular region on the ladder. This correlation, not explained by Ohmae, can only be explained with an account of temporal and spatial continuities. But as Smith implies, the claimed newness of globalization elides the continuities of time: the unequal state of development of various regions is naturalized in cultural difference rather than being seen as a product of the history of colonialism or "development" projects. The deployment of analogy supplements this temporal discontinuity with a spatial discontinuity; in the articulation of a proliferating series of comparable social formations, a kind of global pluralism, the global/localization discourse renders each location independent of every other one rather than a product of its interactions with other locations.

Piore and Sabel analogize their vision of local/communal economic development with historical industrial districts organized through a guild structure and with craft unions in the construction trades, where entry into the union is quite difficult and often based on ethnicity or kinship, but once accepted, the worker has a great deal of job security, jobs being distributed through a collaboration between unions and firms. Likewise they idealize the Jewish- and Italian-dominated garment industry of the early twentieth century in New York. They offer as key contemporary analogues the networks of family firms in the textile-producing areas of Italy and the Japanese zaibatsu, federations of family firms (like the Korean chaebols and Indonesian "cronies" we have heard so much about recently), but also the Japanese kanban just-in-time inventory system, which ties a select group of subcontracting firms to a multinational corporation in a system of outsourcing tightly controlled by the multinational. Though industrial agglomerations run by multinationals might at first seem quite different from networks of family firms, Piore and Sabel explicitly analogize these outsourcing arrangements with familial or ethnic groups in the structures of authority, allegiance, and exclusion through which they are organized. The biggest stretch for them is to include the regions based on new high-tech industries such as Silicon Valley, but again they manage to make the analogy by focusing on the collaborative relations between firms and universities and among the entrepreneurs who went to school together. The rearticulation of nations as cultures in Fukuyama's and Reich's work would seem to make the nation yet another social formation potentially analogous to localities, regions, and identity-based niches, that is, yet another in the series of sites that might be exploited by capitalism, without having regulatory power over capitalism.

Analogy has also been a central feature of Fordist discourse, in the form of the liberal pluralism of the nation-state. The deployment of analogy in the context of global/localization discourse is in many ways continuous with its deployment in the context of the nation-state—in fact, liberal pluralism helped to constitute the communities now exploited by post-Fordist capitalism—however, the global/localization discourse explicitly excludes the nation as the mediator between capital and social formations. The liberal pluralist deployment of analogy, that is, its deployment in the context of contemporary identity political civil rights movements in the United States, has been extensively critiqued; I will start by reviewing some of those critiques as I think they are useful in thinking about global/localization discourse as well.

As Janet Jakobsen has pointed out, analogy can function as a powerful political tool by which, as Laclau and Mouffe argue in *Hegemony and Socialist Strategy*, the articulation of equivalence among social struggles makes those struggles recognizable on the mainstream political landscape, and potentially allies for each other. However, Jakobsen argues, analogy also separates such movements and elides their connections with each other.[11] In "Scattered Speculations on the Question of Value," Spivak critiques Goux's analogy between the idealist predication of the subject (the subject of consciousness) and the materialist predication of the subject (the subject of labor power). She points out that the use of analogy renders these two modes of determination independent of each other (as "exclusive predications," 154) and complete unto themselves (each is posited as an internal continuity). It thus "excludes the fields of force that make [each of] them heterogeneous, indeed discontinuous." And "it is to exclude those relationships between the[m] that are attributive and supportive and not analogical" (156). It is precisely this presupposition of internal continuity and external discreteness that makes analogy problematic both in the context of contemporary social movements and in the global/localization discourse.

In "The Ethics of Analogy," Amy Robinson takes up the common deployment of an analogy between race and sexuality. She points out that the use of the analogy "segregates race and sexuality as objects of analytic and political attention," and "presumes the normative whiteness of the gay subject." Similarly, in "Against

Proper Objects," Judith Butler analyzes the use of an analogy between feminist studies and lesbian/gay studies in the introduction to the *Lesbian and Gay Studies Reader*. Butler argues that the analogy between the two is deployed there in order to establish lesbian/gay studies as an autonomous field; the introduction to the *Reader* asserts that the proper object of G/L studies is sexuality, while the proper object of feminist studies is gender. It thus suggests that sexuality and gender are discrete objects. As Butler points out, this account of feminist scholarship is certainly a slight to the extensive work on sexuality that has been done under the rubric of feminism, even while it would seem to suggest that sexual difference is not a crucial issue for the study of sexuality. Simultaneously, the analogy constitutes women's studies and LGB studies, falsely, as each internally continuous, to use Spivak's term, as somehow complete in itself, which it cannot be if, as Gayle Rubin and so many others have argued, gender and sexuality operate as a sex/gender system, which is itself imbricated in an array of complex social processes.

The analogy articulated among various sites of production and consumption in the global/localization discourse posits those sites as autonomous (excludes the relations between them). Thus when companies assess the advantage of moving factories from the United States to Mexico or Indonesia, where labor is cheaper, the use of analogics naturalizes the differences between labor costs here and there. As Ricardo naturalized differences of national wealth in soil quality, differences in wage rates are now situated in cultural differences (their wage is to their culture as our wage is to our culture). The capitalist process by which Mexican workers are differentiated from U.S. workers is erased in the articulation of a new era of globalization that would seem to discover anew these sites of production and consumption as if they had emerged as different through some authentic and autonomous (internally continuous) cultural process.

The internal continuity presupposed by analogy in the global/localization discourse is guaranteed by explicit recourse to "natural" extra-economic ties of community and kinship. For instance, while Piore and Sabel do acknowledge that communality and kinship are often authoritarian and hierarchical, they claim that family-based community operates as a social safety net because members of a community will not allow others to fall completely out of the community. They are quite clear that the production of exclusion is as important to their communal regionalism as inclusion—they acknowledge that such a safety net can extend only to those who are already members of the community or the system would not work at all—but for community members they suggest a kind of trickle-down theory: the economic prosperity produced through a regime of flexible accumulation should mitigate the social hierarchies that these kinship or culture-defined regions entail.

There is, however, a large body of scholarship that suggests that kinship relations actually define and elaborate economic hierarchies. In her ethnographic study of Italian family firms, Sylvia Yanagisako argues that the ideologies of kinship organizing the ownership and management of the firms as well as the transmission of wealth across generations are complex hierarchies and processes that punish as well as protect various members of the kin network. Piore and Sabel's "self-exploitation" often turns out to mean the exploitation of women and children. And kinship ties among firm owners position as labor those who are not members of the kin group but rather immigrants from southern Italy. Regional or local kinship networks and communities establish not one community of common welfare but rather the boundaries between classes, races, and nations.

Not only are the hierarchies within localities not necessarily mitigated by economic development, but the legitimating naturalness attributed to those hierarchies is rather doubtful as well. Scott and Storper point out that the development of high-tech industries in particular regions has depended on the availability of a highly polarized and nonunionized workforce of highly trained engineers on the one hand, and on the other, impoverished new immigrants. As Saskia Sassen argues in *The Mobility of Labor and Capital*, the "availability" of communities of immigrant labor is produced by the pushing of labor out of its previous locations by new investments of capital in some regions and the pull of work opportunities in others. Likewise, Melissa Wright argues that the discursive production of Mexican femininity by maquiladora owners differentiates women as "untrainable," disposable workers whose declining value as variable capital is opposed to Mexican men, who are constructed as trainable and therefore of increasing value. Wright cites one maquila manager as saying, "It's a cultural thing down here." This discursive differentiation is used to legitimate not only the high turnover rates of women in the factories—women who are employed in the lowest-paying, least skilled, most physically draining and destructive work, women who are used up in their work and are ultimately seen by the managers as waste—but also the extraordinary rash of murders of these women. The women are said to be killed because they are not "good girls" and have thus exposed themselves to the "macho" behavior that is to be expected of Mexican men; the women are rendered as murdered by their own culture. The deployment of "culture," analogically constituted as autonomous in time and space, elides the fact that both the patriarchal binary gender construction and the violations of "good-girl" norms by young women are incited by the presence of the maquilas.

The use of kinship and race to naturalize localities is remarkable because kinship has previously been used primarily to naturalize national formations. Adam Smith and David Ricardo articulated the nation as a social body, and thus an organic, natural unit of wealth. Within such social bodies various participants were said to have various roles to play, roles that were articulated and legitimated precisely by kinship. In *Wealth of Nations* Smith is quite clear about the necessity of what he calls "the distinction of ranks," or sometimes "race," to "the peace and order of society" and thus to economic prosperity. In *The Theory of Moral Sentiments*, he says he sees such distinctions as wisely, naturally, based on birth and fortune rather than wisdom and virtue, the one being easy to see, the other more difficult for the "undistinguishing eyes of the great mob of mankind" to perceive (*Theory*, 226). He argues that our natural respect for wealth and power and our natural distaste but also compassion for poverty and wretchedness serve to maintain this stability, as does our natural desire to maintain at least the existing powers and privileges of our particular subsegment of society (*Theory*, 226, 230). He offers a similarly sentimental account of the coincidence of economy with nation, claiming that we naturally care most about those nearest and dearest, beginning with ourselves, extending to our families and immediate face-to-face communities and then by analogy to those we can imagine as like ourselves. He suggests that the natural limits of our sympathy are the limits of our nation.

For Smith, capitalist productive regimes reiterate the premodern social order. In *Wealth of Nations* Smith articulates his vision of the relation between various groups within society through his theory of value. He proposes a labor theory of value, arguing that what one is willing to pay for an object is the equivalent in money of the labor it would take to produce such an object. Labor for him, however, is not, or does not remain throughout the text, primarily the physical labor of the worker who produces the object; rather, it is the labor of capitalists—who deploy "stock," land, and wage labor—to produce commodities, to whom he credits production: "Those whose capitals are employed in any of these four ways ["cultivation of land, mines, or fisheries," "master manufacturers," "wholesale merchants," "retailers" (*Wealth*, 301)] are themselves productive laborers" (*Wealth*, 303). Value "resolves itself" into the sum of rent, wages, and the profits of stock (*Wealth*, 51). "The whole annual produce of the labour of every country" is composed of rent, the profits of stock, and wages—each element distributed to one of the "three great, original and constituent orders of every civilized society" (*Wealth*, 217, see also 55); landlords must own land and collect rent, capitalists must deploy stock and collect profit, the working class must labor and collect wages. Capital and the capitalist subsume both land and labor, landlords and wage laborers, within a single self-regulating body. Differences between capitalists and wage laborers are either erased, through the abstraction of national statistics, or naturalized, the poor being seen as organs of or parasites on the national body, as nonhuman means of production, or as a distinct race with intrinsically different, and lesser, material needs.[12]

While Smith's and Ricardo's texts work to legitimate the nation as the unit of economic activity, where particular national formations have been inadequate to the task of assimilating and naturalizing the class differences that national (really colonialist) capitalism has produced, strategies of geographic/political reformulation are inevitably proposed or enacted. As David Kasanjian argues, Jefferson imagined the end of slavery as requiring the freed slaves to be exported to their own geographic and governmental space, a nation that would become a colony of the white United States. Spatial dispersal was also an economic and political strategy in the twentieth-century United States. As many urban geographers have argued, David Harvey among them, ethnic and class conflict in urban areas was dealt with through the building of suburbs. This spatial dispersal not only absorbed overaccumulation but allowed various "communities" to elaborate themselves without experiencing the direct conflicts between and within themselves.

In the global/localization discourse, localities and regions are promoted as a solution to the obstacles to capitalism presented by the nation-state. (Ohmae says that "traditional nation states have become unnatural, even impossible, business units" [5].) They are, however, described in ways that are quite similar to Smith and Ricardo's nations. Successful capital accumulation is both the goal and defining feature of a region. Ohmae's use of GNP in addition to culture to delineate the boundaries of regions reiterates the use of statistical abstraction to assimilate the interests of all to that of capital. For Sabel, Piore, and Ohmae, firms rather than labor are the producers of wealth. Class difference is acknowledged but not seen as a problem—as Ohmae explicitly argues, economic success requires that all contribute to the production of wealth, not that all share equally in its distribution (53). Social conflict that might disrupt the flow of capital will be quieted by the rising tide of economic well-being. (In making this point Ohmae specifically refers to "Southern blacks" in the United States, claiming that it was not civil rights legislation but rather the growth of the southern economy that brought them social

84

justice and economic opportunity [120].) Social difference appears only in the marketplace, as the idiosyncratic desire of individual sovereign consumers.

While kinship is a particularly important tool for naturalizing the internal continuity of the social formations necessary to capitalism, part of the power of analogics is that, it seems, they can articulate any social formation as a site of production and consumption. It is crucial in thinking about analogy to recognize that it is relationships being compared and not objects themselves, so, as Robinson points out, the SAT analogy test takes the form of A is to A's domain as X is to X's domain. As Foucault says of the use of analogy in the sixteenth century, "Its power is immense, for the similitudes of which it treats are not the visible, substantial ones between things themselves; they need only be the more subtle resemblance of relations. Disencumbered thus, it can extend, from a single given point, to an endless number of relationships" (21). That it is relations being compared is also crucial to the contemporary use of analogy in that the isolation of the objects in their own domains is key to the autonomy-effect of the deployment of analogy. In fact it is this autonomy-effect that emerges as predominant in the modern period, according to Foucault, when analogy, as the mode of relating one organic structure to another according to a similarity in the relations between the internal elements of that structure, displaces the order of visible identities and differences that characterized the classical age (218). The assimilation of domains—gays are to civil rights as African Americans are to civil rights, or Mexico is to economic development as the United States is to economic development—allows the production of a hierarchy among objects being compared.

Butler suggests that the analogic pairing of feminist studies and gay/lesbian studies, "a binary frame," excludes from consideration other relevant issues such as race and class. I think she is actually wrong here. While analogy and binary logics do work in complicity, she conflates the two much too quickly. Binary logic is a discourse of exclusion, a simple determination of us and them, a mode of self-definition by abjection. Analogics work in precisely the opposite fashion; they include, making the other known. As Robinson argues, the analogy between race and sexuality implies that race is the known term by which we come to know, make familiar, a second, unfamiliar term. It "renders the struggle for racial justice to the past"—race is figured as a "solution (not a problem) in the American landscape." And it moves the inchoate subject (gays and lesbians) to the grounds of the (supposedly) known, choate object, positions the unseemly in relation to the seemly.

The liberal nation-state has operated through the relentless sequencing of binary boundary making and cultural pluralist analogic inclusion of others, who are then subject to oppression within the state. Nayan Shah describes a shift in the early twentieth century with regard to the construction of San Francisco's Chinatown. While it was at first imagined as the site of otherness, a classed, raced, sexualized, opium-infused culture that embodied the forbidden desires of a consolidating white bourgeoisie, it was later transformed into a version of that bourgeoisie itself. The interplay of binary logic and analogy has operated in economic discourse as well. Adam Smith and David Ricardo both describe a world of national economies that are comparable to each other on the basis of their wealth, productive abilities in various industries, and soil quality. They articulate a notion of nations in competition with each other that has persisted up to the present, a notion that sets up a binary division between "us" and "other" nations. But they also initiate a comparative discourse that suggests that nations can be ranked in relation to each other and that some division of productive tasks will be to the advantage of all. While the binary logic that establishes national boundaries was a particularly prominent narrative structure in the era of Fordist nation-based mass production and consumption, in our post-Fordist era of "globalization" and niched production and consumption, analogy has emerged as the dominant narrative structure.

The impetus to renarrate formerly excluded formations as analogically includable can be accounted for by the fact that local particularity is not only complicit with abstraction within capital, but also contradictory. As Stuart Hall says, "capitalism only advances, as it were, on contradictory terrain. It is the contradictions which it has to overcome that produce its own forms of expansion" (29).

Marx's discussion of the relation between value and use value in the circulation process suggests that value (abstraction) is dependent on use value (particularity), which functions as the "material bearer" of value, and thus that use value is complicit with value. The complicity between abstraction and particularity in the global/localization context is in a sense obvious: the international flow of capital depends on an abstract equivalence (and to some extent qualitative similarities) among various sites around the globe, but it also depends on qualitative particular differences. As one does not exchange commodity A for commodity A, one does not move a production plant from site A to site A but rather moves the plant because labor in site B is cheaper, and so on.[13]

But Marx's discussion of the relation between value and use value emphasizes not only or even primarily their complicity; rather, he generally describes them as contradictory or antagonistic: "The simple form of value of the commodity is the simple form of the appearance of the opposition between use-value and value which is contained within the commodity" (vol. 1, 153). In the simple equation of two commodities (x coats = y linen), each commodity can only be either in the role of the relative form or the equivalent but not both. The relative form would seem to express only value, while the equivalent form would seem to express only use value. But in the process of exchange, a given commodity must metamorphose from its appearance as value into use value and vice versa—a thing that is not useful to its owner is sold to someone for whom it does have a use value: "The commodity itself is here subject to contradictory determinations. At the starting point it is a non–use-value to its owner; at the end it is a use value" (207). The realization of capital depends on the resolution of these opposed determinations through successful exchange. Should the joining/metamorphosis of value and use value fail, capital accumulation will fail. For instance, if useless goods are brought to market they will not be purchased; or conversely, if useful goods are not brought to market, they do not participate in the social exchange process, and they will fail to have value. Marx describes these potential failures at length in *Capital*, volume 2, where he discusses the time and space obstacles in the circuits of capital (to the circulation of capital).

The fact that value is an abstraction, that it is what is left when the concrete particularities of a commodity are subtracted, makes it appear to be mobile and dynamic, able to change its form and location at the will of the capitalist. But value can do nothing without embodiment. And this embodiment that enables its movement also weighs it down, obstructs its movement through time and space. In "The Urban Process under Capitalism," Harvey describes overaccumulation (where overaccumulation takes the form of a built environment that is no longer the most efficient environment for capitalism) as a contradiction between value and use value: buildings, transportation infrastructures, and other things that were designed to facilitate the flow of value become encumbrances to that flow and have to be devalued and/or destroyed to free the capital to be invested in new embodiments, new infrastructures (83).

The contradiction between particularity (concreteness?) and abstraction operates not only at the level of the commodity but also in more complex forms such as money and capital. The development of technologies for overcoming the obstructions presented by the necessary embodiment of capital is a history that hardly needs repeating here. Possibly the most interesting development for my purposes is the mobility of labor, which indicates that the contradiction between abstraction and particularity must be resolved for social formations as well as for the built environment.

The obstacles for capital flow presented by social formations are overcome not only through the mobility of labor but also through the discursive shift from binary exclusion to analogic inclusion. This shift is particularly clear with regard to kinship and sexuality. The story about the relationship of kinship structures to capitalism that is familiar to us from the popular culture of Fordism is that productive extended family forms have been undermined by the emergence of capitalism, replaced by a much weaker nuclear family. The Marxist version of this story suggests that capitalism freed laboring subjects from the bonds of hierarchical family structures—allowing the formation of communities that are potentially more freely chosen. This is Marx's story of the shift from feudalism to capitalism. It is also Marx's response, in volume 1 of *Capital*, to mid-nineteenth-century concerns that child labor laws were destroying male control over family members; he suggests that this transformation will lead to a "higher" form of familial relations. This account is taken up by feminists who describe the liberation of young women from their patriarchal families as they left the family farm to go work in factories.[14] And it recurs in D'Emilio's account of the formation of gay identity, which involves likewise the liberation of individuals from their kinship structures when they moved to urban centers created by/for capitalist production. D'Emilio's essay, which leans hard on Zaretsky's work, marks a return of kinship even as it describes its eclipse: Zaretsky argues that as the family was emptied of its productive role it took on instead a compensatory role as the site of reprieve from the public workplace. D'Emilio's essay would suggest this shift of production from domestic to public spheres as the moment of the creation of the ideology of "traditional family."

Zaretsky and D'Emilio account for an ideological investment in "family" as a consequence of the abstraction of production from the family and the relocation of production in the newly distinct public sphere. However, the public space of capital is not as impersonal as their accounts suggest, nor is the family the nonproductive space it appears in the ideology that Zaretsky and D'Emilio simultaneously describe and ascribe to. I would hardly be the first to suggest that kinship formations are an important site of capital: they produce variable capital, that is, labor power embodied in particular laborers;[15] they are the site at which value leaves the circulation process, allowing surplus value to be realized, through the consumption of commodities. And the bourgeois family, at least, is the site of capital formation. On the other hand, while we may think of multinational corporations as highly abstract, impersonal entities with little regard for the particularities of kinship and culture, a number of journalistic and ethnographic studies of capitalist firms large and small suggest just the reverse—that even the largest are often family businesses or businesses owned and managed by a closely knit group of people with multiplex social relationships to each other.[16] The fetishization of family—our ability to forget that our attachments to our families are economic—occurs only in very particular political/ ideological moments.

In the D'Emilio/Zaretsky narrative, the production of homosexuality through the freeing of labor seems to situate homosexuality in the public and constructed realm of capitalism, while the family would seem to represent the (ethical, religious, national) values that seem to lie outside capitalism, to be prior to it. The homo-hetero binary places the heterosexual family on the side of use value, where it operates as a fetish that—like the use value aspect of the commodity—hides its value, its role as a bearer of economic value (capital), by appearing to have an inherent value. Gays, freed from the family—like money-lending Jews—then seem to represent abstract value, abstract capital itself, and become the scapegoats in a romantic or populist anticapitalism where only the abstractness of money and the impersonal corporation are seen as evil.[17]

However, the opposition between gay identity and family that D'Emilio assumes may seem quite dated. Christians seem to have won the ideological battle over "family values" in the sense that gays have entirely given up the fight against family as an oppressive form and have instead joined it, claiming that they too enact family. And gays are addressed as a form of family in the consumer marketplace (Ikea and VW try to sell their products to bourgeois gay couples). This incorporation of gay kinship into capitalist marketing suggests an expanded notion of kinship, where the binary opposition of homo and hetero that subtended a binary opposition between capitalism/value and community/culture/values has been displaced by an analogic discourse articulating all social formations as potential sites of capitalist activity. The principal effect of rearticulating gays as family is to rearticulate the family as value rather than use value—as within rather than against capital.

As I have suggested, family plays a particularly central role in legitimating the localities to be included in capitalism. The task of promoting kinship as the legitimating basis for local and communal economic units while keeping it flexible and expansive is a delicate one, resulting in rather ambivalent and contradictory articulations in the global/localization literature. Piore and Sabel view family proper as the positive model on which the various social arrangements analogized to it should be based. The positives are the loyalty and obedience of workers who view their employers as patriarchs and an easy flow of information among related firm owners. But they also do not limit themselves to "real" families, moving by analogy to all sorts of other collectivities. Ohmae, by contrast, finds family too conservative, constraining the development of desires for a range of consumer goods, and seeks to replace it by the miscegenated kinship of a global melting pot. Crucial to his story of transformation from nationalism to a globalism mediated by regions is the freeing of the next generation of consumers from their familial bonds; the family, he says, is the site at which people are attached to their nations. He describes the experience of Japan, where a breakdown of family values has been happily brought on by capitalism. But, in order to achieve economies of scope, regions must be coherent racially and culturally—race and culture are just the things he says find their home in the family. Fukuyama wants family values but not family itself: while he posits family as the site of socialization in trust, a trust necessary to doing business with non–family members, he says that an over-investment in family will train people to not trust those who are not family members and thus overly constrain potential business relationships.

The resort to kinship is not altogether surprising in this moment, in which it is a commonplace if not fully accurate claim that nation-states have been or are being disempowered as actors in global capital. In political theory and anthropology, as Gayle Rubin noted in her brilliant essay "The Traffic in Women," the common story—a story iterated in classic form by Engels—is that kinship provides the social structure in societies that do not yet have a state. This is a developmental narrative in which modern state formations are seen as surpassing kinship as the technology for social and political cohesion. The notion that nation-states are not about kinship is of course absurd. As Alys Weinbaum has argued, even Engels recurs to an anachronistic "barbarism" as the source of the positive aspects of German nationality, which is to say he gives kinship a role in what was for him a contemporary state-centered social formation. And Foucault's work, while with one hand suggesting that sexuality displaces kinship as the basis for social organization, with the other (and a little help from Stoler), more persuasively suggests that discourses of sexuality and kinship actually operate together to produce white European national bourgeoisies in relation to raced colonial others. However, in the global/localization literature, nations do not appear as modern but rather as premodern obstacles to development.

The troublesome connection of kinship to nationalism provokes a particularly exquisite ambivalence about kinship and family in the representations of the success and failure of the Asian economies. In fact, I suspect that the focus on kinship may well have been motivated by the "Asian miracle." In these texts, all written prior to the "crash," the virtues of Asian family values form an important reference point in an attempt to make the rapid "development" of a number of Asian economies into a model that the already "developed" West might learn from. The crash has provoked a reassessment in the business press. As an article in the *Economist* says,

Now some of the sins laid at the doors of the region's economic systems look suspiciously like Asian values gone wrong. The attachment to family becomes nepotism. The importance of personal relationships rather than formal legality becomes cronyism. Consensus becomes wheel-greasing and corrupt politics. Conservatism and respect for authority become rigidity and inability to innovate. Much vaunted educational achievements becomes rote-learning and a refusal to question authority. ("Asian Values," 23)

This article goes beyond the critique of Asian values that it cites, criticizing the notion that there really are particularly Asian values; it suggests that the promotion of such an idea by Asian leaders was partly a postcolonial backlash against the West and partly an attempt to produce collaboration among Asian nations in an economic and political competition with the West. And certainly Suharto's reference to family values during Indonesia's negotiations with the IMF seems an instrumental nationalist ploy. (According to the *New York Times,* he cited Indonesia's 1945 Constitution, which says, "The economy shall be organized as a common endeavor based upon the principle of the family system" [Mydans].) Whether portrayed as sincere or instrumental, the representation of family values as a form of nationalist resistance to "open" financial and commodity markets (as well as resistance to cutbacks in the social welfare practices that these Asians mistakenly think are due to workers who enact obedience and loyalty based on their understanding of employers as kin) suggests that the Western business press is not so sure that family values are good for globalization after all. An article in the *Times Magazine* interprets Asian values as "traditional values":

These Asian values aren't unique to Asia. When I was a kid growing up in the American South, I used to hear constant paeans to "Southern values." Our families were bigger and warmer than those of the cold dreary Yankees. We were more deferential and polite. . . . European immigrants used to say many of the same things. . . . What united all these traditional cultures was their relative lack of experience with a modern market economy. . . . Asia, for reasons that have nothing to do with Western imperialism and everything

*to do with its own social and economic development, will look more and more like west-
ern Europe and North America. . . . It's called progress, and it is, despite many short-
comings, a good thing. (Mead)*

While contemporary global/localization discourse is critical of family values
where they imply nationalism or an inflexible valuing of a particular set of relationships, these authors do like the idea of kinship as an organic force constitut-
ing—naturalizing—the boundaries and internal coherence of political-economic
formations and they redeploy it to legitimate the communal (regional, local) economic units they promote. The slippage from family to kinship to various fictive
kin relations or modern substitutes for kinship serves to legitimate a broad array
of exclusive and hierarchical economic communities; through the analogy with
kinship, they are posited as expressions of authentic human relationships.

In marking a slippage from kinship to fictive kin I am in some sense making a
false distinction. As Gayle Rubin points out, "a kinship system is not a list of biological relatives. It is a system of categories and statuses that often contradict actual genetic relationships" (169). She goes on to use Lévi-Strauss to argue that kinship systems organize relations not only within but also between social groups.
The global/localization texts, which simultaneously center and decenter family,
working by analogy from family to a wide array of fictive kinship arrangements,
invest in the discourse of family/kinship as a powerful mechanism for generating
social relationships that facilitate the flow of capital but simultaneously keep the
nature of those relations quite flexible. The ambivalence, or flexibility, about family and kinship articulated through this use of analogy is, I would argue, an expression of the fundamental contradiction between use value and value—between
the need for value to be embodied in particular concrete use values and its need
to move freely among such embodiments. The discourse of global/localization
mobilizes family as a mechanism simultaneously vigorous enough to motivate
stable adherence to particular social formations and particular practices of production, consumption, and capital formation, and flexible enough to allow those
formations and practices to vary as needed.

So where does this analysis leave us? The potentially contradictory relation of social formations to the flow of capital might entail a Luddite response, an investment in "tradition." But the costs of such a traditionalism are for me too high.
Like Marx, I think our interventions must take advantage of the ways capitalism
has freed us, as well as the ways we have been exploited. Neither family values nor

nationalism is the answer. Against the elision of the relations between the terms of analogy and the discontinuities within the terms, Spivak argues that discourses of domination (idealist or cultural predications) supplement a chain of value (economic predication) that is, by itself, discontinuous. Homi Bhabha argues that this recognition of supplementarity can interrupt the operation of analogy: "The supplementary strategy interrupts the successive seriality of the narrative of plurals and pluralism . . . the 'many as one.'. . . the supplementary antagonizes the implicit power to generalize" (155). But for me the power of supplementarity is not so much the disruption of generalization as the revelation of complicity, of connections, across sites of value; Spivak argues that rather than seeing race, gender, sexuality, or nation as analogous with (and thus complete in themselves and independent of) class, these discourses supplement the international division of labor. "The complicity between cultural and economic value-systems is acted out in almost every decision we make," she says (166). In marking the supplementary relation of local to global, I hope to disrupt the pacifying analogics among localities and make it possible to see the "politics of difference" (Bhabha, 154), the conflictual, hierarchical interdependence of localities with each other.

This might seem an overly philosophical response to domination and exploitation, but I think it might have a variety of practical applications. It might allow us to imagine new opportunities for political and economic intervention. What, for instance, would come of seeing Piore's two arguments—for the liberatory impact of flexible specialization as well as for its dependence on "communal" and kinship formations—in relation to each other? Over the last few days I have forwarded messages to the gay/lesbian campus listserv about our campus's Students Against Sweatshops protest (the students are in their fifth day of occupation of the president's office as I write). As I expected, someone posted a message objecting to my placing "irrelevant" material on the gay/lesbian list. However, I would suggest (and did on the list) that sweatshops are a GLBT issue. If we understand that the recognition of gays and lesbians in the marketplace in the United States depends on the elaboration of patriarchal relations in Mexican maquilas (and it would be interesting to find out just how the particular products being advertised to us are produced—where are those Ikea tables made? where are the parts for Subarus made?), then it might seem in our interest to support that exploitation, or it might seem in our interest to work against it—wouldn't the elaboration of patriarchy imply the oppression of gay and lesbian maquila workers? Rather than wedding ourselves to capitalism, to the privatization of welfare, health care, and so forth through a movement for gay marriage, might it not make sense for gays and lesbians to abandon a narrowly identitarian framework and see it in "our" interests to join in battles to shift the balance of power against capital?

Notes

1. "Flexibility" is generally characterized as involving just-in-time supplying of both human and material means of production, outsourcing, horizontal management, and diversity management. See Emily Martin's *Flexible Bodies* for a fuller account of the discourse of flexibility.

2. "Post-Fordism" was coined by regulation school theorists, but now is used quite widely and loosely. "Flexible specialization" is Piore and Sabel's term. "Flexible accumulation" is David Harvey's coinage. "Disorganized capital" is Claus Offe's term, but Lash and Urry also describe "the end of organized capitalism."

3. Paul Krugman's critique of the economic discourse of national "competitiveness" in *Pop Internationalism* is another version of this view, as is Reich's critique of "economic nationalism" in *The Work of Nations*.

4. Numerous specific studies show the weakness and dependence of the local within globalization. Amin and Robins question the notion that localization is a coherent or salient tendency within the current economic restructuring. They suggest we are witnessing not the end of mass production but merely increased product differentiation (12). They argue that the phenomenon of localization is itself diverse and is contradicted by countervailing tendencies toward "transnational networks" (8). They cite Castells to argue that the most important effect of the new international economy for localities is their loss of autonomy (28). Peck and Tickell mark the dependence and vulnerability of the local to the global by describing the competition between localities that each hope to attract global capital and the internal conflict within localities.

5. Stuart Hall's two essays in *Culture, Globalization, and the World System* are additional examples of this kind of argument, as is Lisa Lowe's *Immigrant Acts*. Arif Dirlik offers a critique of the celebrations of heterogeneity and local culture found in "postmodern" and "postcolonial" cultural criticism. In "The Global in the Local," Dirlik argues that "to the extent that postmodern criticism fails to account for the totality that is its context, its ideological criticism becomes indistinguishable from an ideological legitimation of the social forms that are the creation of global capitalism" (36; see also his essay "The Postcolonial Aura"). Dirlik does suggest that some (modern, constructed) version of the local might be a site of resistance, but differentiates his notion of the local from the celebrations of diversity found in much cultural studies scholarship. I'm not sure that his argument is really so different from that found in Hall or Lowe and Lloyd,

though his sober emphasis on the role of the local as a supplement to the global is quite useful.

6. While Harvey seems to be criticizing the popular version of the globalization narrative here, a similar critique has been offered with regard to the academic regulation school version. Hirst and Zeitlin point out that the regulation school account can be criticized both as too Marxist and by Marxists for envisioning the establishment of a functionally determined structure instead of describing contestations over an open process.

7. For a critique of the role of heterogeneity to support rather than contest capitalist hegemony, see Miranda Joseph, "The Performance of Production and Consumption."

8. See, for instance, Mander and Goldsmith. For a critique of Romantic anticapitalism, see Postone; Sayre and Lowy; and also chapter 1 of Miranda Joseph, *Community and the Performativity of Capitalism.*

9. See, for instance, Russell Berman.

10. See Amin and Robins.

11. Jakobsen's essay addresses the analogy between Jews and queers. She argues that we need to move beyond an analogic understanding to a recognition of a complicity in the construction of the categories. She points out that the co-articulation of Jews and queers in Cold War rhetoric posited them not as merely analogous but as acting together to subvert America. This Cold War anti-Semitic and antihomosexual discourse, she argues, played a crucial part in postwar racist resurgence, consolidating white supremacy, rendering blacks the visible enemy in contrast to the invisible, Jewish-queer enemies. She hopes that we can appropriate this complicity, this negative articulation of cooperation between Jews and queers, as a potential positive space of alliance.

12. See Poovey.

13. For a fuller discussion of the complicity of use value and value, see chapter 1 of Joseph, *Community and the Performativity of Capitalism.*

14. See Tilly and Scott.

15. See Harvey, "The Body as an Accumulation Strategy."

16. See Barnet and Cavanagh; Yanagisako.

17. See Postone; Joseph, *Community and the Performativity of Capitalism*, chapter 1.

Works Cited

Amin, Ash, ed. *Post-Fordism: A Reader.* Oxford: Blackwell, 1994.

Amin, Ash, and K. Robins. "The Re-emergence of Regional Economies? The Mythical

Geography of Flexible Accumulation." *Environment and Planning D: Society and Space* 8.1 (1990): 7–34.

Appadurai, Arjun. "Disjuncture and Difference in the Global Cultural Economy." *Public Culture* 2.2 (spring 1990): 1–24.

"Asian Values Revisited." *Economist*, July 25, 1998, 23–28.

Barnet, Richard J., and John Cavanagh. *Global Dreams*. New York: Simon and Schuster, 1994.

Berman, Russell A. "Beyond Localism and Universalism: Nationhood and Solidarity." *Telos* 105 (fall 1995): 43–56.

Bhabha, Homi K. *The Location of Culture*. London: Routledge, 1994.

Brenner, Neil. "Global, Fragmented, Hierarchical: Henri Lefebvre's Geographies of Globalization." *Public Culture* 10.1: 135–67.

Butler, Judith. "Against Proper Objects." *Differences* 6.2–3 (1994): 1–26.

Cox, Kevin, ed. *Spaces of Globalization: Reasserting the Power of the Local*. New York: Guilford, 1997.

D'Emilio, John. "Capitalism and Gay Identity." In *The Lesbian and Gay Studies Reader*, ed. Henry Abelove, Michèle Aina Barale, and David M. Halperin. New York: Routledge, 1993.

Dirlik, Arif. "The Global in the Local." In *Global/Local*, ed. Rob Wilson and Wimal Dissayanake. Durham: Duke University Press, 1996.

———. "The Postcolonial Aura: Third World Criticism in the Age of Global Capitalism." *Critical Inquiry* (winter 1994): 328–56.

Fabian, Johannes. *Time and the Other: How Anthropology Makes Its Object*. New York: Columbia University Press, 1983.

Foucault, Michel. *The History of Sexuality*. Vol. 1, *An Introduction*. Trans. Robert Hurley. New York: Random House, 1978.

Fukuyama, Francis. *Trust: The Social Virtues and the Creation of Prosperity*. New York: Free Press, 1995.

Gibson-Graham, J. K. *The End of Capitalism (As We Knew It)*. Cambridge, MA: Blackwell, 1996.

Gordon, Avery. "The Work of Corporate Culture: Diversity Management." *Social Text* 44, 13:3 (fall–winter 1995): 3–30.

Hall, Stuart, "The Local and the Global: Globalization and Ethnicity." In *Culture, Globalization, and the World-System*, ed. Anthony D. King. Minneapolis: University of Minnesota Press, 1997.

———. "Old and New Identities, Old and New Ethnicities." In *Culture, Globalization, and the World-System*, ed. Anthony D. King. Minneapolis: University of Minnesota Press, 1997.

Harvey, David. "The Body as an Accumulation Strategy," *Environment and Planning: Society and Space* 16.4 (Aug 1998): 401–22.

———. *The Condition of Postmodernity.* Cambridge, MA: Blackwell, 1990.

———. "Globalization in Question." *Rethinking Marxism* 8.4 (1995): 1–17.

———. "The Urban Process under Capitalism." In *The Urban Experience.* Baltimore: Johns Hopkins University Press, 1989.

Hirst, Paul, and Jonathan Zeitlin. "Flexible Specialization versus Post-Fordism: Theory, Evidence and Policy Implications." *Economy and Society* 20.1 (February 1991): 1–56.

Jakobsen, Janet. "Queers Are Like Jews Aren't They? Analogy and Alliance in Theory and Politics." In *Queers and the Jewish Question*, ed. Daniel Boyarin et al. New York: Columbia University Press, forthcoming.

Joseph, Miranda. *Community and the Performativity of Capitalism.* Unpublished manuscript, 1999.

———. "The Performance of Production and Consumption." *Social Text,* no. 54 (spring 1998): 25–61.

Kasanjian, David. "Racial Governmentality: Thomas Jefferson and the African Colonization Movement in the United States." *Alternation: Journal of the Centre for the Study of Soutern African Literature and Languages.* 5.1: 39–84.

Krugman, Paul. *Pop Internationalism.* Cambridge: MIT Press, 1996.

Laclau, Ernesto, and Chantal Mouffe. *Hegemony and Socialist Strategy: Toward a Radical Democratic Politics.* London: Verso, 2000.

Lash, Scott, and John Urry. *The End of Organized Capital.* Madison: University of Wisconsin Press, 1987.

Lefebvre, Henri. *The Production of Space.* Trans. Donald Nicholson-Smith. Cambridge, MA: Blackwell, 1991.

Lipietz, Alain. "Post-Fordism and Democracy." In *Post-Fordism: A Reader*, ed. Ash Amin, 338–58. Oxford: Blackwell, 1994.

———. *Towards a New Economic Order: Postfordism, Ecology and Democracy.* Trans. Malcolm Slater. New York: Oxford University Press, 1992.

Lowe, Lisa. *Immigrant Acts: On Asian American Cultural Studies.* Durham: Duke University Press, 1996.

Lowe, Lisa, and David Lloyd, eds. *The Politics of Culture in the Shadow of Capital.* Durham: Duke University Press, 1997.

Mander, Jerry, and Edward Goldsmith, eds. *The Case against the Global Economy and for a Turn toward the Local*. San Francisco: Sierra Club Books, 1996.

Martin, Emily. *Flexible Bodies*. Boston: Beacon, 1994.

Marx, Karl. *Capital*. Vol. 1. Trans. Ben Fourkes. New York: Random House, 1977.

Mayer, Margit. "Post-Fordist City Politics." In *Post-Fordism: A Reader*, ed. Ash Amin, 316–37. Oxford: Blackwell, 1994.

Mead, Walter Russell. "Asia Devalued." *New York Times Magazine*, May 31, 1998, 38–39.

Mydans, Seth. "Crisis Aside, What Pains Indonesia Is the Humiliation." *New York Times*, March 10, 1998, A9.

Offe, Claus. *Disorganized Capitalism: Contemporary Transformations of Work and Politics*. Cambridge: MIT Press, 1985.

Ohmae, Kenichi. *The End of the Nation State: The Rise of Regional Economies*. New York: Free Press, 1995.

Peck, Jamie, and Adam Tickell. "Searching for a New Industrial Fix: The After-Fordist Crisis and the Global-Local Disorder." In *Post-Fordism: A Reader*, ed. Ash Amin, 280–315. Oxford: Blackwell, 1994.

Piore, Michael. "Economic Identity/Sexual Identity." In *A Queer World*, ed. Martin Duberman. New York: New York University Press, 1997.

Piore, Michael, and Charles F. Sabel. *The Second Industrial Divide: Possibilities for Prosperity*. New York: Basic Books, 1984.

Poovey, Mary. "The Production of Abstract Space." In *Making a Social Body*. Chicago: University of Chicago Press, 1995.

Postone, Moishe. "Anti-Semitism and National Socialism." In *Germans and Jews since the Holocaust*. New York: Holmes and Meier, 1986.

Reich, Robert B. *The Work of Nations*. New York: Random House, 1991.

Ricardo, David. *On the Principles of Political Economy and Taxation*. Ed Pierro Sraffa. Cambridge: Cambridge University Press, 1951.

Robinson, Amy. "The Ethics of Analogy." Lecture presented at Stanford Humanities Center, March 20, 1997.

Rubin, Gayle. "The Traffic in Women: Notes on the 'Political Economy' of Sex." In *Toward an Anthropology of Women,* ed. Rayna R. Reiter. New York: Monthly Review Press, 1975.

Sassen, Saskia. *The Mobility of Labor and Capital*. Cambridge: Cambridge University Press, 1988.

Sayre, Robert, and Michael Lowy. "Figures of Romantic Anti-Capitalism." In *Spirits of Fire*, ed. G. A. Rosso and Daniel P. Watkins. Rutherford: Fairleigh Dickinson University Press, 1990.

Scott, Allen J., and Michael Storper. "High Technology Industry and Regional Development." *Regional Science* 112 (1987): 215–32.

———, eds. *Production, Work, Territory: The Geographical Anatomy of Industrial Capitalism.* Boston: Allen and Unwin, 1986.

Shah, Nayan. *Contagious Divides: Epidemics and Race in San Francisco's Chinatown.* Berkeley: University of California Press, 2001.

Smith, Adam. *The Theory of Moral Sentiments.* Oxford: Oxford University Press, 1976.

———. *Wealth of Nations.* Amherst: Prometheus Books, 1991 (1776).

Smith, Neil. "The Satanic Geographies of Globalization." *Public Culture* 10.1: 169–89.

Spivak, Gayatri. "Scattered Speculations on the Question of Value." In *In Other Worlds.* New York: Methuen, 1987.

Stanley, Alessandra. "For Ambitious Entrepreneurs, All Europe Is Just One Nation." *New York Times*, December 24, 1998, A1, 10.

Stoler, Ann Laura. *Race and the Education of Desire.* Durham: Duke University Press, 1995.

Storper, Michael. "Territories, Flows, and Hierarchies in the Global Economy." In *Spaces of Globalization: Reasserting the Power of the Local*, ed. Kevin Cox. New York: Guilford, 1997.

Thrift, Nigel. "A Phantom State? International Money, Electronic Networks and Global Cities." In *Spatial Formations.* Thousand Oaks, CA: Sage, 1996.

Tilly, Louise, and Joan Wallach Scott. *Women, Work and the Family.* New York: Routledge, 1989.

Weinbaum, Alys. "Engels' Originary Ruse: Race, Reproduction and Nation in the Story of Capital." Paper presented at the Pemboke Center, Brown University, Providence, RI, April 1998.

Wright, Melissa. "The Dialectics of Still Life: Murder, Women and the Maquiladoras." *Public Culture,* forthcoming.

Yanagisako, Sylvia. *Culture and Capital.* Unpublished manuscript.

Zaretsky, Eli. *Capitalism, the Family, and Personal Life.* New York: Harper and Row, 1986.

6 Redecorating the International Economy

Keynes, Grant, and the Queering of Bretton Woods

Bill Maurer

John Maynard Keynes is often credited with the creation of the theory of the "national economy," since the components of his *General Theory of Employment, Interest, and Money* (1935) are all economic aggregates measured over a given geopolitical space (Radice 1984:112). Hence Keynes's association with Fordism and Fordist nation-based systems of mass production and mass consumption. Also central to Keynes's *General Theory* was the explicit threat, as he saw it, of external forces of instability. Hence Keynes's arguments for limits on capital mobility, fixed exchange rates, and a model of international order based on economically sovereign nation-states interlinked by trade and guaranteed by a spatialized regulatory order (see Leyshon and Thrift 1997:73–75).

Keynes's emphasis on national macroeconomic planning and international regulation through Bretton Woods bureaucracies like the International Monetary Fund and the World Bank has led critics to equate Keynesianism with the disciplinary aspects of Fordist production systems (Harvey 1990). Yet there is another Keynes in between the lines of the *General Theory*. This is the Keynes of play and magic, the Keynes who wrote that capitalist markets resemble nothing so much as a great "casino," who quipped that the monetary system is "a contrived system of pretty, polite techniques, made for a well-paneled board room and a nicely regulated market" (in Leyshon and Thrift 1997:33), and who compared investing to selecting the winners of a beauty contest. This is the Keynes of Bloomsbury, whose theories of probability and aesthetics, developed alongside the playful interior designs of his lover, Duncan Grant, envisioned an alternative modernity set apart from the bureaucratic apparatus of the welfare state and the naturalized logic of the "free" market. To the well-paneled board room and the nicely regulated market Keynes would contrast the playful dressing-screen and the enjoyment of art in an economy of pleasure.[1]

In analyzing "globalization," writers from across the political spectrum have focused on the breakdown of the post–World War II global economic order, specifically, the breakdown of the Bretton Woods system of capital controls and Keynesian social welfare policies. Neoliberal political leaders have dismissed Keynesianism and the Bretton Woods system as outdated macroeconomic planning and social engineering that supported regimes now seen to hinder "free" markets. Many commentators on both the left and the right have long been suspicious of the normalization of social life that Keynesianism and its attendant Fordist production and consumption practices sought to achieve (see Hayek 1990; Friedman 1960 on the right, as well as Foucauldian critics as in Barry, Osborne, and Rose 1996). However, emerging discourses arrayed against globalization remain critical of Bretton Woods while often seeking to institute controls on capital mobility and reconfigurations of debt and exchange that closely resemble Keynes's original formulations. Ranging from Green Party "alternative currency" movements, to left-wing autonomism, to a host of interests on the right (from the militia movement to calls for the reinstitution of the gold standard), these discourses imagine small autonomous communities that either provide the ground from which to launch an attack on and reformulation of globalization, or constitute a cherished home that must be defended from the global economy.

Debates on the economics of globalization intersect with queer politics in troubling ways. Gay and lesbian identities and communities emerged in tandem with the economic restructuring and social dislocation of Fordism (D'Emilio 1984) and were also subject to and, arguably, produced by the disciplinary practices of the normalizing welfare state. Transformations in Fordism co-occurred with the rise of new social movements like gay liberation. This does not imply that the end of Fordism heralded the end of the regulation of gay identities, or that post-Fordism promises a free play of bodies and pleasures in any necessarily liberatory sense.[2]

Post-Fordism does promise just such a free play of bodies and pleasures, but only within the strictures of a neoliberal market logic that renders all bodies into

101

vehicles of consumer choice and all pleasures into gut-level preferences (Strathern 1992). In critiquing a heteronormativity that only became normative through the governmentalities of the Bretton Woods moment, however, does critical queer scholarship share a vision of person and preference with the very neoliberal logic that currently inspires globalization? To what extent are critical queer perspectives products and promulgators of neoliberal visions of freedom, desire, value, and profit?[3] To what extent does undermining neoliberal logic, in an effort to challenge globalization, also undermine queer criticism? Or, alternately, can the emergence of queer politics and criticism in the post–Bretton Woods moment have the potential to recuperate an alternative Keynesianism that might have been constitutive of another modernity but was a road not taken by the Bretton Woods planners? In other words, can we engage the post–Bretton Woods world without falling into its categorical distinctions between supposed domains like economics and sexuality, and can doing so point toward a new vision for future worlds?

Julie Graham and Katherine Gibson argue persuasively that critiques of contemporary capitalism must not fall into the trap of using for analytical or political purposes the dominant metaphors of capitalism's supposed triumph (Gibson-Graham 1996). As they put it, "the script of globalization need not draw solely upon an image of the body of capitalism as hard, thrusting and powerful. Other images are available, and . . . it is important to draw upon such representations in creating an anticapitalist imaginary and fashioning a politics of economic transformation" (Gibson-Graham 1996:138–39). Revisiting Keynes, I maintain, affords an opportunity to consider alternative representations of capitalism and to think through alternative visions of globalization. This project is important for queer politics because it counters heteronormative language of globalization and suggests possibilities for queer rethinkings of capitalism. It is important for anticapitalist politics because it allows a reconsideration of lost economic alternatives that were available when the global visions of Bretton Woods came into focus (see Ritter 1997:19).

This essay seeks to develop a perspective on globalization, and on alternative possibilities, by claiming the queerness of Keynes's economics through a recuperation of his aesthetics. I am wary of critical approaches to globalization that imagine a future world of capital controls and local autonomy and that rely on troubling notions of community. At the same time, I am skeptical of celebrations of globalization that emphasize the creative possibilities of new technologies like the Internet and new publics like transnational civil societies. Both sets of perspectives often take for granted categories of knowledge, being, space, and time that they share with the object of their critique, and rely on problematic notions of causality and the delineation of domains of "sexuality" and "the economy" (as well as "art," "politics," "gender," and so forth).[4] Ultimately, queer politics and effective challenges to dominant global visions require new categories that are not bound up in bureaucratic rationality, neoliberal market logic, or nostalgic visions of community or autonomy. Focusing on the interplay of Keynes's economics with the interior design of Duncan Grant, this essay reflects on the notion of creative endeavor that underwrote both Bretton Woods and Bloomsbury, in an effort to recover an alternate modernity in response to neoliberal globalization.[5]

The first section of this chapter considers Keynes's theories of aesthetics as they were developed alongside Grant's art and in the wake of G. E. Moore's *Principia Ethica*, a text that had a profound impact on the shape of Bloomsbury art and philosophizing. It then explores connections between Keynes's aesthetics and Grant's post-impressionist interior design, both of which rested on a particular notion of agentive perception and moral action. The second section turns to Keynes's theory of probability, which was a direct outgrowth of his aesthetics and permeates his *General Theory*. The third section specifically addresses the chapter on long-term investment and capital mobility, issues that would preoccupy the Bretton Woods planners. The fourth section explores the alternative modernity expounded by Keynes immediately before and during the Bretton Woods conference of 1944. Bretton Woods established the regulatory and theoretical apparatus of the post–World War II international monetary system in institutions like the International Monetary Fund and the World Bank. I show how Keynes's alternative plan for an International Clearing Union resonated with his theories of probability and aesthetics, and can be viewed as a post-impressionist project in the manner of Grant's interior design. The fifth section reflects on the failures of Keynes's alternate modernity in light of its colonial politics, and considers the economies of eroticism in Grant's colonial themes. In the conclusion, I return to the problem of globalization, the breakdown of the Bretton Woods system, and the possibilities for criticism based on Keynes's and Grant's alternative modernity. This modernity had as its centerpiece a doctrine of nonreductive, nonnatural "organic unity" actively constructed by individuals drawing together disparate objects (localities, points on a canvas, designs in a room) into new, everchanging wholes, and a rejection of the delineation of separate domains of cultural life.

Keynes's Aesthetics: Organic Unities in Theory and Design

As many Keynes scholars have argued, Keynes's economic theories were the outgrowth of his earlier work in aesthetics.[6] Like others in the Bloomsbury circle, Keynes based much of his thinking on G. E. Moore's *Principia Ethica*, published in 1903 when Keynes was a student at Cambridge. Keynes's reading of Moore resulted in several papers on aesthetics, written between 1904 and 1909.[7]

These papers proceeded from Moore's discussion of the relationship between aesthetics and morally correct actions, embodied in his statement that

By far the most valuable things, which we can know or can imagine, are certain states of consciousness, which may be roughly described as the pleasures of human intercourse and the enjoyment of beautiful objects. No one, probably, who has asked himself the question, has ever doubted that personal affection and the appreciation of what is beautiful in Art or Nature, are good in themselves; nor, if we consider strictly what things are worth having purely for their own sakes, *does it appear probable that any one will think that anything else has* nearly *so great a value as the things which are included under these two heads. . . . [But the] mere existence of what is beautiful has value, so small as to be negligible, in comparison with that which attaches to the* consciousness *of beauty. This simple truth may, indeed, be said to be universally recognized. What has not been recognized is that it is the ultimate and fundamental truth of Moral Philosophy. That it is only for the sake of these things—in order that as much of them as possible may at some time exist—that any one can be justified in performing any public or private duty; that they are the raison d'etre of virtue; that it is they—these complex wholes themselves, and not any constituent or characteristic of them—that form the rational ultimate end of human action and the sole criterion of social progress. (Moore 1903:237–38, section 113, original emphases)*

Moore continued, in what became a Bloomsbury slogan, "personal affections and aesthetic enjoyments include *all* the greatest, and *by far* the greatest, goods we can imagine" (Moore 1903:228, section 113, original emphases). These "goods," these things of beauty that cannot be disaggregated into their constituents, form "highly complex *organic unities*," according to Moore (ibid., original emphasis). As Keynes wrote in 1938, reflecting on the influence of Moore on himself and his peers,

Nothing mattered except states of mind, our own and other people's of course, but chiefly our own. These states of mind were not associated with action or achievement or with consequences. They consisted in timeless, passionate states of contemplation and communion, largely unattached to "before" or "after." Their value depended, in accordance

with the principle of organic unity, on the state of affairs as a whole which could not be
usefully analysed into parts. . . . The appropriate subjects of passionate contemplation
and communion were a beloved person, beauty and truth, and one's prime objects in life
were love, the creation and enjoyment of aesthetic experience and the pursuit of knowl-
edge. (Keynes 1949:83)

Keynes's papers on aesthetics considered the nature of these "organic unities" pos-
tulated by Moore, and concerned what he called their "fitness," or ability to generate "good" states of mind. However, the doctrine of organic unities presented a
paradox. The existence of a "bad" object like suffering might be necessary to produce a "good" state of mind like pity, which would inspire good action to relieve
suffering (see Skidelsky 1991:107–8). This paradox might lead to the conclusion
that social reformers ought to create deprivation in order to inspire pity and moral
actions designed to resolve it. But, Keynes maintained, there are ways to create the
good feeling of pity without actively creating situations of suffering or deprivation; for instance, by writing melodramas (Keynes 1906). Melodramas, Keynes
wrote, allow people to "enjoy at second hand, or admire, the noble feelings *with-*
out the evil happening which generally accompany [*sic*] them in real life" (Keynes
1928, quoted in Skidelsky 1991:108).

If the task is to increase "fitness" in objects and ontological categories in order
to increase "goodness" in the world, yet fitness inheres in parts of complex organic
unities, then how does one conduct social reform? Keynes's answer involved a rejection of empiricism, or the belief in the transparency of sense data.[8] Keynes did
not seek to distinguish objects in the world from ontological categories, since all
objects in the world are called forth only in our perception of them. "Aesthetic
feelings," Keynes wrote, "are not directly evoked by the objects themselves but by
the content of our perceptions" (Keynes 1905a, in O'Donnell 1995:102). Keynes
explicitly left aside the question of whether external objects matter at all—in both
a consequential and a substantive sense. "I am not endeavoring to answer the
question of our relation to the external world," he wrote (Keynes 1905a, in O'-
Donnell 1995:102). Our perceptions are relative. "The beauty of some pictures,"
he wrote, "depends a good deal upon the particular method in which we fix them"
(Keynes 1905a, in O'Donnell 1995:103). Furthermore, "it is not beauty but only
the feelings which beauty can create that are good" (Keynes 1905b, in O'Donnell
1995:107). What, then, are the entities that the social reformer must work on in
order to increase goodness?

Keynes deferred the answer onto the agentive aspects of perception. These are

105

ultimately dependent on context and situatedness in a social and aesthetic space. As O'Donnell summarizes, "[b]y adjusting our sense organs and position, we have a certain voluntary control over the perception produced in us. We can see different 'aspects' of a painting depending on how we fix it, and from where we view it" (O'Donnell 1995:107). For Keynes, aesthetic judgments are not based on "mental facts supplied by the senses," but only on "a 'certain selection' of these, made either consciously or instinctively" (O'Donnell 1995:107), to produce a "kind of harmony between our surroundings, as they are presented to us by our senses, our thoughts, and our emotions" (Keynes 1905b, in O'Donnell 1995:109). How is one to determine the best "arrangement" of objects, the best position from which to view objects, or the selection of sense data from which to create harmony? Although Keynes held that "[p]ersons with the finest taste and greatest artistic power see 'the most beautiful grouping' of these facts" (O'Donnell 1995:107), he wavered on the standards of "fine taste" because of his anti-empiricist position on the question of beauty:

> [W]e must refrain from narrowing down too far the fit objects of our senses, and, while it is the delight and duty of all lovers of beauty to dispute . . . concerning tastes, we must not impose on the almost infinite variety of fit and beautiful objects . . . tests and criteria which we may think we have established in that corner of the field which is dearest to ourselves; nor must we fail to see beauty in strange places because it has little in common with the kind of beauty we would strive to create. (Keynes 1905b, in O'Donnell 1995:112)

This emphasis on perception as an active, agentive process found direct expression in the post-impressionist art of Duncan Grant. Post-impressionists rejected techniques like palate mixing in favor of techniques like pointillism, in which the spectator's eye resolves a collection of small dots into color and form depending on the spectator's distance from and position in relation to an object (Reichardt 1988:240).[9] The effect of such painting is to call into question the process of seeing itself, highlight its contingent nature, and exploit "the discrepancy between physical fact and psychic effect" (Alpers, quoted in Reichardt 1988:238–39).[10]

Duncan Grant, together with Vanessa Bell, brought the movement into interior design, working not with a two-dimensional canvas but the three-dimensional space of living areas. Two- and three-dimensional patterns come together in the spectator's field of vision into surprising and playful patterns, the perception of which is dependent on the spectator's position and motion through a room. One of his most important works, his 1949 *Abstract Kinetic Collage Painting with Sound,* or *The Scroll,* combines the play of perception with the motion of the object and the spectator's relative position in relation to it. It is designed to be viewed through a rectangular aperture as the work is unwound vertically off a yarn-winding machine used in craft weaving, while accompanied by music (Watney 1990:39).

The emphasis is decidedly nonfunctional. As one art critic notes, Grant's art served "as an alternative to the precious materials and machined sleekness of the 'heroic' modernism exemplified in the designs of Le Corbusier" (Reed 1988, quoted in Watney 1990:11). Grant's masterwork is not a particular decorative object or painting, but his home, Charleston, where his "pictures, fabrics, pottery and design work in the type of environment for which they were envisaged, as elements of an overall aesthetic involving the artist in every aspect of an interior" (Watney 1990:9). As Angelica Garnett, the daughter of Duncan Grant and Vanessa Bell, wrote, Grant and Bell's artistic project "enabled them to make the imaginative leap from seeing walls, doors and fireplaces as a potentially tasteful background to treating them—like canvases—as an opportunity to make a statement of a very personal nature" (Garnett 1984:71).[11]

Although some maintain that, as a project opposed to modernism, Grant's interiors presented an "escape" from a "life . . . increasingly dominated by machines" into a home-space of "fantasy, imagination, [and] wit" (Todd and Mortimer 1929:28), the work itself undercut the very opposition of home and world central to both modernism and romanticism. Here, Grant was derivative of Vanessa Bell. He relied on elaborate trompes l'oeil that confounded the distinction between interior and exterior space. Many of his paintings play on this distinction. His interiors represent an "increased blurring of the distinction between 'inside' and 'outside'" the picture-space and the home-space (Watney 1990:53). Doors become canvases; canvases become windows; frames enclose other frames, which in turn open out into other picture-spaces, and so on. As Watney summarizes, "Charleston [itself] was lived in very much as an ongoing process of representation. . . . At times it seems almost as if Grant were living inside a picture that he was painting, of himself painting the picture in which he was living" (Watney 1990:53).[12]

Probability and Possibility in Social Action

Keynes carried his ideas about aesthetics forward in his *Treatise on Probability* (1921), which was written during the time of his relationship with Duncan Grant

(1908–1914). In 1908 Keynes and Grant vacationed in the Orkney Islands "and enjoyed many profitable hours on painting and probability" (Hession 1983:55). Grant believed that Keynes's appreciation of painting derived from their pursuits during this trip; "in fact he accepted," Grant wrote, "without me having to point it out, that the painter had a serious job on hand" (Grant, quoted in Skidelsky 1983:198). Keynes's work on probability was to have a profound impact on *The General Theory*, and derives directly from his aesthetics and the concretized embodiment of his theory of aesthetics in the interiors of Duncan Grant.

Recall Keynes's contention that increasing the goodness in the world entails improving upon what he called "fit" objects, which were objects or ontologies about which it was possible to have good feelings. But his notions of fitness and beauty were profoundly anti-empiricist. One could not really grasp hold of a fit object without transforming it, as it was always part of a larger organic unity, and its fitness was a consequence of and a condition for one's perception of it in the first place. Furthermore, one's perception ultimately depended on the object's and one's own position in a broader field, much as perception of Grant's *Scroll* depends on a particular viewing point and process of seeing. According to Keynes, therefore, a fit object is one to which it is possible, *but not necessary*, to have good feelings or a good mental state; it is "defined in terms of a possibility, not [an] actuality" (O'Donnell 1995:100). The claim that fitness is a possibility led Keynes to a redefinition of probability in his *Treatise on Probability*. For Keynes, probability was not about frequencies of phenomena, or statistical description and projection, but rather "the formulation of probability judgments in the broadest sense, with arguments and the process of reasoning" (Moggridge 1992:144; see Skidelsky 1991). Probability referred to "the degree of belief it is rational to entertain in given conditions" (Keynes 1921:4), not the relative frequency of empirically observable phenomena. Probability is by definition a logical, not empirical, problem, according to Keynes, and uncertainty, having no place in logic, has no place in probability. Our belief that our knowledge of the present gives us some purchase on the future is the product of sloppy thinking about the nature of the universe and a consequence of the empiricist fallacy. We have "only the vaguest idea of any but the most direct consequences of our acts" (Keynes 1937:213, in Dow and Dow 1985:49). As Keynes wrote,

The scientist wishes . . . to assume that the occurrence of a phenomenon which has appeared as part of a more complex phenomenon, may be some reason for expecting it to be associated on another occasion with part of the same complex. Yet if different wholes

were subject to different laws qua wholes and not simply on account of and in proportion to the differences of their parts, knowledge of a part could not lead, it would seem, even to presumptive or probable knowledge as to its association with other parts. (Keynes 1921:277)

Keynes's vision of probability thus recalls the Moorean doctrine of organic unities (Carabelli 1985). Also, like Moore's notion of goodness, Keynes's probability is "unanalysable, indefinable, non-natural, [yet] directly perceived or intuitive and objective" (Moggridge 1992:149). It is also, again, profoundly anti-empiricist. As Keynes wrote in the *Treatise*,

If our experience and our knowledge were complete, we should be beyond the need of the calculus of probability. And where our experience is incomplete, we cannot hope to derive it from judgments of probability without the aid either of intuition or of some further a priori principle. Experience, as opposed to intuition, cannot possibly afford us a criterion by which to judge whether on given evidence the probabilities of two propositions are not equal. (Keynes 1921:94)

Elaborating on the doctrine of organic unities, Keynes explicitly contrasted the "atomic," methodologically individualist perspective with an "organic" perspective embodied in his probability. According to the "atomic" perspective, found in the mathematical sciences and in the mathematical social sciences like econometrics,

[t]he system of the material universe must consist . . . of bodies which we may term . . . legal atoms, such that each of them exercises its own separate, independent, and invariable effect, a change of the total state being compounded of a number of separate changes each of which is solely due to a separate portion of the preceding state. . . . Each atom can, according to this theory, be treated as a separate cause and does not enter into different organic combinations in each of which it is regulated by different laws. (Keynes 1921:276–77)

Much of Keynes's argument in the *Treatise* is aimed at the methodological individualism of mathematical approaches to the social sciences, and is a defense of "intuition" as opposed to rational calculation (see Davis 1991, 1994).[13] As he put it in the *Treatise*, "[t]he hope, which sustained many investigators in the course of the nineteenth century, of gradually bringing the moral sciences under the sway of mathematical reasoning, steadily recedes" (Keynes 1921:349). In a later speech, he discredited social science aimed at quantifying human behavior and

109

sentiment, since human beings and human societies are always more than the sum of their parts:

Mathematical Psychics has not, as a science or study, fulfilled its early promise. . . . The atomic hypothesis which has worked so splendidly in physics breaks down in psychics. We are faced at every turn with the problems of organic unity, of discreteness, of discontinuity—the whole is not equal to the sum of the parts, comparisons of quantity fail us, small changes produce large effects, and the assumptions of uniform and homogeneous continuum are not satisfied. (Keynes 1921:262)

The organic perspective, for Keynes, provided insight "not through prior knowledge of 'atoms' but through our interacting with reality, with coming to grips with complex things at their own level of being" (Rotheim 1988:87). Rotheim's statement could also be applied to the post-impressionist artists, whose works aimed to upset a methodologically individualist conception of art. In the individualist conception, an artist creates a work for a viewer. The viewer engages with the work only at the level of a distanced observer casting a critical or appreciative eye. The work itself is inert, an object created and an object to be viewed. For Keynes and the post-impressionists, however, the work was just as much a part of an active, lived reality as the viewer and the artist. It is only through interacting with that reality that the viewer and artist come to grips with the complexity conveyed through the work of art.[14]

How, then, does one go about making a logical probabilistic argument, especially when, given the nature of probability, there may be several logical conclusions to be drawn from a set of premises?

[E]ven if we know the degree of advantage which might be obtained from each of a series of alternative courses of actions and know also the probability in each case of obtaining the advantage in question, it is not always possible by a mere process of arithmetic to determine which of the alternatives ought to be chosen. If, therefore, the question of right action is under all circumstances a determinate problem, it must be in virtue of an intuitive judgment directed to the situation as a whole, and not in virtue of an arithmetical deduction derived from a series of separate judgments directed to the individual alternatives each treated in isolation. (Keynes 1921:344–45)

If not through arithmetical deduction, how do we assess different logical conclusions from the same set of premises in order to guide our action in the world? Keynes relies on a notion of the "weight of argument," which is relative to the amount of evidence that a particular conclusion is probable. Remember that, for

Keynes, the probability of a particular conclusion says nothing about its actuality (what is the likelihood of its coming to pass?) but rather its logic (can we be reasonably sure that conclusion q can be derived from premise p?). New evidence may in fact compel us to think that conclusion q, in actuality, may not occur at all. But that new evidence has increased the *weight* of our argument on which we base our ascription of decreasing actuality (Keynes 1921:77).

Of course, Keynes's notion of "evidence" seems paradoxical here, given the anti-empiricist bent of his other philosophizing. What counts as "evidence"? How can we assess different kinds of "evidence" and measure them against each other? Keynes answers that the problems of measuring evidence are similar to those of measuring probabilities, which may imply that evidence, like probability, is a logical, not empirical, category (Keynes 1921:77–78; see Davis 1991; Rotheim 1988).

If evidence is a logical category, it therefore changes along with changing premises and conclusions. For Keynes, an understanding of temporality was central to assessing the weight of arguments. Conclusions based on an equilibrium model, for instance, ignore the temporality of social life and thus have less "weight" than conclusions based on more organically conceived probabilistic claims. Take the idea of an economic process "tending toward" equilibrium. Joan Robinson, in a lecture on Keynes, notes that this idea confuses metaphors, since it involves "using a metaphor based on space to explain a process which takes place in time" (Robinson 1953:255). As Rotheim points out,

words such as tendency, if used in an equilibrium framework, only have meaning if the concept of equilibrium exists, a priori. One cannot move in time when the language emanates from an equilibrium system, because in the latter we start with an equilibrium, define the appropriate premise structure, and then rest assured that we will return to the equilibrium unscathed. (Rotheim 1988:98).

He continues,

When we move into a framework of time, we start with the premises and move forward as we interact along the way causing us to change our premises and change our path. The two thought processes reflect different, incompatible language structures; between those based on atomistic systems where probabilistic statements are valid, and those which are organic, where uncertainty prevails, and where knowledge of the real, social world evolves in an interactionist configuration. (Rotheim 1988:98)

Keynes's probability thus also introduced a particular notion of time-space, reminiscent of the vertigo of Grant's play with enframing devices in interior design,

111

confusing inside and outside as a person moves through living spaces. Logical relationships are reversible. Therefore, for Keynes, so are probabilistic and evidential ones. As Keynes reflected in his 1938 memoir, in reference to his early philosophizing,

Suppose we were to live our lives backwards, having our experiences in the reverse order, would this affect the value of our successive states of mind? If the states of mind enjoyed by each of us were pooled and then redistributed, would this affect their value? How did one compare the value of a good state of mind which had bad consequences with a bad state of mind which had good consequences? In valuing the consequences did one assess them at their actual value as it turned out eventually to be, or their probable value at the time? (Keynes 1949:87)

We are left in a space-time field like that of one of Duncan Grant's interiors, where inside, outside, frame, and world dissolve into each other and resolve into new patterns depending on the position of the spectator and movement through space-time. Keynes's epistemology, like Grant's design, is based on "using a variety of logical chains . . . with differing starting-points, and taking different parts of the system as exogenous. As a result, the duality of endogeneity and exogeneity loses its universal application and becomes specific to the particular chain of reasoning at hand" (Dow and Dow 1985:59).

This may not seem a very satisfying place to be when the problem is what course of action one should pursue in the process of trying to bring about social change. Keynes's response to this dilemma has to do with a notion of "risk" inherent in any action in the world. "There seems," he writes, "a good deal to be said for the conclusion that, other things being equal, that course of action is preferable, which involves least risk and about the results of which we have the most complete knowledge" (Keynes 1921:347); or "a high weight and an absence of risk increase *pro tanto* the desirability of the action to which they refer" (Keynes 1921:348). Skidelsky summarizes, "[t]he important conclusion for practice is that it is more rational to aim for an immediate good than a remote one, since the first will have behind it both a greater weight of argument and a higher probability of attainment" (Skidelsky 1991:112). As Keynes wrote elsewhere,

it can seldom be right . . . to sacrifice a present benefit for a doubtful advantage in the future. . . . It is not wise to look too far ahead; our powers of prediction are slight, our command over results infinitesimal. It is therefore the happiness of our own contemporaries that is our main concern; we should be very chary of sacrificing large numbers of people for the sake of a contingent end, however advantageous that may appear. . . . We can never know enough to make the chance worth taking. (Keynes, in Skidelsky 1991:114)

Keynes thus articulated a vision of political action and history that is profoundly anti-teleological. This has consequences for both Christian and liberal humanist metaphysics and morality (Skidelsky 1983:153), and, like recent movements in queer criticism, troubles liberal visions of activism and political efficacy.

Queering The General Theory

Keynes's notions of space, time, and probability came together in some of the most important parts of his economics. Chapter 12 of *The General Theory*, titled "The State of Long-Term Expectation," provides an account of the state-of-play of the modern stock market and the raising of capital for enterprise. Investments based on long-term expectations of return, Keynes argued, are not based on forecasts or frequency-based probability judgments, the kind of judgments Keynes was arguing against in the *Treatise*. True to his position in the *Treatise*, he writes that "[t]here is . . . not much to be said about the state of confidence *a priori*" (Keynes 1935:149). "If we speak frankly, we have to admit that our basis of knowledge for estimating the yield ten years hence of a railway, a copper mine, a textile factory, the goodwill of a patent medicine, an Atlantic liner, a building in the City of London amounts to little and sometimes to nothing" (Keynes 1935:149–50). How, then, are expectations made and investments revalued in the course of market trading?

Keynes's answer came straight out of his thinking on aesthetics and probability. "In practice," he wrote, "we have tacitly agreed, as a rule, to fall back on what is, in truth, a *convention*" (Keynes 1935:152, original emphasis). He continued,

The essence of this convention . . . lies in assuming that the existing state of affairs will continue indefinitely, except in so far as we have specific reasons to expect a change. This does not mean that we really believe that the existing state of affairs will continue indefinitely. We know from extensive experience that this is most unlikely. The actual results of an investment over a long term of years very seldom agree with the initial expectation. . . . We are assuming, in effect, that the existing market valuation, however arrived at, is uniquely correct in relation to our existing knowledge of the facts which will influence the yield of the investment, and that it will only change in proportion to changes in this knowledge; though, philosophically speaking, it cannot be uniquely correct, since our existing knowledge does not provide a sufficient basis for a calculated

mathematical expectation. . . . Nevertheless the above conventional method of calcula-
tion will be compatible with a considerable measure of continuity and stability in our af-
fairs, so long as we can rely on the maintenance of the convention. *(Keynes*
1935:152, original emphases)

In other words, the convention that maintains capitalist enterprise is a sort of
collective illusion that the current state of affairs A will continue into the future
state of affairs A_1, and not into an entirely unexpected future state B. We know
full well that this is an illusion. But it serves to bolster our confidence that the
present state of affairs A is a reasonable one—that existing market values of stocks
are appropriate given assets and current yields. It also serves to guarantee a particular vision of stability and order. In effect, Keynes was saying, the capitalist
market is an illusion of our own making, yet it is an illusion with which we can
live quite happily, as long as we stick to the conventions warranting its stability.
Participation in the illusion is like an invitation to Grant's Charleston: come, participate in this world, setting aside any claims to a "reality" behind the illusion;
so long as everyone plays the game according to convention, only goodness will
result.

Convention is upset, however, by certain aspects of the market that encourage
speculation. Keynes made a distinction between investment in the hopes of securing a steady income through regular return, and investment in the hopes of
making a fast buck through an increase in conventional basis of valuation. The
former he termed "enterprise," the latter he termed "speculation." Keynes saw
speculating on stock values, putting one's money into the stock market in the
hopes that a stock itself will increase in value over the short term, as a form of gambling, rendering the capitalist economy into a great "casino" (Keynes 1935:159).

Chapter 12 is highly critical of logic of speculation as opposed to logic of enterprise. People speculate, Keynes believed, because capitalist markets have made
what he termed a "fetish" of "liquidity," or the belief that one's money should be
able to move and be convertible into any manner of investment quickly and easily. Liquidity, of course, is the cornerstone of contemporary globalizing processes.
Liquidity only makes sense, Keynes argued, when people are able to approach the
market as a gambling operation, and not as a social process designed to increase
goodness in the world by helping enterprise accumulate the necessary capital for
its endeavors, while distributing profit and risk. Because of the way the market is
currently organized, Keynes wrote, "it is not sensible to pay 25 for an investment

of which you believe the prospective yield to justify a value of 30, if you also believe that the market will value it at 20 three months hence" (Keynes 1935:155). Speculation need not be harmful when it merely consists of "bubbles on a steady stream of enterprise" (Keynes 1935:159). But things get out of hand "when enterprise becomes the bubble on a whirlpool of speculation. When the capital development of a country becomes a by-product of a casino, the job is likely to be ill-done" (Keynes 1935:159). "These tendencies" toward speculation "are a scarcely avoidable outcome of having successfully organised 'liquid' investment markets" (Keynes 1935:159).

Liquidity encourages investors to make unwise choices. It masks the morally correct relationships of investment, which, for Keynes, are relationships that constitute community over time, not relationships that garner particular individuals wealth in the short term. The issuing of shares in corporate enterprise, Keynes wrote, leading to the separation of ownership from control (cf. Berle and Means 1932), has created a whole class of people whose involvement in the stock market is not based on commitment to enterprise but on daily (or hourly) revaluations of stock (Keynes 1935:150–51). "It is as though a farmer, having tapped his barometer after breakfast, could decide to remove his capital from the farming business between 10 and 11 in the morning and reconsider whether he should return to it later in the week" (Keynes 1935:151). "Thus," Keynes wrote, "certain classes of investment are governed by the average expectation of those who deal on the Stock Exchange as revealed in the prices of shares, rather then by the genuine expectations of the professional entrepreneur" (Keynes 1935:151). Furthermore, the process of investment on the stock market leads individuals, not actually to assess the productive potential of any given enterprise, for instance, but rather to anticipate other investors' choices and gain advantage over them.

Keynes chose the example of beauty competitions to illustrate this logic:

professional investment may be likened to those newspaper competitions in which the competitors have to pick out the six prettiest faces from a hundred photographs, the prize being awarded to the competitor whose choice most nearly corresponds to the average preferences of the competitors as a whole; so that each competitor has to pick, not those faces which he himself finds prettiest, but those which he thinks likeliest to catch the fancy of the other competitors, all of whom are looking at the problem from the same point of view. It is not a case of choosing those which, to the best of one's judgment, are really the prettiest, nor even those which average opinion genuinely thinks the prettiest.

115

We have reached the third degree where we devote our intelligences to anticipating what average opinion expects average opinion to be. (Keynes 1935:156)

Like sexuality and gender, then, investment decisions are performances that are always made in relation to others. Investment/desire is triangulated through third and fourth and *n*th parties.[15]

Keynes clearly valued a kind of entrepreneurialism that may have been, by the 1930s, a product of an earlier era, if not a complete myth working to justify capitalist expansion. This is the myth of the capitalist-patriarch concerned with industry and enterprise for community betterment and not merely profit. Keynes's chapter on long-term investment makes sense only in the context of his belief that capitalism ultimately should serve communities—or, more precisely, "civilization" itself—not individuals. Keynes also reified "society" in his vision of an ethically good capitalist system. The argument rested on a particular model of ethical and appropriate action in the world that came straight from his aesthetics and probability theory. People should act to increase goodness by increasing the fitness of objects and ontologies in organic unities. There is no other moral way to act. Investment, thus, like enterprise, should be undertaken with these goals in mind. The fact that it did not indicated, to Keynes, that people must be persuaded to see the moral content of their decisions and actions.

Keynes provided no specific formula for encouraging people to see that their investments ought to be bound up in an ethic of community. He did, however, write that "[t]he spectacle of modern investment markets has sometimes moved me towards the conclusion that to make the purchase of an investment permanent and indissoluble, like marriage, except by reason of death or other grave cause, might be a useful remedy for our contemporary evils" (Keynes 1935:160). But such a prospect, he continued, would foreclose the good, productive possibilities of liquidity—just as marriage forecloses the good possibilities of "personal affections and aesthetic enjoyments." If the individual investor is assured that his investments are "liquid," and he can convert them to cash at any time, than he will be "much more willing to run a risk" (Keynes 1935:160), and encourage more investment. Human beings, Keynes believed, contained what he called "animal spirits" that urge them to movement, change, and risk:

Most . . . of our decisions to do something positive, the full consequences of which will be drawn out over many days to come, can only be taken as a result of animal spirits— of a spontaneous urge to action rather than inaction, and not as the outcome of a weighted average of quantitative benefits multiplied by quantitative probabilities. (Keynes 1935:161)

Furthermore, these animal spirits could be harnessed toward the creation of good-ness in the world, especially when they are combined with hopes for the future and when they help mitigate fears of failure.

It is safe to say that enterprise which depends on hopes stretching into the future ben-efits the community as a whole. But individual initiative will only be adequate when reasonable calculation is supplemented and supported by animal spirits, so that the thought of ultimate loss which often overtakes pioneers, as experience undoubtedly tells us and them, is put aside as a healthy man puts aside the expectation of death. (Keynes 1935:162)

Here is Keynes as a high modernist and humanist, fully believing that in put-ting aside fears and accepting the illusion of the continuation of the present state of affairs into the future, human beings will maintain the conventions necessary to maintain order, while increasing goodness through entrepreneurial and moral progress. At the same time, here is Keynes as a member of Bloomsbury, accepting a nonquantifiable, probabilistic reasoning based on a vaguely hinted at notion of intuition that reveals the illusion of a future to be just that—an illusion, an arti-fice based on convention, a collective leap into the unknown. We cannot worry too much about the actual future that may come to pass, since that future is al-ways unknowable.

We should not conclude from this that everything depends on waves of irrational psy-chology. . . . We are merely reminding ourselves that human decisions affecting the fu-ture, whether personal or political or economic, cannot depend on strict mathematical ex-pectation, since the basis for making such calculations does not exist; and that it is our innate urge to activity which makes the wheels go round, our rational selves choosing where we can, but often falling back for our motive on whim or sentiment or chance. (Keynes 1935:163)

Contingency occupied a powerful place, then, in Keynes's philosophy of moral action. And that contingency was the logical corollary to his vision of organic uni-ties. In arguing against reformers who would suggest action for the good of the many in the uncertain future, Keynes quipped, "this *long-run* is a misleading guide to current affairs. *In the long run* we are all dead" (Keynes 1923:65).

The International Clearing Union: Designing Modernity

*The decadent international but individualist capitalism, in the hands of which we found
ourselves after the war, is not a success. It is not intelligent, it is not beautiful, it is not
just, it is not virtuous—and it doesn't deliver the goods. In short, we dislike it and are beginning to despise it. But when we wonder what to put in its place, we are perplexed.*
—Keynes 1933:760–61

The economic program that Keynes developed in the years around World War II
had as its centerpiece the two proposals that, together, have come to define "Keynesianism": the state should have primary responsibility for directing the domestic economy; and international trade and finance should be politically controlled
(Crotty 1983:59). Many of Keynes's pronouncements in the 1930s and 1940s bear
the stamp of the model of the domestic economy that has been rejected by neoliberal political leaders in the 1980s and 1990s. They also strike a chord with contemporary arguments against the globalization of markets. For instance, in his
essay "National Self-Sufficiency," Keynes sounds very much like people on the
protectionist right as well as on the autonomist left:

*a greater measure of national self-sufficiency and economic isolation among countries
than existed in 1914 may tend to serve the cause of peace rather than otherwise. . . . [L]et
goods be homespun wherever it is reasonably and conveniently possible, and, above all,
let finance be primarily national. (Keynes 1933:758)*

Keynes here, and in his call for the "euthanasia of the rentier" (Keynes 1935:376)
and the diminishment of interest rates to zero through state management and
control of capital, may be more reminiscent of feudal discourses on usury and
trade than modern bureaucratic ones. Recall Martin Luther's injunctions against
trade in exotic luxury goods and nonlocal textiles (Luther 1520:481). Eric
Helleiner (1996) aptly terms contemporary movements for local monetary autonomy through local currencies a kind of "neo-medievalism."

Put in the context of his aesthetic theory and his probability theory, however,
Keynes's writings on the currency controls and the domestic economy would support neither feudal imaginations nor the bureaucratic calculus of the modern welfare state. Rather, they demonstrate, first, the species of contingency that ani-
mated his thinking on social action in the world, and second, a failure of analytical language to describe the future world he was envisioning. Parts of "National
Self-Sufficiency" read like passages out of the *Treatise on Probability*; for instance,

"the new economic modes, toward which we are blundering, are, in the essence of their nature, experiments. We have no clear idea laid up in our minds before-hand of exactly what we want. We shall discover it as we move along" (Keynes 1933:768). Much as Grant's interior design was a process of discovery through movement and no small measure of experiment and blundering, Keynes's discourse on economic transformation relied on a recognition of contingency and a faith in the human combination of intuition and animal spirits to reframe problems in the process of trying to solve them.

At the same time, Keynes came up against the limits of modernist discourses. His writings on exactly how to manage investment, currency control, interest rate reduction, and full employment frequently contain references to hybrid entities, Keynes's attempt to move among the discursive possibilities of the modern world that bounded state, market, public, private, domestic, international, and other do-mains. In trying to move through these categories, Keynes leaned heavily on the notions of goodness derived from his aesthetics, and appeals to justice and beauty:

progress lies in the growth and recognition of semi-autonomous bodies within the State— bodies whose criterion of action within their own field is solely the public good as they understand it . . . bodies which in the ordinary course of affairs are mainly autonomous within their prescribed limitations, but are subject in the last resort to the sovereignty of the democracy expressed through Parliament. (Keynes 1926:313–14)

These semiautonomous, semipublic bodies are nowhere clearly defined. Yet in his concrete proposals for the international monetary order, proposed as Britain was going heavily into debt to the United States to finance the war against Germany, Keynes put forward a model for just such a body in the form of an International Clearing Union. The plans for the Clearing Union formed the basis for discussion in the years immediately preceding the Bretton Woods conference in 1944.[16] Indeed, Bretton Woods itself can be read as a rewriting of Keynes's proposal to ben-efit the United States and redesign the modernity Keynes had just begun to envi-sion. Earlier, he had written,

I now envisage as a possibility of the near future the separation of the countries of the world into two groups, one of which will continue to adhere for a time to a rigid gold stan-dard and the other of which will aim at some form of price stability whilst maintaining a definite but non-rigid relationship with gold. For example, I allow my mind to play with the idea of a currency union which might embrace the British Empire, Japan, South Amer-ica, Central Europe and Scandinavia with a common currency unit, the value of which would be kept stable within (say) 5 per cent of the norm more or less (i.e. within a total range of 10 per cent) in terms of a composite commodity made up of the principal articles of international trade in which the adherents to the new currency unit were chiefly interested. . . . Furthermore, there would at all times be a defined, but not invariable, relationship between the new unit and gold. (Keynes, in van Dormael 1978:31–32)

In their later drafts, Keynes's Clearing Union proposals provided for exchange controls on all international transactions, which would be handled by the Clearing Union. The CU's unit of account, which Keynes termed "bancor," would serve as an international numeraire and would be the ultimate reserve asset. Each country would be granted a quota of the Clearing Union's assets pegged to its national imports and exports, and could draw against this quota. Debtor countries would not be allowed to borrow more than their quota, but at the same time creditor countries would not be allowed to maintain an account balance larger than their quota (Eckes 1975:67–68). Furthermore, members of the Clearing Union would not be able to convert one reserve asset into another. They could convert in one direction only—into bancor. Bancor "would exist only on the clearing union's books and would merely shift from one account to another within the union" (Eckes 1975:66). The goal was to equalize balances of payments internationally, so that finance would serve what Keynes called "enterprise," not "speculation." Keynes was especially concerned that the world's exceptionally wealthy would move their assets with "the speed of the magic carpet" (Keynes 1940:31) to countries with less restrictive financial policies, and Keynes sought to head this magic movement off at the start (Moggridge 1992:673). Keynes discovered here, as well, a means for financing international operations like an international police force, postwar relief organizations, buffer stock schemes to stabilize commodity prices, and so forth (Moggridge 1992:674).

Keynes's plans were grand indeed, and, to many of his contemporaries, too vague to be practical. Yet what others observed as ill-defined can be readily seen to derive from Keynes's aesthetics and theories of probability, as well as the epistemology of post-impressionism. Keynes wrote, "The management of an international standard is an art and not a science, and no one would suggest that it is possible to draw up a formal code of action, admitting of no exceptions or qualifications, adherence to which is obligatory on peril of wrecking the whole structure. Much must necessarily be left to time and circumstance" (Keynes, in Moggridge 1986:70). The project hinged on perspective, position, and experimentation (see Mini 1990:154). Bancor, for instance, was based on the belief that international currency exchanges exist to serve enterprise, which will generate exports and increase income, spurring imports. Bancor would facilitate long-term investment over short-term speculation. As a central unit of account held in a central, international organization, it would reflect and embody the organic unity of the whole international capitalist system. And it would emerge in practice, over time, without a set plan governing it but rather borne of experimentation and of active participation in the lived reality of international trade. Here, as in other writing, Keynes laid his faith in a class of "international civil servants" (Keynes, in Moggridge 1986:79) to manage the Clearing Union. The vision was of cosmopolitans who continually reposition themselves so that they can capture the whole, and, for instance, revalue bancor from the resolution of international payments and currencies exchanges, much as a viewer resolves the dots of a pointillist painting into forms and images. These international civil servants would be like Grant's artist-viewers, thrown into a reality that they continually construct and reconstruct. "Decision-makers [would] organise their perceptions and their expectations around [several] world views, or paradigms" (Dow and Dow 1985:60), not one. Since "what is exogenous within one approach, or line of reasoning, is endogenous within another," social reformers could "tackle each question from a variety of angles, with a variety of methods" (Dow and Dow 1985:62).

While the Clearing Union plan was an important starting point for the Bretton Woods negotiations, its key features were utterly transformed as the plan became the blueprint for the International Monetary Fund and Bank for Reconstruction and Development, or World Bank. The United States was in a position to dictate the terms of these institutions, for reasons I cannot go into here (but see Crotty 1983; Helleiner 1994; Strange 1986; Leyshon and Thrift 1997). Most important here, however, was the United States' success in securing for the U.S. dollar the key position in the new international economy as the unit of account, instead of Keynes's proposed international currency unit. In practical terms, this meant that the United States "was liberated from the disciplining power of money because balance-of-payments difficulties could be countered simply through an expansion of domestic credit" (Leyshon and Thrift 1997:72). Replacing Keynes's proposed bancor with the U.S. dollar meant grounding international monetary arrangements in one version of the "real," as if it were a painting with one unchangeable vanishing point from which all perspective is derived, rather than an interior designed to confound any efforts at perspective.

The U.S. negotiating team also succeeded in setting conditions to members' access to their quota with the Fund. This meant that the Fund could actively interfere with member nations' domestic policies—a theme all too familiar as we look back on the Bretton Woods institutions' structural adjustment programs. Unlike Keynes's proposal, which required that creditor countries' surpluses in the Clearing Union be reinvested in productive enterprise elsewhere, under Bretton Woods creditor countries were under no obligation to contribute to overseas investment. They could very much go their own way, like the "legal atoms" Keynes derided in his probability theory, without having to account for their place as parts of an organic whole.

Thus, Bretton Woods took Keynes's Clearing Union plan and subverted some of its most radical elements. It did so by turning the post-impressionist ever-changing masterwork into a realist bureaucratic enterprise. There would be no international civil servants revaluing the unit of account in an ever-changing process of experimentation and engagement with complex lived realities. Nor would that unit of account be the result of the sort of perspective-shifting endeavor of moving through one of Duncan Grant's interiors. Rather, it would be the product of one perspective, that of the United States. The Fund would not be a passive force, either, merely balancing accounts against one another to ensure enterprise on a world scale in accord with individual member countries' specific interests. Rather, the Fund would actively interfere in member countries' internal affairs, enforcing frugality and thrift and at the same time encouraging speculation and capital flight. There would not be the multifaceted perspective of diversely positioned international civil servants; rather, the perspective of one member country, the United States, whose money served the dual function of a national currency and an international standard of account, would aspire to become the only available point of view.

We Have Never Had an Alternate Modernity?

There are many reasons to be wary of Keynes's Clearing Union proposal, of course, not the least of which is the poorly delineated notion of cosmopolitanism it relied on. There was a dark underbelly to that cosmopolitan vision, too, which crept into Keynes's thinking on international monetary orders beginning with his first book on the subject, written in 1913, *Indian Currency and Finance*, and culminating in his contributions to the Bretton Woods conference. Where Keynes's aesthetics failed him, he fell back on familiar discourses of bourgeois nationalism and colonial nostalgia in their most antimodern, Romantic form.

His pronouncement at the end of *Indian Currency and Finance*, that "India, so far from being anomalous, is in the forefront of monetary progress" (1913:182), is reminiscent of Mr. Cameron in Virginia Woolf's play *Freshwater*, who sought "truth" in India, and, like other anti-industrialists of the era, celebrated colonial subjects' alternative "truths" without accounting for their colonial subjection (Woolf 1935). Keynes's book studiously ignores the imperial politics of early-twentieth-century India. Indeed, there are no "Indians" in the book—except for the "Indian tax-payer," who appears in a sarcastic passage about an imaginary member of Parliament, with little knowledge of India, worrying "that some cosmopolitan syndicate of Jews was not fattening at the expense of the ryots of India, whose trustee he had often declared himself to be" (Keynes 1913:101–2). At these moments, Keynes sounds, at best, a good deal like the contemporary "neo-medievalists" described by Helleiner (1996). At worst, he sounds like an anti-Semite. This points up some of the failures of the discursive possibilities opened up by Bloomsbury.

Keynes's proposals for the Clearing Union had their origins in the plans for the establishment of a central clearing bank to handle German reparations payments after World War I. The Bank for International Settlements (BIS), set up in 1929 to serve national central banks' collaboration and cooperation on international capital transactions like the German reparations, was not a credit bank, but a clearing bank (Eckes 1975:18). Hjalmar Schacht, the German central banker from 1926 to 1930, and later finance minister under Hitler from 1934 to 1937, had proposed an international credit bank for all international financial transactions. Keynes had paid close attention to Schacht's proposals, which resonated with Nazi ideas about a new Reich encompassing Europe, centered on Germany, based on supposedly national principles of sentiment and spirit. Keynes shared with Schacht a distrust of interest and capital mobility, and commented favorably on Schacht's proposal for the return of barter to international trade. From Schacht, Keynes acquired the idea of "discarding the use of a currency having international validity and substitute for it what amounted to barter, not indeed between individuals, but between different economic units" (Keynes, in van Dormael 1978:33). "In this way," Keynes wrote, "Schacht was able to return to the essential character and original purpose of trade whilst discarding the apparatus which had been supposed to facilitate, but in fact was strangling it" (Keynes, in van Dormael 1978:33).

That "essential character" and "original purpose" that were being "strangled" by financial apparatuses hark back to classic discussions in the West about usury and the supposed deviousness of bankers, discussions ranging from Aristotle to Luther to Hitler. Keynes praised "those reformers, who look for a remedy by creating artificial carrying-costs for money through the device of requiring legal-tender currency to be periodically stamped at a prescribed cost," who "have been on the right track" (Keynes, in Mini 1990:162).[17] The rate of interest held back "the possibilities of civilization" itself (Mini 1990:163). Here, Keynes tapped into the same Romantic and anti-Semitic rhetoric animating Nazism. This illustrates one of the failures of his analytical discourse. Unable to conceptualize what a radical alternative to the "decadent international but individualist capitalism" he decried might look like, Keynes fell into the familiar "antimodern" modernity of the Reich, giving his call for the "euthanasia of the rentier" a chilling cast.

Keynes's probability theory, together with his aesthetics of "fitness," aimed to circumvent modernity's rational calculus and to discredit the possibility of bureaucratic planning. His theoretical apparatus attempted to replace the methodological individualism of neoclassical economics with an organic, much more Continental, and perhaps more mystical conception of social reality and the place of social action in the world. Keynes's theoretical orientation also led him away from the orthodox high-modern variants of Marxism circulating at midcentury. As he recounts in his memoir, speaking of his Bloomsbury circle of friends,

[We] escaped from the Benthamite tradition. But I do now regard that as the worm which has been gnawing at the insides of modern civilisation and is responsible for its present moral decay. We used to regard the Christians as the enemy, because they appeared as the representatives of tradition, convention and hocus-pocus. In truth it was the Benthamite calculus, based on an over-valuation of the economic criterion, which was destroying the quality of the popular Ideal. Moreover, it was this escape from Bentham, joined with the unsurpassable individualism of our philosophy, which has served to protect the whole lot of us from the final reductio ad absurdum of Benthamism known as Marxism. We have completely failed, indeed, to provide a substitute for these economic bogus-faiths capable of protecting or satisfying our successors. (Keynes 1949:96–97)

Keynes's project also left him open to utopianism. And this particular utopian vision ultimately subverted the radical potential of his theorizing. In criticizing convention while attempting to use conventions to guide society, Keynes and his compatriots fell back on a dominant modern version of the opposition between reason and convention, modernity and tradition, civilized and primitive, conscious and unconscious. This is clear in his discussion of the "animal spirits" leading humans to favor action over inaction. But listen to Keynes reflect on what he considered with hindsight to be his youthful naïveté regarding reason and unreason:

We were among the last of the Utopians . . . who believe in a continuing moral progress by virtue of which the human race already consists of reliable, rational, decent people, influenced by truth and objective standards, who can be safely released from the outward restraints of convention and traditional standards and inflexible rules of conduct, and left, from now onwards, to their own sensible devices, pure motives, and reliable intuitions of good. . . . In short, we repudiated all versions of the doctrine of original sin, of there being insane and irrational springs of wickedness in most men. We were not aware that civilisation was a thin and precarious crust erected by the personality and the will of a very few, and only maintained by rules and conventions skillfully put across and guilefully preserved. (Keynes 1949:99)

Or, again: "The attribution of rationality to human nature, instead of enriching it, now seems to me to have impoverished it. It ignored certain powerful and valuable springs of feeling" (Keynes 1949:101).

World War II and its aftermath jarred Keynes and shook his faith in animal spirits simply trundling along getting things done. Now, these spirits could be seen capable of motivating the darkest of passions sitting just beneath the surface of human reason. Keynes's later reflections sound downright Freudian, as when he wrote in his memoir that he and his Bloomsbury colleagues went through life "as water-spiders, gracefully skimming, as light and reasonable as air, the surface of the stream without any contact at all with the eddies or undercurrents underneath" (Keynes 1949:103).

The tendency toward filling the gaps of his modern vision with the hegemonic modernity's others was present in his work from the start, as it was in the work of Duncan Grant. Keynes's thinking on matters of finance and currency grew from his experience in the Indian civil service and his work on Indian currency reform (Keynes 1913). Grant's interiors were inspired, in part, from his voyages to Italy and Turkey, where he encountered an East that worked its way into Charleston and Grant's own self-perceptions through erotic self-portraiture.[18] Their attempts to construct an alternate modernity did not shield them from the intense pull of the dominant modernity through its self-constructed others, and led Keynes, at least, to consider gazing down the "alternative" modern paths of National Socialism.

The Probabilities of Queering Globalization

[D]isembodied spirits will be cold creatures and we must hope for the resurrection of the body. —Keynes 1908, in O'Donnell 1995:116

Keynesianism was fundamentally inspired by the orientalism, classism, and aesthetic sensibilities of early-twentieth-century England. At the same time, however, Keynes articulated a discourse that might have provided another model for modernity and for the postwar international economic order. Excavating that model may help provide new possibilities for responding to globalization in ways that do not replicate the terms of the Bretton Woods world, while avoiding the neoliberal celebration of markets and individualism or the frightening invocations of "community" that critiques of Bretton Woods often incite.

Like Keynes, critics on the left and the right often locate their opposition to globalization—which is really shorthand for the breakdown of Bretton Woods institutions—in an imagined local community, bound in time and space, made up of individuals connected by commonality of interest and sentiment. For many gays and lesbians, this can be a terrifying place in which to locate oneself. The Bloomsbury vision of cosmopolitanism and a perspective-shifting experimentalism may hold more promise. Keynes's methodology depended on "several, parallel, intertwined and mutually reinforcing" logical chains, none of which is objective or positivist but rather contingent and partial (Dow and Dow 1985:59, quoting Stohs 1983). His Clearing Union would have been an international yet translocal organization, linking diverse entities into an overarching pattern that changes depending on the position from which it is viewed, much like one of Duncan Grant's interiors. Perhaps, too, it is the sort of model we have already created for ourselves, in our own translocal communities. This model may only need to be set in motion to new purposes—purposes not explicitly about "sexuality" or the "economy," but about challenging the taken-for-granted domains of contemporary and past modern discourses.

Keynes and Grant offer "alternative scripts or inscriptions of sexual/economic identity" (Gibson-Graham 1996:139). Keynes's Clearing Union, for example, might well have been the sort of (organizational) "body" invoked by Gibson-Graham and Elizabeth Grosz. This is a body "that is permeable, that transmits in a circuit, that opens itself up rather than seals itself off, that is prepared to respond as well as to initiate" (Grosz 1994:201, quoted in Gibson-Graham 1996:139). This body, Grosz maintains, "would involve quite a radical rethinking of male sexual morphology" (Grosz 1994:201, quoted in Gibson-Graham 1996:139). The Clearing Union might have metamorphosed into a body strikingly different from contemporary capitalist morphologies.

Whether it might have done so for good or ill, I cannot say. Making explicit Keynes's designs, however, exposes the probabilistic nature of those possibilities that *have* been realized, suggesting that ultimately the apparatus of Bretton Woods, and its breakdown, was never a foregone conclusion. After all, even with the benefit of hindsight, political economists are still hard put to come up with consistent explanations of the collapse of the Bretton Woods system. Perhaps their failure reveals that the system was never quite systemic, was always a little nervous, and always contained unrealized potential, though this has been hidden, as behind a dressing-screen. It also suggests that there may be other possibilities as yet unexplored, to redesign, and to redecorate.

Notes

I would like to thank Duran Bell, Tom Boellstorff, Jim Ferguson, Julie Graham, Marcia Klotz, Liisa Malkki, Mark Moore, Sheila O'Rourke, Richard Perry, and Tamara Teghillo for useful comments and conversations as this essay was taking shape. I would also like to thank members of the Critical Theory Institute at the University of California, Irvine, for their careful reading of the essay, and the editors of this volume for their support and encouragement. All errors or inconsistencies are my responsibility alone.

1. I refer throughout this essay to an "alternative modernity," not an alternative capitalism, since Keynes did not specifically address some of the core features of market capitalism, like wage work, and since his monetary proposals did not challenge the money form itself—at least, not money as a method of payment or measure of wealth (but see the discussion of "bancor," his proposed unit of account, below). As I note in the conclusion, however, I do believe that Keynes's visions might have metamorphosed capitalism as we know it. For the purposes of this essay, I would also like to sidestep the substantial debates around the non-interchangeability of historical "modernism" and "modernity" as a cultural condition or logic.

2. Such arguments would rely on assertions about causal relationships between economics and sexualities as putatively separate spheres or cultural domains. Part of my project is to demonstrate the utter impossibility of making such claims of autonomy, and of making the kinds of causal arguments that rely on the relative autonomy of

separate cultural domains like "economics" and "sexuality" (Yanagisako and Delaney 1995).

3. See also Gibson-Graham 1996 on constructions of desire in globalization narratives.

4. See Yanagisako and Delaney 1995.

5. My method parallels Nathaniel Berman's work on aesthetic modernism in the logic of interwar reconstruction (Berman 1995) and Peter Galison's work on logical positivism and Bauhaus architecture (Galison 1990).

6. As Rod O'Donnell, a leading Keynes scholar, writes of this period in Keynes's career, "aesthetics was not of minor interest in the pre-1914 period but was *one of the foremost preoccupations of his early philosophizing*" (O'Donnell 1995:97, original emphasis).

7. I lean heavily on the so-called new Keynes scholarship in this essay. As Robert Skidelsky writes, summarizing the thrust of this scholarship, Keynes's beliefs about political and economic planning are seen as "expressions of his beliefs about ethics and probability developed before the First World War" (Skidelsky 1991:104).

8. As he wrote in his paper on melodramas,

our object is not the optically obvious; we seek by signs and symbols to make known the workings of the spirit. We endeavor to convey through the medium of the eyes and ears not what the eyes and ears immediately perceive, but what of the immaterial and intangible parts of men it is by their means possible to suggest. Mental events compose the essence of the play; they must be actual and real to the minutest flicker of feeling, the subtlest suggestions of changing sentiment. (Keynes 1906, in O'Donnell 1995:113)

9. Sheila O'Rourke (personal communication) points out that Georges Seurat's use of pointillism engaged both "scientific" theories of color and perception and, beyond formal technique, subject matter evoking alienation, the disciplining practices of industrial capitalism, child labor, the division of the world into public and private, and so on—a critique that resonates with Keynesian economic thought.

10. I do not have space here to review the post-impressionist movement in English art more thoroughly, or the signal importance of Vanessa Bell on the careers of both Keynes and Grant. The following texts have been very helpful to me in thinking through connections between post-impressionism and Keynes: Harrison 1981; Anscombe 1981; Turnbaugh 1987; Watney 1980, 1990. Roger Fry provided much of the intellectual inspiration and exhibition space for post-impressionism, and a more complete account of the connections between Keynes's philosophy of aesthetics and the post-impressionist movement would have to consider Fry's writings on art; see Fry 1920, 1996. Grant was deeply influenced by Fry after hearing him give a lecture at

Vanessa Bell's house in 1910 (Skidelsky 1983:252), as was Bell (Anscombe 1981, chap. 2). Bell and Fry were romantically involved around the same time that Bell and Grant spent more and more time painting together (1912–1914) (Anscombe 1981, chap. 2).

11. The relationship between Grant and Bell, together with Angelica's birth and subsequent denials of Angelica's paternity, makes for a fascinating story (Garnett 1984). Of interest especially, given the argument of this essay, is Angelica's anger at her parents' denial of the "truth" of her "origins." Angelica seems to have sought out the sorts of "truths" that Bloomsbury aesthetics and Keynes's economics aimed to destabilize.

12. I cannot review here the extensive debate in art history and criticism on perspective, although such debate is clearly relevant to the topic at hand. See Panofsky 1991; Steinberg 1972; and Greenberg 1986 for the canonical positions.

13. It is also aimed at Christian morality, as Skidelsky notes (1983:153).

14. This emphasis on agentive perception is what makes Keynes's and Moore's "organic" unities not simply another naturalization of social life; this is not Durkheim's functionally integrated social organism, for instance. Durkheim's conception (and that of others who naturalized social orders with organic metaphors) really took the metaphors to their limit—society *was* an organism, it was not merely like an organism, and its parts were functionally integrated into a larger whole. The parts did not construct the whole through their agentive interaction with it; the whole was not an art project, but a natural object.

15. See Sedgwick 1985; I am indebted to Richard Perry for this connection.

16. See Keynes's papers on the Clearing Union collected in volume 25 of the *Collected Writings of John Maynard Keynes.*

17. Compare the contemporary alternative global system of Islamic finance; Chapra (1985) makes the same distinction between speculation and investment as Keynes did. Islamic financial practice also imposes a special tax on capital that sits idle (*zakah*).

18. Sheila O'Rourke comments (personal communication) that walking through the Grand Bazaar, the Blue Mosque, and other Turkish sites may have afforded Grant an experience in "constantly changing perspective and perception. The walls of these structures are covered with Ottoman tiles that are decorated with very busy little designs that create an optical effect not different from that of pointillism to the moving spectator. Walking through the decorated maze of the Bazaar . . . would parallel the experience of walking through Grant's interiors." This is a fascinating observation that space constraints forbid me from exploring here, but that leads me to reflect further on resonances between Grant, Keynes, and modernist Islam. I would like to thank Sheila O'Rourke for this comment, and for her careful reading of this essay.

References

Anscombe, Isabelle. 1981. *Omega and After: Bloomsbury and the Decorative Arts*. London: Thames and Hudson.

Barry, Andrew, Thomas Osborne, and Nikolas Rose, eds. 1996. *Foucault and Political Reason: Liberalism, Neo-Liberalism and Rationalities of Government*. Chicago: University of Chicago Press.

Berle, A., and G. C. Means. 1932. *The Modern Corporation and Private Property*. New York: Macmillan.

Berman, Nathaniel. 1995. "Modernism, Nationalism, and the Rhetoric of Reconstruction." In *After Identity: A Reader in Law and Culture*, ed. Dan Danielsen and Karen Engle, 229–50. New York: Routledge.

Carabelli, Anna. 1985. "Keynes on Cause, Chance and Possibility." In *Keynes' Economics: Methodological Issues*, ed. Tony Lawson and Hashem Pesaran, 151–80. London: Croom Helm.

Chapra, M. Umer. 1985. *Towards a Just Monetary System*. Leicester: Islamic Foundation.

Crotty, James R. 1983. "On Keynes and Capital Flight." *Journal of Economic Literature* 21:59–65.

Davis, John B. 1991. "Keynes's Critiques of Moore: Philosophical Foundations of Keynes's Economics." *Cambridge Journal of Economics* 15:61–77.

———. 1994. *Keynes's Philosophical Development*. Cambridge: Cambridge University Press.

D'Emilio, John. 1984. "Capitalism and Gay Identity." In *Powers of Desire: The Politics of Sexuality*, ed. A. Snitow, C. Stansell, and S. Thompson, 100–113. New York: Monthly Review Press.

Dow, Alexander, and Sheila Dow. 1985. "Animal Spirits and Rationality." In *Keynes' Economics: Methodological Issues*, ed. Tony Lawson and Hashem Pesaran, 46–65. London: Croom Helm.

Eckes, Alfred E., Jr. 1975. *A Search for Solvency: Bretton Woods and the International Monetary System, 1941–1971*. Austin: University of Texas Press.

Friedman, Milton. 1960. *A Program for Monetary Stability*. New York: Fordham University Press.

Fry, Roger. 1920. *Vision and Design*. New York: Meridian, 1956.

———. 1996. *A Roger Fry Reader*. Ed. and intro. Christopher Reed. Chicago: University of Chicago Press.

Galison, Peter. 1990. "Aufbau/Bauhaus: Logical Positivism and Architectural Modernism." *Critical Inquiry* 16:709–52.

Garnett, Angelica. 1984. *Deceived with Kindness: A Bloomsbury Childhood*. London: Chatto and Windus.

Gibson-Graham, J. K. 1996. *The End of Capitalism (As We Knew It): A Feminist Critique of Political Economy*. Oxford: Blackwell.

Greenberg, Clement. 1986. *The Collected Essays and Criticism*. Ed. John O'Brian. Chicago: University of Chicago Press.

Grosz, Elizabeth. 1994. *Volatile Bodies: Towards a Corporeal Feminism*. Bloomington: Indiana University Press.

Harrison, Charles. 1981. *English Art and Modernism, 1900–1939*. New Haven: Yale University Press.

Harvey, David. 1990. *The Condition of Postmodernity: An Enquiry into the Origins of Cultural Change*. Cambridge, MA: Blackwell.

Hayek, F. A. 1990. *Denationalisation of Money: The Argument Refined*. London: Institute of Economic Affairs.

Helleiner, Eric. 1994. *States and the Reemergence of Global Finance: From Bretton Woods to the 1990s*. Ithaca: Cornell University Press.

———. 1996. "International Political Economy and the Greens." *New Political Economy* 1 (1):59–77.

Hession, Charles. 1983. "Keynes, Stratchey, and the Gay Courage to Be." *Challenge* 36 (4):53–59.

Keynes, John Maynard. 1905a. "Miscellanea Ethica." Selections used here are quoted from O'Donnell 1995.

———. 1905b. "A Theory of Beauty." Selections used here are quoted from O'Donnell 1995.

———. 1906. "Shall We Write Melodramas?" Selections used here are quoted from O'Donnell 1995.

———. 1908. "Prince Rupert or Prince Henry?" Selections used here are quoted from O'Donnell 1995.

———. 1913. *Indian Currency and Finance*. Collected Writings of John Maynard Keynes. Vol. 1. London: Macmillan.

———. 1921. *Treatise on Probability*. Collected Writings of John Maynard Keynes. Vol. 8. London: Macmillan.

———. 1923. *Tract on Monetary Reform*. Collected Writings of John Maynard Keynes. Vol. 4. London: Macmillan.

———. 1926. "The End of Laissez-Faire." In *Essays in Persuasion*, 312–22. New York: Harcourt, Brace.

———. 1928. Letter to F. Lucas, 19 April 1928. In Skidelsky 1991.

Keynes, John Maynard. 1933. "National Self-Sufficiency." *Yale Review* 22 (4):755–69.

———. 1935. *The General Theory of Employment, Interest, and Money*. New York: Harcourt, Brace, 1964.

———. 1937. "The General Theory of Employment." *Quarterly Journal of Economics* 51:209–13.

———. 1940. *Activities, 1940–1944: Shaping the Postwar World—The Clearing Union*. Collected Writings of John Maynard Keynes. Vol. 25. London: Macmillan.

———. 1949. "My Early Beliefs." In *Two Memoirs*, 78–103. Intro. David Garnett. New York: Augustus M. Kelley.

Leyshon, Andrew, and Nigel Thrift. 1997. *Money/Space: Geographies of Monetary Transformation*. London: Routledge.

Luther, Martin. 1520. "An Appeal to the Ruling Class of German Nationality as to the Amelioration of the State of Christendom." In *Martin Luther: Selections from His Writings*, ed. John Dillenberger, 403–85. Garden City, NY: Anchor Books.

Mini, Piero V. 1990. *Keynes, Bloomsbury, and* The General Theory. London: Macmillan.

Moggridge, D. E. 1986. "Keynes and the International Monetary System, 1909–46." In *International Monetary Problems and Supply-Side Economics*, ed. Jon S. Cohen and G. C. Harcourt, 56–83. London: Macmillan.

———. 1992. *Maynard Keynes: An Economist's Biography*. London: Routledge.

Moore, G. E. 1903. *Principia Ethica*. Cambridge: Cambridge University Press, 1993.

O'Donnell, Rod. 1995. "Keynes on Aesthetics." In *New Perspectives on Keynes*, ed. Allin F. Cottrell and Michael S. Lawlor, 93–121. *History of Political Economy*, annual supplement to volume 27. Durham: Duke University Press.

Panofsky, Erwin. 1991. *Perspective as Symbolic Form*. Trans. Christopher S. Wood. New York: Zone Books.

Radice, H. 1984. "The National Economy: A Keynesian Myth?" *Capital and Class* 22:111–40.

Reed, Christopher. 1988. "Bloomsbury Art: Re-imagining the Domestic." Ph.D. diss., quoted in Watney 1990.

Reichardt, Jasia. 1988. "Op Art." In *Concepts of Modern Art*, ed. Nikos Stagnos, 239–43. London: Thames and Hudson.

Ritter, Gretchen. 1997. *Goldbugs and Greenbacks: The Antimonopoly Tradition and the Politics of Finance in America, 1865–1896*. Cambridge: Cambridge University Press.

Robinson, Joan. 1953. "Lecture Delivered at Oxford by a Cambridge Economist." *Collected Economic Papers*, Vol. 4.

Rotheim, Roy J. 1988. "Keynes and the Language of Probability and Uncertainty." *Journal of Post-Keynesian Economics* 11 (1):82–99.

Sedgwick, Eve Kosofsky. 1985. *Between Men: English Literature and Male Homosocial Desire*. New York: Columbia University Press.

Skidelsky, Robert. 1983. *John Maynard Keynes*. Vol. 1, *Hopes Betrayed, 1883–1920*. New York: Viking.

———. 1991. "Keynes's Philosophy of Practice and Economic Policy." In *Keynes as Philosopher-Economist*, ed. R. M. O'Donnell, 104–23. London: Macmillan.

Steinberg, Leo. 1972. *Other Criteria: Confrontations with Twentieth-Century Art*. New York: Oxford University Press.

Stohs, M. 1983. "'Uncertainty' in Keynes' *General Theory*: A Rejoinder." *History of Political Economy* 15:87–91.

Strange, Susan. 1986. *Casino Capitalism*. London: Blackwell.

Strathern, Marilyn. 1992. *After Nature: English Kinship in the Late Twentieth Century*. Cambridge: Cambridge University Press.

Todd, Dorothy, and Raymond Mortimer. 1929. *The New Interior Decoration: An Introduction to Its Principles and International Survey of Its Methods*. London: Batsford.

Turnbaugh, Douglas Blair. 1987. *Duncan Grant and the Bloomsbury Group*. Secaucus: Lyle Stuart.

van Dormael, Armand. 1978. *Bretton Woods: Birth of a Monetary System*. London: Macmillan.

Watney, Simon. 1980. *English Post-Impressionism*. London: Studio Vista.

———. 1990. *The Art of Duncan Grant*. London: John Murray.

Woolf, Virginia. 1935. *Freshwater: A Comedy*. New York: Harcourt, Brace, Jovanovich, 1975.

Yanagisako, Sylvia, and Carol Delaney, eds. 1995. *Naturalizing Power: Essays in Feminist Cultural Analysis*. New York: Routledge.

Commodity Capitalism and Transformations in Gay Identity

Ann Pellegrini

> We're here, we're queer, we're not going shopping.
>
> —Queer Nation

I want to begin with some of the usual, but not for that reason any less sincere, disclaimers as to the provisional status of the claims—a series of hunches, really—unfolded here. In what follows, I am interested in tracing two narratives of transformation: (1) from industrial capitalism to postindustrial or commodity capitalism; (2) from homosexuality as minority identity to homosexuality as "alternative lifestyle." Much of my argument depends on, even as it criticizes, John D'Emilio's much-reprinted "Capitalism and Gay Identity"and Donald M. Lowe's *The Body in Late-Capitalist USA*. Both D'Emilio and Lowe offer historical accounts that emplot the relations between homosexuality and capitalism. Indeed, though in different ways and with somewhat different emphases, both men seem to narrate capitalism as the very emplotment of homosexual identity.

It will be clear that I find much that is persuasive and helpful in both D'Emilio's and Lowe's studies. Yet, in setting the word "narrative" up front—as in "narratives of transformation"—I mean also to mark my own skepticism about the adequacy (as theory or history) of their accounts, even as I retell them.[1] I hope, however, that I will be repeating with a difference. With a lesbian difference, perhaps?

The Story So Far

One way of writing the history of gay identity and gay liberation in the twentieth century is to say, with Amy Gluckman and Betsy Reed, in their introduction to *Homo Economics: Capitalism, Community, and Lesbian and Gay Life*, that "social and economic policies [e.g., antidiscrimination statutes, domestic partner benefits provided by major corporations and universities, targeting of lesbian and gay consumers by corporate America] are *following* cultural shifts and beginning to accommodate lesbian and gay life."[2] Of course, economic relations have also been *productive* of "lesbian and gay life" and of growing, if still uneasy, social tolerance of homosexuality.

The point I mean to stress here is that economic policies have not simply followed on developments in lesbian and gay identity, but have been also in some way generative. So the accommodation—between market and identity, and between economic openings and social tolerance—goes both ways. Yet it remains an open question, one I cannot settle here but one on which I want to provoke discussion, what the relationship is between legal and social rights, on the one hand, and economic recognition and consumptuary opportunities, on the other. That is, what is the relationship between being addressed as *consuming* subjects (and gay men and lesbians are being so addressed, openly addressed *as* gay men and lesbians for the first time) and becoming full *social* subjects, subjects, that is, of rights? To the extent that the discourse of rights was, at its emergence, marked by property relations (rights as a kind of private property), perhaps this form of social address—in which capitalism reaches out to queer consuming subjects—is the very fulfillment of rights and, thus, a fulfillment that can only disappoint. Yet might these consuming subjects also queer capitalism?

In his important essay "Capitalism and Gay Identity," historian John D'Emilio argues for the implicature of modern gay identities in the evolution of industrial capitalism from the eighteenth century forward.[3] D'Emilio points out how the expansion of capital and rise of wage labor (in which the laborer owns his/her ability to work and can sell his/her labor power, his/her use value) radically transformed (1) the structure and functions of the family, (2) the ideology of family life, and (3) the meaning of "heterosexual relations" (469). "Heterosexual relations" is D'Emilio's term (469), and it is an unfortunately mystifying one, smuggling in a set of claims we might want to open up rather than decide in advance. By it, however, he means that technology of sex that results in natal reproduction, a technology we misrecognize as nature when we refer to it, simply, as "sexual intercourse" or, still more simply, as just "sex."

Here I am thinking with Henry Abelove's marvelous arguments regarding the invention of foreplay in the long eighteenth century.[4] This was not an invention of a heretofore unknown set of practices and pleasures so much as the reorganization and reconstruction of a tradition of very diverse cross-sex sexual behaviors as merely preliminary to the real thing, "sexual intercourse so-called" (Abelove, 340). Such a reorganization is, as Abelove observes, an "important passage in the making of modern heterosexuality," a making that raises one act above all others in the field of the sexual.

As wage labor spread and the production of goods became socialized, D'Emilio argues, sexuality was released from the "imperative" of penis-in-vagina-sex-with-seminal-emission for the purpose of producing more and more children. In separating sexuality, as sexual pleasure, from procreation, wage capital creates the conditions whereby some women and men can organize and experience their personal lives around their erotic attraction to their own sex.

To be sure, this transformation and the possibilities of sexualized self-affirmation it helped to produce happened unevenly and were mediated by differences in region, gender, race and ethnicity, religion, and national status. For example, although both men and women were drawn out of the household economy and into the wage labor force, for women of a certain class, working for wages usually stopped upon marriage (when they began working for free). It was not the rise of wage labor per se that allowed for elaboration of lesbian identity, but twentieth-century transformations in sex roles and the breakdown in the sexual division of labor, changes that enabled middle-class women to work outside the home and attain some economic independence from men (Gluckman and Reed). As Miranda Joseph has argued, the unevenness of the elaboration of (homo)sexual identity and the meaning of family indicates that family and sexual identity have been articulated through racializing and patriarchal logics and not simply through the logic of capital.

D'Emilio makes clear that the growing separation between sexual pleasure and procreation did not break the hold of the family. Instead, family becomes invested as that place alone in which emotional sustenance can be achieved, a buffer zone from the hard realities of economic struggle. Stripped of one kind of economic justification, family gains some others: It will occupy one side of a new structural opposition between production (coded as male) and social reproduction (coded as female). It will be the provenance of the emergent and newly idealized middle-class heterosexual couple. The invention of homosexuality was also, then, the invention of heterosexuality, and family has shifted from site of production to site of consumption.

The family idealized under modern forms of U.S. capitalism is thus caught in a series of contradictions. On the one hand, changes in the organization of labor and capital undermined the family by taking away its economic rationale; on the other, family has become enshrined as emotional and psychic glue, the place where our need for stability, love, affection is nurtured, and the only place where it can be nurtured and satisfied. The privatized nuclear family fits well with capitalism. Production occurs outside the family home, but the products of socialized labor (i.e., products of wage labor outside the household) belong to the owners of private property.

As D'Emilio argues, despite the fact that child rearing has been progressively socialized, with the great majority of children being educated outside the home and by persons who are not their parents, there is still a stress on child rearing and reproduction as essentially private tasks and rights. Children belong to their parents (unless they are the children of poor people). To be sure, every society needs structures for reproduction and childbearing and for the reproduction of social life. But there is no one necessary way to do family or kinship, no necessary ties between natal reproduction and social reproduction, no one way gender and sexuality have to be organized and lived.

Ideologically, capitalism drives people into heterosexual families and keeps them there (or tries to). Each generation comes of age having internalized heterosexual intimacy as the model for human relationship. But materially, capitalism knocks the legs out from under the family, by reducing the family's capacity to be self-sufficient, and thus weakens the bonds that formerly kept families together. Paradoxically, then, people come to experience instability and insecurity in the very place they have been taught to expect and receive emotional happiness. This paradox helps to make sense of the scapegoating of lesbians, gay men, heterosexual feminists, so-called welfare queens, and anyone else who is seen to undermine "family values." But whose family and whose family values? This is a question to which I will return below.

Gay identity too is enmeshed in ongoing contradictions. Gay men and lesbians owe much of our newfound freedom to "economic trends." Wage labor helped to create an "*escape route* from heterosexual family life" (Gluckman and Reed, xiii; emphasis added). Yet openly gay people still face occupational segregation and discrimination, which may hit lesbians and gay men of color more heavily. The

137

array of disincentives includes lost jobs, fewer promotions, discrimination in housing and banking and health care. As Gluckman and Reed note, many gay people are forced to choose between being openly gay and having access to a wider array of occupations (7). So capitalism has been among the conditions enabling the emergence and development of gay identity, but it has also helped to generate and reproduce, via links to an ideology of heterosexuality, conditions whereby gay people are disenfranchised.

Increasingly, however, corporations, universities, and city governments are offering domestic partnership benefits to their lesbian and gay employees. (That these benefits are usually restricted to same-sex couples, since cross-sex couples can and "should" marry, dulls this cutting edge, *if* it is a cutting edge at all.) There are major marketing efforts to target gay and, to a lesser extent, lesbian consumers. Marketers, gay and straight, generate data that purport to show the high disposable income of gay men and lesbians. Never mind the fact that these data mistake the incomes of readers of high-end gay magazines for the incomes of all gay men and lesbians, in a move that indicates just how intertwined are citizenship and consumption, these data are re-cited by gay newspapers and even some lesbian and gay rights organizations to show what good citizens we are and can't we have our rights too.[5]

As a strategy for courting corporate America, it seems to have worked: more and more companies have developed ad campaigns that represent readably gay or lesbian images. As Gluckman and Reed note, Absolut vodka is the ur-case here. Others work the line by pitching to both heterosexual and queer consumers at once, relying on the latter's ability to read between the lines and the former's—what?—commitment to denotation. (I continue to marvel at the profitable ignorance of heterosexuality. Innocent of any reading but one, the straight consumer covers his ass in a hermeneutics of plausible deniability.)

However, as a political strategy the recitation of high-earning, high-spending, double-income gay and lesbian consumers has only courted disaster. Opponents of gay rights point to the same distorted data to make their case that gays already have, if anything, more rights than anyone else. In a time of large-scale social and economic changes, the rhetoric of "special rights" draws much of its persuasive power from the very statistics some gay organizations have been so busily promoting. Cases in point: Overlooked Opinions (a gay marketing organization) received requests for data on gay income from the Colorado attorney general's office. The request was issued while Colorado was preparing to defend the constitutionality of Amendment 2 before the Supreme Court (Gluckman and Reed, 6) Although Colorado lost that case, and Amendment 2 was overturned, in his ,cathing dissent Justice Antonin Scalia too cited claims of "high disposable" income as reasons to uphold Amendment 2 and, with it, the logic of special rights.

But what accounts for the new willingness of some companies to chase gay dollars? Is it simply a case of tolerance winning the day, or does it suggest that capitalism can accommodate gay identity without fundamentally undermining its structuring inequalities? As Gluckman and Reed argue, corporations have calculated that the benefits of pitching to gay and lesbian consumers may outweigh the risks of enraging conservative groups and their constituents. But this risk must be recalculated with each product. Companies such as Absolut or Calvin Klein, which do not serve a conservative, family-oriented constituency, are more likely to reach out to and for gay dollars (6). However, do not hold your breath for Proctor and Gamble to do a marketing campaign for diapers featuring Melissa, Julie, and baby makes three.

The right is not alone in privileging some kinds of families over others. Even D'Emilio's analysis recapitulates an antagonism between family and homosexuality. He produces a homosexual coming-out narrative that seems to require a coming out of family, as the homosexual subject leaves family of origins behind. So, for example, when he notes that "among working-class immigrants in the early twentieth century, closely knit kin networks and an ethic of solidarity placed constraints on individual autonomy that made gayness a difficult option to pursue" (471), he implies that leaving family behind is a nonnegotiable condition of gay identity. Gluckman and Reed sound this theme of disconnection as well, when they narrate the way economic changes have opened an "escape route from heterosexual family life." But isn't this to articulate gayness with or even as whiteness? It would certainly seem to place racialized or working-class queers between rock hudson and a hard place. But what if some ways of doing kinship are not dispensable? What if some ways of doing kinship actually provide different possibilities for elaborating queer desires and doing queer identities? We need to see the ways such accounts (and I hope it will be clear just how valuable I find D'Emilio's essay) yet narrate homosexual identity and community formation through an unmarked whiteness. What's more, in suggesting a misfit between homosexuality and family as "we" know it, they potentially reproduce what they would critique.

From Identity to Lifestyle?

Let us recall, with Foucault, that the deployment of sexuality "has to be seen as the self-affirmation of one class rather than the enslavement of another."[6] Far from attempting to "disqualify or nullify" the sex of those whom they would dominate, Foucault argues, the bourgeoisie turned their sights on themselves, focusing in ever and expanding detail on "that aspect of themselves which troubled and preoccupied it more than any other, begged and obtained its attention, and which it cultivated with a mixture of fear, curiosity, delight, and excitement" (123–24). Crucially, "what was formed was a political ordering of life, not through an enslavement of others, but through an affirmation of self" (123). This new disciplinary regime of sexuality helped to generate and affirm middle-class identity. It was also generative of new norms of health (with its contrary, disease), new techniques of individuation with a concomitant specification of individuals (42–43), as well as a renewed and sexualized form of interiority/individuality for all.

In his gloss on Foucault, Donald M. Lowe suggests that this new disciplinary sexuality fits well with an earlier moment in capitalism, industrial capitalism, which worked through the structural oppositions production/social reproduction, public/private, male/female, and outer/inner, and privileged the first term of each of these binary pairs.[7] However, Lowe goes on to argue that the collapse of the structural opposition between production and social reproduction, under what he calls "the hegemony of exchangist practices," requires a rethinking of Foucault's model of sexuality. If disciplinary sexuality accommodated industrial capitalism, in late capitalism, sexuality has been transformed "from a disciplinary to a consumptuary phenomenon" (Lowe, 127). He concludes, "We now have a very different sexuality" (127).

On what does Lowe base these suggestions? First, technological advances, such as the pill and other forms of contraception, have helped to disjoin sexual pleasure from natal reproduction for the population as a whole, and not just for those individuals who did not participate in sexual acts that could result in natal reproduction in the first place. What's more, not only can there be sexual pleasure without reproduction, but there can now be natal reproduction without any sex at all: through, for example, in vitro fertilization, alternative insemination, and gestational surrogacy. Second, separated from social and natal reproduction, Lowe argues, sexuality becomes a sign and a site to animate late-capitalist consumption. You can sell sex, and you can sell to it. "The result," he writes, "is a sexual *lifestyle*, as distinct from the bourgeois assumption of an interiorized sexual *identity*" (127; emphases added).

He develops his thesis in most detail around the case of *male* homosexuality, theorizing a shift from the identity orientation of an emergent homosexual minority in the 1960s (an incorrect periodization, by the way) to the emergence of "gay culture" in the 1970s as an "alternative lifestyle." Via practices of consumption and economic self-organization, Lowe argues, "an urban male homosexual minority with sufficient income transforms itself into the gay lifestyle" (135). He goes on, "Gays display themselves as consumers of clothing, holidays, theater and cinema, restaurant meals, cosmetics, and household goods" (137), lifestyle indicators familiar to Overlooked Opinions as well. In turn, and surprisingly, the patterns of consumption identified with gay men are then picked up and sold as avant-garde trends (137).[8] In part, this is because a subculture's stylistic innovations may be the first things seen by the media.

Lowe implies that the commodification of gayness as lifestyle bars politics. However, it seems to me that commodification is not the end of politics, need not amount to depoliticization, but may actually constitute the starting point for contemporary lesbian and gay politics in the United States. Rather than nostalgically yearning for lesbian and gay identities unmarked by commodity capitalism, what if we acknowledged that lesbian and gay identities have always been in some way marked by capitalism, and so too have heterosexual identities (though we rarely speak of heterosexuality as any identity at all)?

What and whose losses does such nostalgia wishfully regret? "What is lost," Donna Haraway argues in another context, "is often virulent forms of oppression, nostalgically naturalized in the face of current violation."[9] We just cannot disarticulate lesbian and gay identities from capital, even as we must move to get as sharp a critical purchase on the relations between capital and any sexual identity at all. What's more, to suggest this is *not* to think (homo)sexuality as detritus or, to use a less charged term, epiphenomenon of capital. If, as Miranda Joseph has argued, there is nothing new about the intimacy of capital and community formation, to the relay capital-identity-community, we might then reply, "So what?" This is not the end of politics, homosexual, gay, queer, or otherwise, but among its operating conditions and constraints.

Although I am intrigued by some of Lowe's suggestions, which seem to me to make sense of the new homo shopping network, nonetheless I think he has not taken sufficient account of the persistence of disciplinary models of sexuality. Disciplinary sexuality has not gone quietly into the night, but rather seems to

141

operate side by side with the new consumptuary model he outlines. The flap over the presidential penis illustrates many of Lowe's claims regarding the commodification and valorization of previously relatively autonomous terrains of non-exchangist practices (e.g., social reproduction, political-administrative functions of the state, and other sites of reciprocal social relations). Politics has been hypersexualized. But, at the same time, don't the apparently endless speculations over Bill Clinton's sexual conduct, speculations that have been elevated into criminal investigations, also mark the holdover of a disciplinary sexuality? The tensions between these two models both illustrate *and* energize renewed ideological disputes over the meaning of family, the role and place of women, and the morality of homosexuality and other so-called alternative lifestyles. These disputes are themselves also displacements of economic anxieties, as queers of all sorts get blamed for the economic changes that have reshaped and destabilized the cultural landscape.[10]

Moreover, I am troubled by the exemplary status of homosexuality—male homosexuality—in Lowe's study. (Lesbianism seems to have no status at all, as if lesbians are the abject of capital.) He is quick to point out that everyone is caught up in this new dynamic, not just homosexuals. But homosexuality is the only detailed example he offers of this shift from identity to lifestyle. This is not a neutral decision. My concern here is less a case of policing Lowe's examples; if you cannot give a "positive" example, do not cite us at all. Rather, it seems to me that he can only generate this theory around homosexuality because the description cum reduction of homosexuality to a matter of lifestyle choice only is a ready-made example. In the discourse of heteronormativity, gays have lifestyles, everyone else (an everyone else that need not be further identified because we know who and what we are) has lives. But is gayness understood as an "alternative lifestyle" by self-identified gay men and lesbians? Much of the continuing appeal of and to identity on the part of gay men and lesbians has to do with precisely the dismissals the language of lifestyle enacts.

I must mark too Lowe's curious lesbian lacuna, a blank spot that is hardly his alone. Witness Daniel Harris's annoying *Rise and Fall of Gay Culture*, in which lesbians are but a shadow in Harris's tale of gay assimilation. Yet what sense are we to make of the apparent hypervisibility of lesbians (or what passes for lesbianism) in popular culture? From films to TV to mainstream magazines like *People*, *Time*, and *TV Guide* (that weather vane of cultural consciousness), images of lesbians and lesbianism are being produced, consumed, and circulated like never before. We need to distinguish between (at least) two modes of hypervisibility: what I would call the representation (and stereotypification) of bad subjects and the representation and selling of consumable objects. For "bad subjects," think gay men; for marketable, consumable objects, think lesbians. Or, rather, think "lesbians." (Arguably, the cancellation of *Ellen*, one year after its famous coming-out episode, suggests the volatility of the schematic I have just presented. It may well be that *Ellen* and the actress with whom the show was identified, Ellen DeGeneres, crossed from marketable object to bad subject when the show refused to adopt the point of view of the heterosexual viewer, refused, that is, to portray lesbianism as other.)

Whose is the face of perverse public sexuality? The alleged perversity of gay male sexuality means that it is always and only too public by far. But what of lesbian sexuality? Is it seen as any sexuality at all? And, where it is, sexuality for whom, pleasure for whom? We need to think at the intersections of sexuality and gender if we are to make sense of the paradoxical scene of lesbianism, in which a Larry Kramer (some of whose best friends are, or at least know, lesbians) can cite the "lesbian difference" as a way to discipline and normalize gay men. Kramer is not the only man (nor even the only gay man) overcome with a passion for lesbians, of course. Witness Howard Stern. Frankly, I prefer Stern's hetero-fantasy of lesbians. At least his lesbians have sex—with other women, even.

In another place I have written about the way the sign "lesbian" is being circulated as a wedge against politicizing and publicizing the sexual:

Mainstream representations of lesbians are the picture of a properly self-regulated public face, in fact, of a public face so well disciplined that the sexual can be politely passed over. This is the closet as public spectacle. Stripped of its sexual and political sting, this lesbianism for public consumption—call it Lesbianism Lite—points back towards the private by representing the domestic as ideal.

In this either/or scenario, stereotyped images of lesbians get pitted against stereotyped images of gay men. Sanitized and celibate, lesbian images are fit for home consumption, with no parental advisory required. And that's exactly the point. In the end, what these "positive" images of lesbianism affirm is the wish that gay men be more like lesbians and disappear even, or especially, when in public.[11]

There is no neat solution to the paradoxes—of economy, of representation, of sexual politics or identity—queer subjects currently find and make ourselves in. Yet the messiness of the present might be something to be valued, rather than

143

abruptly foreclosed. In suspending an ending—of the project of criticism as of politics—I hope to leave the matter (and materializations) of doing homosexual (into gay and lesbian and queer) "identities" under commodity capitalism open for and toward another writing, another future.

Notes

Earlier versions of this essay were presented at a joint meeting of the seminars on Post-National Studies and Feminist Literary Theory and Culture at the Center for Literary and Cultural Studies, Harvard University; and as part of "Queer Publics, Queer Privates," a two-day conference at New York University. I am grateful to Kalpana Seshadri-Crooks, Lynne Layton, and Andrea Walsh for inviting me to speak to their CLCS seminars, and to Carolyn Dever, Phillip Brian Harper, Lisa Duggan, and José Muñoz, who invited me to NYU. Mary Poovey's gracious response to my paper at the latter occasion helped me to see some of the issues presented in this published version more clearly. Finally, the concerns that animate this essay have emerged, in part, out of some collaborative writing and thinking I have been doing with Janet R. Jakobsen.

1. For a related critique of the way capitalism gets narrated, see Miranda Joseph, "Telling Tales, Exploitation, and Domination; or Narrating Post-Fordism" (paper presented at "Queer Globalization/Local Homosexualities: Citizenship, Sexuality, and the Afterlife of Colonialism," Center for Lesbian and Gay Studies, City University of New York, April 24, 1998).
2. Amy Gluckman and Betsy Reed, eds., *Homo Economics: Capitalism, Community, and Lesbian and Gay Life* (New York: Routledge, 1997), xi–xii; emphasis added. Further references to this anthology will appear in the main text.
3. John D'Emilio, "Capitalism and Gay Identity," in *Powers of Desire*, ed. Ann Snitow, Christine Stansell, and Sharon Thompson (New York: Monthly Review Press, 1983); reprinted in *The Lesbian and Gay Studies Reader*, ed. Henry Abelove, Michèle Aina Barale, and David M. Halperin (New York: Routledge, 1993), 467–76. Page numbers cited in the main text refer to the version of the D'Emilio essay published in *The Lesbian and Gay Studies Reader*.
4. Henry Abelove, "Some Speculations on the History of 'Sexual Intercourse' during the 'Long Eighteenth Century' in England," in *Nationalisms and Sexualities*, ed. Andrew Parker, Mary Russo, Doris Sommer, and Patricia Yaeger (New York: Routledge, 1992), 335–42. Further references to this article will appear in the main text.
5. For an important critique of these data, see M. V. Lee Badgett, "Beyond Biased Sam-

ples: Challenging the Myths on the Economic Status of Lesbians and Gay Men," in Gluckman and Reed, *Homo Economics*, 65–71.

6. Michel Foucault, *History of Sexuality,* vol. 1: *An Introduction* (New York: Vintage, 1978), 123.

7. Donald M. Lowe, *The Body in Late-Capitalist USA* (Durham: Duke University Press, 1995).

8. See also Dane Clark, "Commodity Lesbianism," in Abelove, Barale, and Halperin, *The Lesbian and Gay Studies Reader.*

9. Donna Haraway, "Manifesto for Cyborgs," in *Feminist Social Thought: A Reader,* ed. Diana Tietjens Meyers (New York: Routledge, 1997), 519.

10. Some of us like the destabilization of gender and sexual certainties, of course. Some others of "us," also homosexual, do not. The regime of discipline and punish has found adherents among self-identified homosexuals too. Here's one self-appointed guardian of homonormativity, Jonathan Rauch, professing new rules of conduct in the pages of the *New Republic*: "If gay marriage is recognized, single gay people over a certain age should not be surprised when they are disapproved of or pitied. That is a vital part of what makes marriage work. It's stigma as social policy. If marriage is to work, it cannot be merely a 'lifestyle option'" (May 6, 1996).

11. Ann Pellegrini, "Lesbianism Lite," *New York Blade*, October 24, 1997, 27.

Part 3

DIASPORIC QUEER IDENTITIES

8   Local Sites/Global Contexts

The Transnational Trajectories of Deepa Mehta's *Fire*

Gayatri Gopinath

In 1995 a group of Indian immigrant businessmen in New York City known as the FIA (Federation of Indian Associations) denied both SALGA (the New York–based South Asian Lesbian and Gay Association) and Sakhi (an anti–domestic violence women's group) the right to march in the annual New York City India Day parade. The two activist organizations were banned from the parade, which celebrates India's independence from the British in 1947, on the grounds that both groups were, in essence, "anti-national."[1] In 1996, however, the FIA allowed Sakhi to participate while continuing to deny SALGA the right to march. The FIA, as self-styled arbiter of communal and national belonging, thus deemed it appropriate for women to march as "Indian women," even perhaps as "feminist Indian women," but could not envision women marching as "Indian queers" or "Indian lesbians."

This particular configuration of gender, sexuality, and nation was echoed in the recent riots in Bombay and New Delhi prompted by the release of the 1996 film *Fire*. The film, made by the Indian Canadian director Deepa Mehta, depicts a lesbian relationship between two sisters-in-law in a middle-class, joint family household in contemporary New Delhi. In December 1998 local theaters in various urban centers in India were stormed by dozens of activists from the Shiv Sena, a Hindu right-wing organization that forms the militant wing of the Hindu

149

nationalist government currently in power. The Shiv Sena justified their actions by claiming that lesbianism is an affront to Hinduism and "alien to Indian culture."[2] Prior to the riots, the Indian media had made similar criticisms, claiming that the film had "very weak links to the true Indian milieu."[3] In other words, both the mainstream media and the extremist Hindu nationalist movement used the charge of inauthenticity (the notion that the film wasn't "truly Indian") to disavow both its queer content and its diasporic origins.

It is this conflation of "queer" and "diaspora," and the construction of both as impure and inauthentic within a hegemonic diasporic and nationalist imaginary, that I interrogate throughout my larger project on race, gender and sexuality in South Asian diasporic cultural production. Juxtaposing the controversies surrounding the India Day parade in New York City and the release of *Fire* in Bombay and New Delhi makes clear the ways an Indian immigrant male bourgeoisie (embodied by the FIA) reconstitutes in the diaspora the contemporary nationalist discourses of communal belonging in India (most blatantly espoused by the Shiv Sena). Both the FIA and the Shiv Sena interpellate "India" as Hindu, patriarchal, middle-class, and free of homosexuals. Furthermore, the conduct of both the FIA and the Shiv Sena makes explicit how hegemonic nationalist discourses, reproduced in the diaspora, position "woman" and "lesbian" as mutually exclusive categories to be disciplined in different ways. Within patriarchal nationalist and patriarchal diasporic logic, the "lesbian" can exist only outside the "home" as household, community, and nation, whereas the "woman" can exist only within it.

My project examines how the gendered and sexualized discourses of bourgeois and religious nationalism in South Asia are reproduced in the diaspora through different religious, political, and economic structures, as well as through particular cultural practices. The ideological linkages that can be traced between immigrant communities in the diaspora and nationalist discourses in South Asia demand that we see these disparate sites as crucially connected, interdependent, and mutually constitutive. Indeed, as I hope to make clear, the concepts of nation and diaspora must always be placed in relation to one another. Furthermore, I would argue that fixed, essentialized concepts of national and diasporic identity are most fruitfully contested from a "queer diasporic" positionality. The concept of queer diaspora functions on multiple levels. First, it situates the formation of sexual subjectivity within transnational flows of culture, capital, bodies, desire, and labor. Second, queer diaspora contests the logic that situates the terms "queer" and "diaspora" as dependent on the originality and authenticity of "heterosexuality" and "nation." Finally, it disorganizes the dominant categories within the United States for sexual variance, namely, "gay and lesbian," and it marks a different economy of desire that escapes legibility within both normative Indian contexts and homo-normative white Euro-American contexts.

The necessity of producing a queer diasporic framework becomes particularly apparent when we try to make sense of the ways a film like *Fire* travels across multiple national sites and accrues multiple audiences in the process of such travel. *Fire* is but the latest example of films dealing with sexuality and sexual identity that are produced by Asian diasporic filmmakers and that have an increasingly global circulation. For instance, Ang Lee's 1993 film *The Wedding Banquet* (which has as its protagonist a gay Taiwanese businessman living in New York) gained huge audiences in Taiwan, the United States, and other international markets. In his reading of *The Wedding Banquet*, Mark Chiang argues that the film "cannot be read solely from within the frameworks of national culture, either Chinese or American, but must be read across them in a transnational analysis that attends to the local and global."[4] Similarly, the politics of *Fire*'s reception in India, the United States, and Canada raises questions of how queerness, as represented and circulated through diasporic cultural forms, becomes legible within a variety of competing and contradictory discourses: first, within developmental narratives of gay and lesbian identity in Euro-American contexts; second, within a discourse of religious nationalism in India, which is reproduced in the diaspora; and third, within liberal humanist discourses in both India and the diaspora. Rather than engaging in a close reading of *Fire*, I will instead trace the ways the film's representation of female homoerotic desire signifies very differently within these various discourses.

In his critique of the globalization of lesbian and gay politics and identity, the anthropologist Martin F. Manalansan IV notes that within the rhetoric of certain international gay organizations, "*gay* gains meaning according to a developmental narrative that begins with an unliberated, 'prepolitical' homosexual practice and that culminates in a liberated, 'out,' politicized, 'modern,' 'gay' subjectivity."[5] Deepa Mehta's 1996 film *Fire* both adheres to and challenges this developmental narrative of gay and lesbian identity, which underlies dominant Euro-American discourses on non-Western sexualities. The film opens with a scene of the adult protagonist Radha's memory/fantasy of herself as a young girl, sitting beside her parents in a wide open field of yellow flowers. Her mother urges the young Radha to "see the ocean" lying just beyond the landlocked field: "What you can't see you can see, you just have to see without looking." This scene, with its exhortation to "see" without looking, to "see" differently, recurs and resonates throughout the

151

film, and suggests an analogy with the ways in *Fire* interrogates the notion that the proper location of lesbianism is within a politics of visibility in the public sphere. However, the film's counterhegemonic representation of queer female desire is undercut and complicated by its own history of production, distribution, reception, and consumption. Funded largely with Canadian money, *Fire* had circulated from 1996 to 1998 mostly at international film festivals in India, Europe, and North America and had a lengthy art house release in major U.S. cities. Thus prior to its release in India in November 1998, it was available to a limited audience in India but gained a significant South Asian diasporic viewership as well as a mainstream lesbian and gay audience in the United States and Canada. Given the trajectory of the film's reception, it is worth asking how the film has become available and legible to its diasporic and international audiences.

Fire takes place in the middle-class neighborhood of Lajpat Nagar, in New Delhi, and tells the story of the burgeoning love and desire that emerge between Radha (Shabana Azmi) and her new sister-in-law Sita (Nandita Das), in a joint family household. Mehta quickly establishes the familiar familial violences and compulsions that inhabit the household: the women do most of the labor for the family business while their husbands ignore or abuse them. Radha's husband, Ashok, is tender and attentive not to Radha but to his guru, with whom he spends all his free time and who preaches sexual abstinence, while Sita's husband, Jatin, is too preoccupied with his "westernized" Chinese girlfriend to attend to Sita. The two women eventually turn to each other for sex and emotional sustenance.

Mehta rather conventionally frames the dilemma of her heroines as one in which "modernity," with its promise of individual freedom and self-expression, pulls inevitably against "tradition," which demands that the women adhere to the roles prescribed to them as good Hindu wives and remain chaste, demure, and self-sacrificing. Indeed, their very names bespeak these roles. In Hindu mythology, Radha is the devoted consort of the god Krishna, who is famous for his womanizing; together Radha and Krishna symbolize an idealized, transcendent heterosexual union. Sita, the heroine of the Hindu epic *Ramayana*, proves her chastity to her husband, Ram, by immersing herself in fire, and thus represents the ideal of wifely devotion and virtue. The image of Sita emerging unscathed from her *agni pariksha*, or trial by fire, is the inescapable motif around which the women's lives revolve throughout the film: for instance, the background noise in their daily lives is the popular serialization of the *Ramayana*, which plays incessantly on the television. Das's Sita, however, refuses to inhabit the overdetermined role of her legendary namesake: with her penchant for donning her husband's jeans instead of her heavy silk saris, and her willingness to pursue her attraction to Radha, she becomes the emblem of a "new India" and its promise of feminist self-fulfillment. Conversely, the stultifying effects of "tradition" are embodied in the character of Biji, the mute, paralytic grandmother who keeps a disapproving eye on the activities of her daughters-in-law.

The dichotomies through which the film is structured—between Biji and Sita, saris and jeans, silence and speech, self-denial and self-fulfillment, abstinence and desire, tradition and modernity—implicate it in a familiar teleological narrative of progress toward the individual "freedom" offered by the West, against which "the non-West" can only be read as premodern. Indeed, a number of U.S. critics have used the film as an occasion to replay colonial constructions of India as a site of regressive gender oppression, against which "the West" stands for enlightened egalitarianism.[6] Within the dominant discursive production of India as anterior to the West, lesbian or gay identity is explicitly articulated as the marker of full-fledged modernity. After Ashok spies the two women in bed together, Sita comments to Radha, "There is no word in our language to describe what we are to each other," to which Radha responds, "You're right; perhaps seeing is less complicated." U.S. film critics, most notably Roger Ebert, have taken this exchange (as well as Mehta's own pronouncement in the press notes that "Indians don't talk about sex") as proof of the West's cultural superiority and advanced politicization: "Lesbianism is so outside the experience of these Hindus that their language even lacks a work for it."[7] Indeed, almost all mainstream U.S. reviewers stress the failure of "these Hindus" to articulate lesbianism intelligibly, which in turn signifies the failure of the non-West to progress toward the organization of sexuality and gender prevalent in the West.[8] To these critics, ironically, lesbian or gay identity becomes intelligible and indeed desirable when and where it can be incorporated into this developmental narrative of modernity.

Because *Fire* gains legibility within such narratives for at least some North American, non–South Asian viewers (both straight and gay), it is helpful to resituate it within discourses of non-heteronormative sexuality that are available to Indian and South Asian diasporic audiences. Indian critics have noted that *Fire* is based on the 1942 short story "The Quilt," by the Urdu writer Ismat Chughtai.[9] Reading the film through the story provides an alternative to the tradition-modernity axis by foregrounding the complex model of queer female desire suggested by the film but foreclosed by its mainstream U.S. reception. Restoring "The Quilt" as an important intertext to *Fire* underscores the film's critique of colonial constructions in which non-Western sexualities are premodern and in need of

153

Western political development, and challenges dominant Indian nationalist narratives that consolidate the nation in terms of sexual and gender normativity. Furthermore, tracing the convergences between *Fire* and "The Quilt" reveals the ways a geographically and culturally "rooted" national text ("The Quilt") is translated and transformed into a mobile, diasporic text (*Fire*) that is in turn consumed within the national space (India). These multiple movements demand that we rethink the conventional distinction between "diaspora" and "nation": the nation is marked by diasporic movement just as the diaspora becomes a part of the nation.[10]

Chughtai's story depicts the lesbian relationship between a sequestered wife and her female servant/masseuse in an upper-middle-class Muslim household. The narrator tells of their curious activities as she remembers having seen them through the eyes of her childhood self. Every night, the young girl is alternately fascinated by the servant's relentless massaging of the wife's body and alarmed by the energetic contortions of the two women under the quilt. Memory in the text does not evoke a narrative of nostalgia in which "home" is imagined as a site of subjective wholeness or originary, heterosexual identity; rather, the narrator remembers the domestic arena of her childhood self as the site of complicated, nonnormative arrangements of pleasures and desires. The anti-nostalgic narrative radically destabilizes conceptions of the domestic as a site of compulsory heterosexuality, while the decidedly partial knowledge afforded by the child's gaze allows Chughtai to resist naming the women's homoerotic relationship within prescribed frameworks as "lesbian" or "homosexual." This resistance is not so much a failure to articulate queerness as an acknowledgment of the inadequacy of such articulation in expressing the range and complexity of non-heteronormative sexual practices and allegiances as they emerge within sites of extreme heteronormativity. Indeed, in the story female homoeroticism is simply one form of desire within a web of multiple, competing desires. While the servant, the wife, and the girl circulate within a particular female homosocial-homoerotic economy, there are similarly uneven male homosocial-homoerotic economies in the text: the husband, for instance, has a penchant for entertaining young boys. Queer desire, then, is quilted into the very fabric of the heterosexual, hierarchical configurations of the domestic arena.

Chughtai's depiction of queer female desire at the interstices of rigidly heterosexual structures is echoed in *Fire*, as it details the ways desire is routed and rooted in the space of the home. In the film, the men in the family access pleasure and fantasy through "escape hatches" from the strictures of conjugal heterosexual domesticity. Ashok, for instance, immerses himself in the homosociality of religious discipleship, Jatin trades in porn videos and escapes into sex with his exotically "other" Chinese girlfriend, while the servant Mundu (who nurses an unrequited love for Radha) masturbates to pilfered porn videos in front of Biji. Male desire, blocked by the officially sanctioned gender and class arrangements of the home, nevertheless emerges and is gratified. Radha and Sita, however, are shut out of such economies of desire; they, like Biji, must mutely witness men's pleasure, fantasies, and desire while being denied their own.

For Radha and Sita, as for the women in Chughtai's story, queer desire becomes a means of extricating oneself from patriarchal heteronormativity by creating alternative circuits of pleasure and fantasy. While some critics suggest that *Fire*'s depiction of lesbian sexuality capitulates to the familiar notion of lesbianism as merely a reaction to failed heterosexual marriages,[11] I would argue that, at least in the middle-class urban Indian context that Mehta details, it is from within the very fissures of rigid heteronormativity that queer female desire emerges. The attraction between Radha and Sita is enabled by those spaces of female homosociality that are sanctioned by normative sexual and gender arrangements. Whether rubbing oil into each other's hair or massaging each other's feet during a family picnic, the women exploit the permeable relation and slippages between female homosociality and female homoeroticism. Similarly, *karva chauth*, a North Indian ritual in which "dutiful" wives fast at home to ensure their husbands' well-being, is transformed from a female homosocial activity into an intensely homoerotic one, as the two women dress up in silk saris and gold jewelry for each other's pleasure.

By depicting the privatized, seemingly sanitized "domestic" space as a site of intense female homerotic pleasure and practice, both "The Quilt" and *Fire* interrogate the teleological Euro-American narrative according to which lesbian sexuality must emerge from a private, domestic sphere into a public, visible subjectivity. Both suggest that female homoerotic desire looks and functions differently in an Indian context than in Euro-American social and historical formations. Thus one critic's assessment that *Fire*'s depiction of lesbian sexuality is "extremely tame by Western standards" must be read as symptomatic of the very narrative that the film reiterates and revises.[12] In *Fire*'s "modernized" version of "The Quilt," however, the two women eventually leave the confines of the household rather than continue to exist within it, as Chughtai's characters do. Thus *Fire*, coming fifty years after "The Quilt," is available for recuperation within (and bears the marks of) the narrative of sexual emancipation and public visibility circulated by

155

contemporary international lesbian and gay politics even as it provides a critique of this narrative.

In its representation of the complicated and wild desiring relations between women in the seemingly "traditional" space of the home, "The Quilt" directly confronts notions of proper Indian womanhood upon which anticolonial nationalist ideologies depend.[13] Similarly, *Fire*'s representation of female homoerotic desire within the home and its rejection of the image of Sita as the ideal Hindu woman challenge contemporary Hindu nationalist ideologies that rely on Hindu women's sexual purity and sanctity as a means of ensuring group solidarity and vilifying Muslim minorities. Queer desire in the film functions (albeit obliquely) as a modality through which the women resist a complicity with the project of Hindu nationalism and its attendant gender and sexual hierarchies. Within the film's logic, escaping heterosexuality is synonymous with escaping the violence of Hindu nationalism: the few moments where the two women are seen together outside the home take place in explicitly non-Hindu spaces such as mosques and tombs. Indeed, the film ends with a shot of the two women in an Islamic shrine, having finally left the confines of the household.

It is precisely *Fire*'s implicit critique of Hindu nationalism that prompted the Shiv Sena to ransack theaters showing the film in December 1998; as one Shiv Sena member said of the film's depiction of the two women having sex, "this scene is a direct attack on our Hindu culture and civilization."[14] Interestingly, Indian liberals both in India and in the diaspora have been quick to counter the charge of perversion and obscenity leveled at the film from the Hindu right by seizing upon the film's strategy of disarticulation and nonspecification. This liberal humanist defense argues that the film is not about lesbianism at all, given that it refuses to name its heroines as lesbians; rather, this argument holds, lesbian desire in the film functions allegorically, and merely stands in for larger, more important issues such as women's emancipation as a whole.[15]

The problematic nature of this liberal humanist defense of *Fire* was particularly evident at a screening of Mehta's new film, *Earth*, that I attended in New York City in December 1998. Mehta was supposed to be present at the event but was unable to do so since she had flown to India to defend *Fire* from the Shiv Sena attacks. Mehta's producer, David Hamilton, apologized for the director's absence and alluded to the *Fire* controversy by suggesting that the film had raised the ire of Hindu nationalists because of the way it addressed issues of "artistic freedom, choice, and women's equality." Hamilton was at least in part taking his cue from the filmmaker Deepa Mehta herself, who has repeatedly defended the film by arguing, "Even though *Fire* is very particular in its time and space and setting, I wanted its emotional content to be universal. The struggle between tradition and individual expression is one that takes place in every culture. The story had a resonance that transcended geographic and cultural boundaries."[16]

These are curious evaluations of the outburst against *Fire* given that the Shiv Sena has directed its outrage very specifically at the lesbian relationship between the two women, and worse still, at the fact that the film locates this lesbian relationship within the confines of Hindu familial domesticity. As Bal Thackeray, the leader of the Shiv Sena, complained recently, "why is it that lesbianism is shown in a Hindu family? Why are the names of the heroines Radha and Sita and not Shabana or Saira?"[17] In the same vein, a senior government official in Maharashtra offered the following argument as justification for the banning of the film: "if women's physical needs get fulfilled through lesbian acts, the institution of marriage will collapse, and the reproduction of human beings will stop."[18] As both these comments amply demonstrate, the extreme anxiety that the film provokes among the Hindu right stems from a recognition of the threat that its representation of queer desire in the home poses to the Hindu nationalist project. What are we to make, then, of the disavowal of queerness on the part of so-called progressive defenders of the film, and their recasting of its queer content in terms of a feminist desire for self-determination?

This collapsing of queerness into feminism, along with the subsequent elision of queerness altogether, is echoed in some recent feminist scholarship on gender and sexuality in South Asia. Feminist work on South Asia has been crucial to my project on queer diasporas since it allows us to identify the legacies of gender and sexual ideologies that were first consolidated within the anticolonial nationalist movement in India in the late nineteenth and early twentieth centuries. These constructions of gender and sexuality have taken on new forms and meanings in the contemporary moment within state and religious nationalisms in South Asia, as well as within South Asian immigrant communities in the diaspora. Feminist historians of colonialism such as Kumkum Sangari and Sudesh Vaid have compellingly argued that from its inception, anticolonial Indian nationalism was predicated on the regulation and surveillance of women's sexuality. Attention to the construction of a private, middle-class, "respectable" sexuality in the formation of bourgeois nationalist subjectivities, as articulated by these critics, has been taken up in more recent work by South Asian feminist scholars analyzing contemporary religious nationalisms in South Asia.[19] Kamala Bhasin, Ritu Menon, and others have demonstrated how anticolonial nationalism in colonial India and

157

religious nationalism in contemporary South Asia intersect around the deployment of sexual and gender ideologies that harness women's sexuality (their sexual
conduct and reproductive capacity in particular) to the propagation of the com-
munity/group/nation. This strand of feminist scholarship on South Asia has been
profoundly instructive in showing how women's bodies become the site on which
the borders of male supremacist religious and national collectivities are drawn. Yet
such work is also marked by a curious lack of attention to the production and deployment of heterosexuality and homosexuality within these collectivities. A recent instance of this particular blind spot in South Asian feminist theorizations of
nationalism and sexuality is apparent in Kumari Jayawardena and Malathi De
Alwis's anthology, *Embodied Violence: Communalising Women's Sexuality in South
Asia*.[20] The collection is especially strong in exploring the various means by which
women's sexuality has historically been disciplined and controlled under religious
nationalist movements. However, the contributors fail to adequately articulate the
ways one of the most powerful methods of disciplining and controlling female
sexuality within such movements has been the prescription of state-sanctioned
heterosexuality as the structure within which female nationalist subjects are
housed. Given that this particular collection, as well as the other works I have
cited above, recognizes that sexuality historically secures the grounds for the production of gendered colonial, bourgeois nationalist, and religious nationalist subjects, it is somewhat surprising that even such recent attempts to specifically consider the imbrication of discourses of nationalism and women's sexuality still presume the heterosexuality of the female subject. Women's sexual autonomy, as
imagined by these critics, never extends beyond the boundaries of heterosexuality; indeed, the possibility that there may exist other forms of non-heteronormative subjectivities that challenge the logic of such nationalisms is never addressed.
By not examining the existence and workings of alternative sexualities within
dominant nationalisms, such analyses ultimately leave intact the very structures
of gender and sexual subordination that they seek to critique and dismantle.

Furthermore, this strand of South Asian feminist scholarship has been unwilling to identify the ways the contemporary nationalisms in South Asia that they
critique are supported and strengthened by an immigrant bourgeoisie in the diaspora. The Shiv Sena and other Hindu nationalist organizations in India receive
huge amounts of funding from immigrant organizations in Britain, Canada, and
the United States. The violent hostility of religious nationalists in India toward a
diasporic film like *Fire* underscores the urgent need for feminists both in India and
in the diaspora to extend their scope of analysis in two directions: first, to view

heterosexuality and contemporary religious nationalisms as overlapping structures of domination; and second, to move beyond the nation-state in order to account for the transnational circuits that both prop up *and* challenge contemporary nationalisms.

Indeed, the organizing that has taken place between South Asian queer activist groups in the United States and lesbian groups in India around the *Fire* issue speaks to the ways transnational circuits of commerce and culture are also being mobilized in the service of alternative visions of community, home, and nation. The activist links forged between the New York–based SALGA and the Delhi-based Campaign for Lesbian Rights, for instance, create a potent counterdiscourse that challenges the violent nationalist rhetoric of the Hindu right on the one hand, and the liberal humanist subsumption of non-heteronormative sexualities on the other. In their press releases immediately following the attacks against *Fire*, SALGA activists explicitly drew lines of connection between the rights of sexual minorities and the advocacy of artistic freedom and anticommunalism: "Supporting lesbian rights in India currently is the only option for our government if it is committed to putting an end to communalism, anti-secularism and the forms of fundamentalism that threaten the lives of our constitutionally protected minorities."[21] By consistently reinserting sexuality back into the arguments in defense of the film, queer activists in both India and the United States demanded that sexuality be seen as central to issues such as anticensorship and anticommunalism that have long concerned leftist organizers in India. Furthermore, the transnational political mobilization produced by queer organizations in India and the United States makes clear the ways it is precisely from a queer diasporic positionality that some of the most powerful critiques of religious and state nationalisms are taking place.

The recent events around the release of *Fire* in India force us to consider the function of popular culture as a site of both "promise and peril,"[22] a site of both the subversion of nationalist ideologies and the reiteration of homophobic sentiments. *Fire* gains multiple and contradictory meanings as it circulates within India, within the South Asian diaspora, and within film festival circuits and theaters in Europe and North America. While the film may on one hand pose a potent challenge to right-wing Hindu nationalism in India, it both resists and plays into dominant developmental narratives of modernity as it travels outside India. I have focused on *Fire* in particular since it is emblematic of the ways South Asian diasporic texts travel along increasingly complex trajectories of production and reception. The violent debates that have surrounded *Fire* demand that we develop

159

frames of analysis supple enough to account for these transnational movements and the various discourses of gender and sexuality to which they give rise.

Notes

An earlier version of this article was published as "On *Fire*," film/video review, *GLQ* 4.4 (1998): 631–36.

1. The official reason given by the FIA for excluding SALGA and Sakhi was that both groups used the term "South Asian" rather than "Indian" in their names.

2. Quoted in *The Hindu*, 14 December 1998.

3. Quoted in *The Hindu*, 16 February 1998.

4. Mark Chiang, "Coming Out into the Global System: Postmodern Patriarchies and Transnational Sexualities in *The Wedding Banquet*," in *Q&A: Queer in Asian America*, ed. David Eng and Alice Hom (Philadelphia: Temple University Press, 1998), 375.

5. Martin F. Manalansan IV, "In the Shadows of Stonewall: Examining Gay Transnational Politics and the Diasporic Dilemma," in *The Politics of Culture in the Shadow of Capital*, ed. Lisa Lowe and David Lloyd (Durham: Duke University Press, 1997), 487. An earlier version of this essay appeared in *GLQ* 2 (1995): 425–38.

6. E.g., one critic writes that "*Fire* is a plea for women's self-determination that . . . will probably strike viewers in this country as a bit obvious." Walter Addeago, "*Fire* Cool to State of Marriage in India," *San Francisco Examiner*, 26 September 1997, C7. Similarly, other critics describe the film as taking place within the "suffocatingly masculine" and "pre-feminist" culture of contemporary India. See, e.g., Owen Gleiberman, "Take My Wife: *Fire*, a Tale of Illicit Lesbian Love in India, Evokes the Early Days of American Feminism," *Entertainment Weekly*, 12 September 1997, 110.

7. Roger Ebert, "*Fire* Strikes at Indian Repression," *Chicago Sun Times*, 17 September 1997, 38.

8. See Margaret McGurk, "Tradition Broken in Indian Tale of Forbidden Love," *Cincinnati Enquirer*, 16 January 1998, W26; and Bill Morrison, "Women on the Verge of a Cinematic Breakthrough," *Raleigh News and Observer*, 21 November 1997, WUP10.

9. Shoma Chatterjee, "One Sita Steps beyond the Lakshmanrekha," *Calcutta Telegraph*, 12 January 1997. See Ismat Chughtai, *The Quilt and Other Stories*, trans. Tahira Naqvi and Syeda Hamid (New Delhi: Kali for Women, 1990).

10. I further elaborate this relation between diaspora and nation in Gayatri Gopinath, "Bombay, U.K., Yuba City: Bhangra Music and the Engendering of Diaspora," *Diaspora* 4.3 (1995): 303–21.

11. Ginu Kamani, "Interview with Deepa Mehta," *Trikone Magazine* 4.4 (October 1997): 11–13.

12. Brian D. Johnson, "Forbidden Flames," *McLean's Magazine*, 29 September 1997, 86.

13. Various feminist critics have argued that anticolonial nationalism in India consti- tuted itself through the construction of the Indian woman as a "modern" national sub- ject who nevertheless acted as "the guardian of national culture, indigenous religion and family traditions." See, for instance, Kumari Jayawardena, introduction to *Femi- nism and Nationalism in the Third World* (London: Zed Books, 1986), 14.

14. "Hindu Militants Stage Lesbian Film Attacks," *BBC News Online*, 3 December 1998.

15. "Attacks on *Fire* Due to Lack of Vision, Says Sathyu," *Times of India,* 3 February 1999.

16. Www.zeitgeistfilms.com/current/fire/fire.html.

17. "Thackeray's Terms," *The Hindu*, 14 December 1998. Radha and Sita, as I discussed, are names drawn from Hindu mythology, while "Shabana" and "Saira" function in Thackeray's statement as generic Muslim names as well as specific references to Sha- bana Azmi (the star of the film) and to the wife of actor Dilip Kumar, who was vocal in his support of the film.

18. *BBC News Online*, 9 December 1998.

19. Kumkum Sangari and Sudesh Vaid, introduction to *Recasting Women: Essays in Colonial History*, ed. Kumkum Sangari and Sudesh Vaid (New Delhi: Kali for Women, 1989), 10.

20. Kumari Jayawardena and Malathi De Alwis, eds., *Embodied Violence: Communalising Women's Sexuality in South Asia* (New Delhi: Kali for Women, 1996).

21. SALGA Press Release, "Lesbian, Gay and Progressive South Asians Support Secular- ism, Freedom of Expression and Lesbian Rights in India," January 1999.

22. George Lipsitz, *Dangerous Crossroads: Popular Music, Postmodernism and the Poetics of Place* (New York: Verso, 1994), 7.

9   Dancing *La Vida Loca*

The Queer Nuyorican Performances of Arthur Avilés and Elizabeth Marrero

Lawrence M. La Fountain-Stokes

If in the not-so-distant past it was commonplace (albeit erroneous) to speak of Puerto Rico and its Diaspora as separate and distinct entities in a relationship of marked inequality—one in which the island was privileged as a "pure" or "authentic" space while the migrant population and its communities were seen as "tragically flawed" or deficient—current discourse on Puerto Rican culture has shifted significantly toward acknowledging the profound interconnection between the two and the rich social, political, and cultural importance of both. Terms such as "commuter nation," "airbus" or "guagua aérea," "transnation," and "translocality," for example, have become popular as theorists and artists such as Juan Flores, Ramón Grosfoguel, Frances Negrón-Muntaner, Julio Ramos, and Luis Rafael Sánchez, who hail from both sides of the "charco" or oceanic divide, employ them in reference to the particular condition of Puerto Rican society and culture of our times.[1]

Diverse sectors on the island, ranging from the traditional and rearticulated left to the "postmodern pessimists" (as Luis Fernando Coss has referred to leading "postmodern" intellectuals), are presently engaged in projects of national redefinition that posit the Diaspora in a central position and, in wider terms, seek to understand the relationship between Puerto Rico and the United States in more nu-

anced ways, as more than simply a Manichean colonial relationship of subjuga-
tion. Unfortunately, this is sometimes done without a concomitant effort to
bridge out to the Diasporic populations themselves, or (with rare exceptions) to
engage scholars and artists who work and/or reside outside the island. In the
United States, on the other hand, Puerto Rican populations are engaged in
processes of cultural adaptation and change that have transformed the nature of
categories of ethnic identity, shifting the key geographic referent from the island
of Puerto Rico to locations in the United States in which Puerto Rican culture
thrives; artists and intellectuals there, whose views have often been challenged by
Puerto Rican and U.S. critics alike, are particularly invested in redefining and
widening the terms of discussion.

These phenomena have significant if often unacknowledged implications for
the study and analysis of Puerto Rican homosexualities. Processes of circular and
one-way migration, including that of U.S. gays and lesbians to Puerto Rico, as well
as media, activist, and political influence and intervention, shape and affect current configurations of desire and the possibilities of identity affirmation. Yet it is
still only a select group of people who openly recognize the centrality of questions
of sexual orientation to understanding the larger social sphere; in many cases, the
attention gays and lesbians receive is mostly negative, as in conservative and fun-
damentalist groups' efforts to maintain the criminal legal status of sodomy in
Puerto Rico and prohibit gay marriage, legal protection, or institutionalized equal
rights, or simply in the disavowal of this concern from dominant discussions.[2]

In this essay I explore the interconnections between Puerto Rican migration
and homosexuality as they are articulated in the cultural production of Arthur
Avilés and Elizabeth Marrero. Their New York–based dance-theater work and its
aesthetics of appropriation offer significant insights for a revision of Puerto Rican
and American culture, and can particularly inform and expand debates in Puerto
Rico and in the United States on postmodernity and national culture. Previously
these have focused, for example, on issues like the appropriateness of Madonna's
use of the Puerto Rican flag during a show on the island; postmodern critics argue
that this episode disqualifies and belittles nationalist revindications, which they
consider highly suspect. Yet, while postmodern Puerto Rican culture on both
sides of the Atlantic challenges static notions of national identity, it does not necessarily renounce or disengage from it; rather, it postulates new configurations—
in the case we will study, one that is inclusive of nonnormative sexualities and of
the Diasporic community. Let us not forget how, in the case of Puerto Rico, national identity has often been predicated or understood in terms of isolation or

163

"insularity" (following Antonio S. Pedreira's 1934 *Insularismo*), a posture that implied an island-centered, Hispanicized, Spanish-language–centered culture, while dominant U.S. culture has also seen itself as predominantly Anglo-Saxon or European and English-language based. To renounce these closed visions is not to renounce the possibility of other, more encompassing articulations of the national. The significance of alternative positions can hardly be stressed enough, particularly in a moment of rampant and sometimes violent homogenizing nationalisms that are accompanied by the unrestrained expansion of U.S. global capitalism, and particularly of its cultural industry, which threatens to wipe out and/or assimilate difference as nothing more than a market tool. In a sense, what Arthur Avilés and Elizabeth Marrero offer is a distinct (sexualized, working-class–based, linguistically plural) ethno-national production that can be viewed polyvalently as American and Puerto Rican, and that defies closed notions of these cultures in terms of language, medium, and referentiality while at the same time resists easy assimilation. But let us turn back, if only briefly, to earlier stages of Puerto Rican Diasporic cultural production that served as fundamental moments in the definition of a new "translocal" Puerto Rican experience, and that will allow us to more fully understand Avilés's and Marrero's work.

The 1952 New York City premiere of *La carreta*, one of the most celebrated plays of the closeted homosexual writer René Marqués,[3] consolidated a tradition of reflecting on the Puerto Rican experience (and particularly that of the Diasporic population) through drama and performance.[4] This effort, which remains active up to our days, was started by musicians and songwriters such as Rafael Hernández and Noel Estrada, whose compositions ("Lamento borincano" and "En mi Viejo San Juan," respectively) gave voice to the nostalgia and longing of earlier migrations;[5] it extends from the narrow confines of traditional theaters to the streets and public and private spaces occupied by everyday people, rap and salsa singers, performance poets, muralists, graffiti artists, and the like.

For the last thirty years or so, and particularly in the 1990s, this Puerto Rican Diasporic performative tradition has included gay, lesbian, bisexual, and transgender exponents who have openly addressed the implications of their sexual orientation. Other artists, who do not publicly identify their sexual orientation as such but who nevertheless explore the theme, set an important precedent; these include Piri Thomas in his novel *Down These Mean Streets*, Miguel Piñero in his celebrated play *Short Eyes*, and Pedro Pietri's occasionally ambiguous, playful poetic and dramatic retorts, as analyzed by Arnaldo Cruz-Malavé (1997). There is at present a genuine critical mass of openly self-identified queer cultural producers, including Eduardo Alegría, Janis Astor del Valle, Brenda Cotto, Mariposa, Jorge Merced, Charles Rice González, Alberto Sandoval, and Emmanuel Xavier. To this list, comprising artists who write and/or present their work in "legitimated" theatrical or performance venues, we could also add drag queens such as Laritza Dumont, the recently deceased Lady Catiria, and Jeannette Alexander, or sex trade workers or erotic dancers who are, in their own right, queer Diasporic Puerto Rican performers.[6]

This essay will focus on the postmodern aesthetics of appropriation of two artists whose work stands out in terms of its sophistication, playfulness, and originality: dancer/choreographer Arthur Avilés and performer Elizabeth Marrero. Arthur's dance-theater work has been described in the *New York Times* as follows:

Mr. Avilés is emphatic: "I have no problem being someone who came after [choreographer] Bill [T. Jones]." But then, for [Arthur], the issue of originality is moot. He has taken the post-modern principle of appropriation to its extreme: he openly copies, everything from Disney movies to whole dances from Martha Graham, José Limón and even Mr. Jones. "If I see something I like, why shouldn't I use it, especially if it inspired me?," he reasons. "Originality is dead, but inspiration is alive. I put myself into that artwork and see what it does for me." (Daly, 12)

In a declaration fit for a Brazilian anthropophagic modernist, the carnivorous Bronx consumer-artist and transformer of myriad cultures Arthur Avilés declares to the world his aesthetics of collage, pastiche, and bricolage. In consonance with the observations of Néstor García Canclini regarding much recent Latin American cultural production from the borderlands, Arthur Avilés incorporates disparate elements, ranging from classic American modern dance choreographies to mass-media cinematographic productions and literary masterpieces, and filters all of these through a Bronx-centered Nuyorican or New York–Rican gay (and with his first cousin Elizabeth Marrero, lesbian) optic: an unabashed aesthetics of material and cultural consumption, in which everything is up for the taking, in which an absence or distance from traditional Puerto Rican culture and history is subsumed by the juxtaposition of popular and daily practices of the ghetto with high and low art.

Who are Arthur Avilés and Elizabeth Marrero? What are their cultural productions about? Arthur Avilés was born in Queens in 1963, one of eight children of working-class Puerto Rican parents who emigrated from the island's countryside as adolescents during the 1950s. Elizabeth Marrero was born in the Bronx the same year as Arthur but comes from a smaller family; she is the youngest of three children. Although their mothers are sisters, they had radically different upbringings: in Arthur's house, everything Puerto Rican was frowned upon; as he puts it, his home was a constant battlefield in which American values and customs were presented as superior even while Puerto Rican traditions and habits were followed. This explains why Arthur does not speak much Spanish. Elizabeth, to the contrary, grew up in an environment in which the value of Puerto Ricanness was instilled, where Spanish was spoken, and where people were not embarrassed of their heritage or willing to downplay it for the sake of achieving the "American Dream."

The difference between these immigrant experiences is summarized in the program notes to their "dance play" *Arturella* in the following way: "Nuyoricans [are] children of Puerto Rican parents who were born in New York and know the island's language and culture, [while] New York–Ricans [are] children of Puerto Rican parents who were born in New York but are estranged from the island's language and culture."

At eighteen, Arthur went to Bard College, where he majored in theater and dance. Having excelled at sports in high school, including wrestling, diving, and gymnastics, and being very graceful and agile have contributed to make him one of the most outstanding Latino modern dancers currently performing in the United States.[7] He became particularly well-known during his eight years as one of the main dancers of the Bill T. Jones/Arnie Zane Dance Company, from 1987 to 1995;[8] during this period, he also choreographed and presented his own work.[9] In 1995 Arthur decided to establish his own group, the Arthur Avilés Typical Theatre, and for the last several years, he has based his work at BAAD, the Bronx Academy of Art and Dance, in Hunt's Point, the Bronx. BAAD is an art and dance space founded by Avilés and his partner, Charles Rice-Gonzales.[10]

Elizabeth's training could not be more different. Up until only recently a trust administrator at Chase Manhattan Bank, she began to collaborate with her cousin in 1990 with purely amateur credentials; her incredible acting skills, powerful stage presence, varied facial, bodily, and emotional repertoire, and boundless talent for comedy have made her an essential participant in Arthur's productions, a true collaborator in the fullest sense. During their performances, Arthur's brilliance is in the dancing, while Elizabeth often speaks in hilarious nonstop monologues; yet, as befits dance-theater, both engage in a variety of activities.

Arthur and Elizabeth's nine years of collaborations have resulted in a corpus characterized by a recurrent cast of characters, comprising a "typical" Nuyorican/New York–Rican family, who adopt different personalities but often have the same or similar names. Elizabeth is thus Maeva, a usually irrepressible, loud Latina mother with many children; Arthur is Arturo, the oldest son, "el nene lindo" or "el rey de la casa"; other characters include Blanquita, a beautiful, blue-eyed blond sister who always receives praise and can do no wrong, and Trigueña, the darker sister, who is always caught up in her irrepressible sexuality and blamed for all the ills that accost the family. The cast members, which resemble a *commedia dell'arte* or Cuban *teatro bufo* troupe, often shed their roles during their performances to interpret other characters, crisscrossing gender, class, and racial lines; in *Arturella*, for example, Elizabeth plays four different people: Maeva, Evil Step Maeva, Fairy God Maeva, and King Maeva.

The cousins' first collaboration, performed in 1991, was called, appropriately enough, *Maeva: A Typical New York–Rican's Ensalada.*[11] Arthur and Elizabeth's most recent pieces, *Arturella* (1996) and *Maeva de Oz* (1997), are rewritings of Walt Disney's *Cinderella* and MGM's *The Wizard of Oz*, respectively. In the first, Arturo (who becomes Arturella) is a poor New York–Rican orphan who lives with his evil stepmother Maeva and her many children in the Bronx and who dreams of going to the princeso's quinceañero or sweet-fifteen birthday party.[12] In the second, Elizabeth plays Maevacita and Maeva as versions of Dorothy, a lesbian Nuyorican who is only able to come out of the closet with the help of her faithful dog Arturoto, as they wander down the Bruckner Expressway in their search for Nuyorrico, a utopian space of liberation that combines elements of New York and Puerto Rico within a socially progressive environment.[13]

The Naked Puerto Rican Faggot's Body

One of Arthur Avilés's distinguishing features, besides his penchant for wearing women's dresses on stage, is his proclivity for dancing naked, a modality which he already explored while with Bill T. Jones.[14] In pieces such as *Intoxicating Calm*, premiered in Cannes, or *A Puerto Rican Faggot from America* (both choreographed and performed by Avilés), the dancer's naked body becomes the instrument for the exploration of dance as movement divorced from what some believe is an extraneous element: costume.[15] Of course, the impact or effect of his naked body goes beyond a mere distillation of movement in and of itself, and immediately brings myriad other associations, ranging from Hellenic ideals and aesthetics to debates on liberty of expression and pornography. It is, after all, in pornography and in the sex trade where the naked Puerto Rican Diasporic male gay body is most commonly exhibited for public consumption, often for a non–Puerto Rican audience.[16]

Arthur's muscular, sinewy, naked body, displayed as a sexualized, healthy, de-siring object in an age of AIDS, signals an affront to those who would like to keep Puerto Rican homosexuality in the closet, or to those who advocate for a "nor-malized," sterile, and conservative family-oriented gay agenda. Such is the case surrounding the controversy at Hostos Community College in the Bronx in 1996, when Arthur presented *Arturella*, where he was told the day of the premiere that he could not dance naked, even though he had advised the college with months of anticipation of his intended plans. Despite their warnings, the performance went on as scheduled.[17]

In *Arturella*, nakedness can be read as a symbol of social defiance, of the indi-vidual stripped of or placed outside social hierarchies and conventions; it is a sign of punishment, but also serves as an affirmation of identity. When Mickey Ratón (Gus from the Disney film) first appears, caught in a trap, he is naked; he is in a "state of nature," so to speak, differentiated from humans by a lack of clothing.[18] Arturella is naked while bathing at the beginning of the play and ends up naked when his evil stepsisters Anacleta and Chancleta rip his dress to shreds so that he cannot go to the princeso's ball. He is naked when the fairy godmother Maeva finds him, and when his madrina's spell breaks, after the clock strikes twelve. The nude body is a sign of the artifice of social convention but also of how it is used to enforce rigid social stratification; nudity is also the provocative revealing of the secret withheld by social masks and propriety.

In *Arturella*, the play between drag and nakedness serves to construct a gay Nuyorican desiring body, whose ultimate wish will be fulfilled when he joins an-other male, the princeso. The waltz scene at the ball, transformed by music (re-worked disco tracks and an Afro-Latino conga drum) and dance (Puerto Rican so-cial forms—the *danza*—rather than European styles), consolidates this project of self-creation and affirmation, one that Ann Cooper Albright has identified as re-current in this period, in which "more and more dancers and choreographers are asking that the audience see their bodies as a source of cultural identity—a physi-cal presence that moves with and through its gendered, racial, and social mean-ings" (xxvi). This is certainly the case in Arthur's performance.

Schizophrenia and Queer Diasporic Identities

In *Maeva de Oz*, the lesbian subject is not constituted through gender-"inappro-priate" clothing or nakedness, nor is lesbian desire signaled by the dancing of two women together.[19] Rather, *Maeva de Oz* is a dance-theater piece that relies on verbal discourse and occasional visual markers to create a lesbian Puerto Rican consciousness. The frustrations of the young Maeva (Dorothy) as she confronts the world of adults who do not understand her and who are too busy to help culminate during the tornado, when she runs into the closet (rather than into her bedroom, as in the film) for shelter. In addition to the flying cows and knitting grandmother from the film's oneiric sequence, a large cardboard gun and a syringe (carried by Kurokos, or silent actors dressed in black, as in the Kabuki theater) appear as signifiers of the Bronx's reality. And instead of waking up in Munchkinland, she awakens in Nuyorrico, a place somewhere beyond the Bruckner Expressway that allows for a different formation of self to arise. "I have a feeling we're not in the South Bronx anymore," she tells her faithful dog companion Arturoto and the audience at that moment, a statement that is profoundly revealing of the difficulties produced by the rigid institutionalized homophobia that the Puerto Rican community has carried with it across "el charco" in the Diaspora, and of how *new* social spaces are required.

Maevacita's process of achieving personal maturity is signaled through a visual change: both the filmic projection and her clothes go from black and white to color; the background is in fact a television rainbow-like color grid. The transformation of the costumes, which were created by Liz Prince, is very notable: Maevacita begins with a hand-painted black and white checkercloth dress, and ends up with a shiny, irregular, yellow- and blue-squared one. Arturoto's costume also changes, from black and white to golden. One of the clearest indications of the lesbian nature of this change is that Maeva receives rainbow-colored ankle ribbons, much like Arturella (who receives them instead of glass slippers). In a funny culminating speech shortly after coming out of the closet, she affirms that it is not necessary to be ugly or bad to be—not a witch, as in the film, but rather—a lesbian.

Just like in *Arturella*, Maeva simultaneously represents a number of the characters from the film: in this case, the aunt and uncle, the evil neighbor Mrs. Gulch, the three farmhands, the fortune teller, Glinda the Good Witch, and the Wicked Witch of the West. These characters are presented as schizophrenic dimensions of herself. As a result, the character acquires a particular depth and complexity that make her especially interesting: sometimes shy, sometimes brash, sometimes good, sometimes bad. Maeva negotiates these different aspects of the self in an attempt to become a coherent individual. The possibly pathological implications of this confusion in turn convey the reality of many queer individuals who must camouflage their identity due to fear or for safety and social acceptance, and reflect on the unfortunately disproportionate rate of mental illness in the working-class, ghetto-confined, Diasporic Puerto Rican population.

An unfortunate effect of having Elizabeth play all the roles of the story except that of Toto the dog is that it sometimes becomes difficult to follow the action, particularly if the spectator is not familiar with the cinematographic referent. Both *Arturella* and *Maeva de Oz* (and its continuation, *Dorothur's Journey*) require intimate knowledge of the Disney and MGM films for full comprehension of the plots.[20]

It is legitimate to question why there is such a difference in approach to the constitution of gayness in *Arturella* and lesbianism in *Maeva de Oz*, as well as such different end results. In the first, a celebration of a youth's body and depiction of his encounter with adversity culminate in a traditional storybook love affair. In the second, the individual child's quest ends in a process of self-identification and consciousness-raising, a coming-to-be as a liberated individual, but not in a celebration of the lesbian body or of lesbian relationships. I believe that the difference in these pieces has to do with the divergent film models followed, with the particularities of Arthur and Elizabeth's training and skills, and with the possibly different meanings of a naked female body on stage.[21] It may also have to do with the fact that, while the creative process often occurs in tandem, Arthur ultimately controls the artistic direction of the pieces. Also, the *topos* of Nuyorrico in *Maeva de Oz* works as a utopian space of liberation, a conceit absent from *Arturella*. I find both pieces satisfactory but am aware that some people are not pleased with these differences.

The performances of Arthur Avilés and Elizabeth Marrero represent a radical new form of Puerto Rican Diasporic cultural production, a dramatic departure not only from representations such as that of Marqués but even from those of other Nuyorican artists such as Nicholasa Mohr, Abraham Rodríguez, Jr., and Janis Astor del Valle, who have also attempted to represent the Bronx in their work. They do not correspond neatly to any of the categories that Juan Flores offers in his essays on Nuyorican cultural consciousness, but rather seem more closely associated to Latino and Latin American hybrid productions such as those of Luis Alfaro, Coco Fusco, and Guillermo Gómez-Peña, or the Puerto Ricans Javier Cardona and Pepatián, formed by island choreographer Merián Soto and visual artist Pepón Osorio (Flores, 182–95). Avilés and Marrero's postmodern aesthetic engages in a polyvalent critique of and reverence for traditional classic forms, such as canonical American modern dance, and of mass-media texts, yet it does this within the Bronx context, one that is rich in associations of Nuyorican cultural production.

Most significantly, their commitment to a Latino community in the Bronx means that a significant number of the productions I have listed are presented in community centers and other locations that are accessible to their desired audience. In this sense, Avilés and Marrero's work is a radical departure from traditional modern dance, an elite form performed for select groups, and becomes a popular theatrical or performance modality, whose aspirations are to critically present and reflect on the reality of Nuyoricans and New York–Ricans, and gay and lesbian ones in particular. At the same time, their work radically challenges limited, "insularist" visions of Puerto Rican and American culture, and also challenges "pessimist" postmodern views that see a need to disidentify with or deny all possibilities of nationalist affirmation. By questioning both narratives of authenticity and narratives of cultural superiority, Avilés and Marrero contribute to the reformulation of Puerto Rican and American culture, in its widest sense, as a space of liberation.

Notes

I wish to thank Marcial Godoy for suggesting the clever title, which alludes, of course, to Ricky Martin's hit 1999 English-crossover song, "Living la Vida Loca." I also wish to thank Arnaldo Cruz-Malavé for his insightful observations.

1. In addition to the work of these authors, see volume by Torre et al.
2. See my dissertation, La Fountain (1999), for extensive consideration of these and other relevant issues.
3. See Arnaldo Cruz-Malavé (1995) regarding René Marqués's homosexuality.
4. See Márquez and Fiet's description of the importance of *La carreta* in the establishment of the New York Puerto Rican theater scene. According to them, the first Puerto Rican drama written about immigrant life was Fernando Sierra Berdecía's 1937 *Esta noche juega el jóker*, first presented in 1950. Fiet (1997) offers a survey of artists whose work spans the island and mainland at the present time.
5. Ruth Glasser's history of early immigrant musicians and the role of music in their communities is a fundamental reference.
6. José (Keke) Rosado follows similar patterns of inclusiveness regarding Puerto Rican queer performance in his article in *Conjunto*.
7. See Dunning (1989) for more biographical information and discussion of his training. Nieves and Rose also offer interesting biographical details.
8. In addition to being a principal dancer, after Arnie Zane's death, Avilés became Bill

T. Jones's lover. Jones describes their personal and professional relationship in *Last Night on Earth* (see 191–92, 228–30). During this time, Avilés won a Bessie from the New York Dance and Performance Award Committee (1988–1989). For reviews of his work with Jones, see Dunning (1989, 1991) and Tobias.

9. See Anderson (1989, 1991), Lewis, Solomons, Sulcas, Supree, Zimmer (1993, 1995).

10. Arthur has stated that the reason the company is named "Typical Theatre" is that one of its goals is to reclaim the cultural and social practices that have been maligned by dominant-class outsiders as "stereotypical," restoring their pertinence to the community and processing them in light of their positive and negative traits.

11. See Solomons for a review of this piece.

12. See Dunning (1996) for a review of *Arturella*.

13. See Gladstone for a synopsis of *Maeva de Oz* and what has now become *Dorothur's Journey*, and La Fountain (1997) for a review of the piece.

14. See, for example, the 1988 photograph of *Absence* in Jones (187).

15. Sulcas comments, "Arthur Avilés . . . caused a sensation . . . with *Intoxicating Calm*, an alternately composed and rollicking solo that he danced entirely nude, with Calibanesque glee. Occasionally addressing the spectators (who experienced their own form of "nudity" as house lights were kept on) with noises or gestures between thinly textured dance phrases, Avilés was interestingly, and not merely childishly, provocative in raising the issues of sex, gender, life, and death" (98).

16. It is interesting to know that Avilés has, in fact, not only danced in erotic businesses in New York City as a means of earning his sustenance, but also been arrested and spent a short time in jail for it (Arthur Aviles, interview by author, 22 April 1998). The number of pornographic films and magazines that focus on Latino men is too large to mention in their totality. Important film production companies include Latino Fan Club and Kristen Bjorn Productions; magazines include *Machismo*, *Latin Inches*, and *Hombres Latinos*.

17. See Dunning (1996).

18. One of the most curious aspects of the Disney film is that Cinderella dresses all the mice and birds, but not the dog or the cat. This unusual behavior seems to make her appear as a "nicer" person, who takes an interest in small, formerly "wild" critters that she "domesticates" herself.

19. Curiously, the dance performances of the Puerto Ricans Ñequi González and Alicia Díaz, of the group En la Brega, do suggest a type of female bonding or relationship (such as lesbianism) expressed through corporal movement. According to Ñequi, this is not the stated intent of their piece, but she admits that it is a possible interpretation

(personal communication). See, for example, *En camino* and *Tomas desde adentro* (performances, Princeton University, 28 Mar. 1998).

20. *Dorothur's Journey*, a companion piece to *Maeva de Oz*, has Arthur as Dorothy incorporate the other characters of the film: the scarecrow, the tin man, the lion, and the wizard, who all become part of his costume. In this piece, which is strongly centered on a seventies disco aesthetic, there is no dialogue, and the plot is constructed exclusively through dance.

21. One can think of 1970s and 1980s feminist film theoreticians' positions (Laura Mulvey's in particular) regarding the impossibility of representation of female images outside a patriarchal, objectifying male gaze. While these debates are by now somewhat outdated, the controversy against female pornography (defended by Andrea Dworkin and Catharine MacKinnon, for example) and in favor (espoused by Camille Paglia and Susie Bright) is still quite active.

Works Cited

Albright, Ann Cooper. *Choreographing Difference: The Body and Identity in Contemporary Dance*. Middletown, CT: Wesleyan University Press; Hanover, NH: University Press of New England, 1997.

Alegría, Eduardo. *Spookiricans*. Performance, P.S. 122, New York City, May 1997.

Anderson, Jack. "In New Works, Laughter, the Alphabet, and Old Saws." *New York Times*, 25 Sept. 1991, C18.

———. "New Works from 4 Choreographers." *New York Times*, 12 Nov. 1989, 72.

Astor del Valle, Janis. *Fuschia*. Performance, Nuyorican Poets Café, New York City, April 1996. In *Intimate Acts: Eight contemporary Lesbian Plays*, ed. Nancy Dean and M. G. Soares, 85–110. New York: Brito and Lair, 1997.

———. *I'll Be Home para la Navidad*. In *Torch to the Heart: Anthology of Lesbian Art and Drama*, ed. Sue McConnell-Celi, 97–113. Red Bank, NJ: Lavender Crystal, 1994.

———. *Where the Señoritas Are*. In *Torch to the Heart: Anthology of Lesbian Art and Drama*, ed. Sue McConnell-Celi, 82–96. Red Bank, NJ: Lavender Crystal, 1994.

Avilés, Arthur. *Arturella*. Performance, Repertory Theater, Hostos Community College, Bronx, New York, 1–2 Nov. 1996.

———. *Dorothur's Journey*. Performance, American Crafts Museum, New York City, 15 Mar. 1998.

———. *Intoxicating Calm*. Performance, Cannes International Dance Festival, Cannes, France, 1993.

Avilés, Arthur. *Maeva: A Typical New York–Rican's Ensalada*. Performance, Dance Chance Series, Dance Theatre Workshop, New York City, 24–27 Jan. 1991.

———. *Maeva de Oz*. Performance, Point Community Center, Hunt's Point, Bronx, New York.

———. *A Puerto Rican Faggot from America*. Performance, Food for Thought, Danspace Project, New York City, 11 Oct. 1996.

Cinderella. Walt Disney Studios, 1949.

Coss, Luis Fernando. *La nación en la orilla (respuesta a los posmodernos pesimistas)*. San Juan: Punto de Encuentro, 1996.

Cotto, Brenda. *Motherlands*. Performance, Boston, May 1996.

Cruz-Malavé, Arnaldo. "Towards an Art of Transvestism: Colonialism and Homosexuality in Puerto Rican Literature." In *¿Entiendes? Queer Readings, Hispanic Writings*, ed. Emilie Bergmann and Paul Julian Smith, 137–67. Durham: Duke University Press, 1995.

———. "'*What a Tangled Web!*': Masculinidad, abyección y la fundación de la literatura puertorriqueña en los Estados Unidos." *Revista de crítica literaria latinoamericana* 45 (1997): 327–40.

Daly, Ann. "When Dancers Move on to Making Dances." *New York Times*, 6 Apr. 1997, C12+.

Dunning, Jennifer. "Arthur Avilés's Life in Dance: Nonstop Exhilaration." *New York Times*, 24 Mar. 1989, C3.

———. "New Spin on 'Cinderella': Prince Finds a Dream Guy." *New York Times*, 5 Nov. 1996, C16.

———. "New Works for a Benefit." *New York Times*, 31 May 1991, C3.

Fiet, Lowell. "El teatro puertorriqueño: Puente aéreo entre ambas orillas." *Conjunto* 106 (May–Aug. 1997): 55–59.

Flores, Juan. *Divided Borders: Essays on Puerto Rican Identity*. Houston: Arte Público, 1993.

García Canclini, Néstor. *Culturas híbridas: Estrategias para entrar y salir de la modernidad*. Mexico: Grijalbo, 1990.

Gladstone, Valerie. "Avilés in Oz: Nuyorican Choreographer Gets to the Point." *Village Voice*, 13 May 1997, 95.

Glasser, Ruth. *My Music Is My Flag: Puerto Rican Musicians and Their New York Communities, 1917–1940*. Berkeley: University of California Press, 1995.

Jones, Bill T., and Peggy Gilespie. *Last Night on Earth*. New York: Pantheon, 1995.

La Fountain, Lawrence. "Arthur Avilés y *Maeva de Oz*." *Claridad* (San Juan, PR), 22–28 Aug. 1997, 26.

174

———. "Culture, Representation, and the Puerto Rican Queer Diaspora." Ph.D. diss. Columbia University, 1999.

Lewis, Julinda. "Reviews: Performance Mix." *Dance Magazine* 64.6 (June 1990): 68.

Márquez, Rosa Luisa, and Lowell A. Fiet. "Puerto Rican Theater on the Mainland." In *Ethnic Theatre in the United States*, ed. Maxine Schwartz Seller, 419–46. Westport, CT: Greenwood, 1983.

Merced, Jorge. *El bolero fue mi ruina.* Performance, Teatro Pregones, Bronx, New York, February 1997.

Negrón-Muntaner, Frances, and Ramón Grosfogel, eds. *Puerto Rican Jam: Essays on Culture and Politics.* Minneapolis: University of Minnesota Press, 1997.

Nieves, Evelyn. "Fund Provides Window into the American Dream." *New York Times*, 14 June 1992. Reprint.

Piñero, Miguel. *Short Eyes.* New York: Hill and Wang, 1975.

Rosado, José O. "Seis piezas 'liminales' de la 'nueva' nueva dramaturgia puertorriqueña." *Conjunto* 106 (May–Aug. 1997): 50–54.

Rose, David James. "Coming Out, Standing Out." *Hispanic*, June 1994, 44–48.

Sánchez, Luis Rafael. *La guagua aérea.* San Juan: Cultural, 1994.

Sandoval, Alberto. *Side Effects.* Performance, Mt. Holyoke College, South Hadley, Massachusetts, 1993.

Solomons, Gus J. "Go Go Latino." *Village Voice*, 12 Feb. 1991, 84.

Sulcas, Roslyn. "Reviews: Festival International de Danse." *Dance Magazine* 67.3 (Mar. 1993): 97–99.

Supree, Burt. "Belly Up: Arthur Avilés and Jody Oberfelder-Riehm." *Village Voice*, 19 June 1990, 111–12.

Tobias, Tobi. "Heaven Can Wait." *New York*, 12 Dec. 1994, 98.

Torre, Carlos Antonio, Hugo Rodríguez Veccini, and William Burgos. *The Commuter Nation: Perspectives on Puerto Rican Migration.* Río Piedras: University of Puerto Rico, 1994.

The Wizard of Oz. Dir. Victor Fleming. MGM, 1939.

Xavier, Emanuel. "Motherfuckers." In *Best Gay Erotica 1997*, ed. Richard Labonté, 112–16. Pittsburgh: Cleis, 1997.

———. *Pier Queen.* New York: Pier Queen Productions, 1997.

Zimmer, Elizabeth. "Dance: Arthur Avilés and Stephane Vambre." *Village Voice*, 3 Jan. 1995, S2.

———. "West Side Stories." *Village Voice*, 7 Sept. 1993, 80.

10 Syncretic Religion and Dissident Sexualities

Roberto Strongman

This essay presents a dissatisfaction with certain strains of thought within the po-litical discourse on sexual orientation produced by economically and racially priv-ileged segments of the gay and lesbian movement in the United States. I argue that the exportation of these knowledges on sexual orientation has a universalizing and homogenizing effect that erases culturally distinct and politically enabling gender differences and options in poorer populations and among communities of color worldwide. I also discuss an equally disturbing trend within scholarly dis-course that polarizes U.S. and Latin American homosexualities to an extremely re-ductive and essentialistic simplicity. My main argument consists of an investiga-tion of the Afro-Catholic syncretic cults of the Americas—Santería, Vaudou, and Candomblé—as sites of local knowledge that can serve as cultural arsenals in the resistance to these hegemonic discourses and as places in which Latin American homosexual identities can find the construction materials necessary to continue developing without total absorption by the hegemony of the mainstream gay and lesbian movement in the United States.

One of the most important reevaluations taking place in queer communities of color, in both Latin America and its diasporic population in the United States, in-volves a generalized realization that the promise of liberation of the North American gay, lesbian, transgender movement is implicated in the project of U.S. hegemonic control through the bodies of its citizens. The work of U.S.-based gay human rights organizations in Latin America, aside from attaining security and asylum for victims of sexual orientation discrimination in many countries, has had the effect of emplotting Latin America as culturally backwards in comparison to what is presented as the more enlightened and progressive United States. For instance, the work of the San Francisco–based International Gay and Lesbian Human Rights Commission (IGLHRC) often involves the judicial defamation of the countries of origin of asylum seekers. This has been required to constitute the main line of argument in immigration judicial proceedings after the February 3, 1986, ruling of U.S. immigration Judge Robert Brown, in which he granted Fidel Armando Toboso's request to withhold his deportation to Cuba on the basis that Toboso fit the definition of a refugee by virtue of being "a member of a particular social group (homosexuals)" who feared persecution from the Cuban government.

Further, the indiscriminate imposition of such gender categories as "gay" or "lesbian" without questioning the culture-specific conditions that gave rise to them in the United States and their noncorrespondence to local Latin American categories is an act of cultural hegemony that the wealthier United States imposes on its neighbors in the hemisphere. The rhetoric of the gay and lesbian human rights movement in the United States unites under the single category of "gay" such different sexual categories as an Indian *hijra* and a Mexican *joto*. Moreover, as U.S. cultural products are exported, often by the demand of other cultures around the world, U.S. categories of sexual orientation start to subsume local modes of sexual alterity.

Aware of the role of translation as a mechanism for the stabilization and homogenization of identities, even as it begins, this essay must confront the problematic nature of language. How is it possible to strive for the construction of more local gay, lesbian, queer Latin American identities when the very terms "gay," "lesbian," and "queer" have been manufactured elsewhere? Therefore, it seems more appropriate to speak of Latin American homosexualities than, for instance, a Latin American "gay" or "lesbian(a)" identity. Nevertheless, because of the current usage in Latin America of the U.S.-fabricated terms "gay," "lesbian(a)," "queer" to refer to some types of Latin American homosexualities—especially among the U.S.-influenced upper classes—I will be using those labels throughout the essay. I will also be using more native designations for same-gender sexualities. As a rule, I will use the sexual label that the subject referred to is likely to use in identifying him/herself according to his/her geographical, linguistic, and class position.

The paradoxical scenario in which a liberational movement among a privileged population translates into a situation of hegemonic domination for another population group is not altogether new. In fact, the problematic displayed in the domination of the U.S. gay, lesbian, queer identities over Latin American native forms of alternative genders is strongly reminiscent of an earlier discussion in the 1980s of Western feminism as a colonizing force. Chandra Talpade Mohanty's important essay "Under Western Eyes" presents how the writings of Western women on women of color construct a monolithical third world woman and how this representation is equivalent to a form of discursive colonialism. As if anticipating our debate on gay, lesbian, queer politics in Latin America, Mohanty writes, "As a matter of fact, my argument holds for any discourse that sets up its own authorial subjects as the implicit referent, i.e., the yardstick by which to encode and represent cultural Others. It is in this move that power is exercised in discourse" (55). In much the same way as Western feminists writing about women of color in India and Africa applied to them developmental models that positioned women of color as "lagging behind" the road to progress and emancipation, so do Western gay/lesbian/queer scholars often carelessly defer to such inefficient and dangerous models of cultural comparison without reflecting on the distorted evaluations that their privileged perspectives are prone to make. Statements such as "Such countries are in a *pre-gay* situation" (Lacey 8) abound in queer U.S. internationalist discourse. Even for a writer like Dennis Altman who, conscious of his positionality as a "privileged, white, Australian, gay intellectual, with access to considerable resources" (418) and critical of the application of the notion of development cross-culturally in the writings of other scholars (426), still falls into the trap of dangerously prejudiced comparisons. Speaking of the cultural transformations taking place currently in Asian countries with respect to sexual orientation, Altman writes, "Yet a certain blurring of the sex/gender order may not be that different from developments in the West . . . which prevailed in the *early stages* of homosexual consciousness in Europe" (emphasis mine) (421). In the Asia of the late 1990s, Altman sees "parallels with the West of several decades ago" (422), such as a form of macho-hustler aesthetics that reminds him of John Rechy's novel of the early 1960s *City of Night* (423).

Altman's essay is suffused with a paternalistic desire toward his informants. Altman's repeated references to the "young Asian men" who make up his pool of informants, for whom "an older western man will often be cast in the role of protector" (423), raise suspicions as to the nature of the relation between researcher and informant and of Altman's perception of himself in such a relationship. Joseph Carrier's essay "Miguel: Sexual Life History of a Gay Mexican American" raises similar suspicions. Carrier's detailed description of his informant's sexual practices makes one wonder exactly which methods of data collection were employed in his study. His description of Miguel as a "trim, good-looking man of average height and build with large, beautiful dark brown eyes and straight black hair" (211) is permeated with a sensuality that could be questionable under the traditional code of ethics of the field of anthropology.[1] In highlighting this, I do not strive to bring censure to any sexual involvement between informant and researcher. Rather, I hope to foreground the asymmetry of power between informant and researcher and explore how this replicates the dominating "global gaze" of U.S. gay/lesbian/queer politics in Latin America and other economically impoverished areas of the world.

Mohanty's "Under Western Eyes" continues to be of use to me in thinking about the issue of gender-minority representation in scholarship, especially in instances in which the distorted representation is enacted by a member of the community s/he is describing. Mohanty writes,

Similar arguments can be made in terms of middle-class urban or working class sisters which assumes their own middle-class culture as the norm, and codifies working-class histories and cultures as Other. Though, while this essay focuses specifically on what I refer to as "Western feminist" discourse on women in the third world, the critiques I offer also pertain to third world scholars writing about their own cultures, which employ identical analytical strategies. (52)

Mohanty's essay appears to me to be at its most suggestive point here as she stops short of saying what appears to be the logical conclusion of her thinking: that class outranks ethnicity, nationality, and geography as the most important criterion in determining the perspective of the researcher toward his or her subject of study. It being so, academics, as middle-class citizens in the United States, are prone to make problematic assumptions about subjects of study who are beneath them in the economic stratification of society. And it is not uncommon to find academics of color who, like Tomás Almaguer—a Chicano—replicate much of the problematic discourse that his White-American colleagues produce. In line with other researchers such as Joseph Carrier and Roger Lancaster, Almaguer makes a distinction between U.S. and Latino homosexualities by presenting the former as "egalitarian" and the latter as based on a *"pasivo/activo"* model. Unlike the egalitarian model, in which sexual partners are able to exchange roles, in the *pasivo/activo* model the sexual roles of inserter and insertee are rigidly established and set. While the insertee or *pasivo* role is stigmatized, the inserter or *activo* is not, and is not thought of as a homosexual.

Anthropologists are very often trained and expected to create a representation of the other as exotic and rare by highlighting differences and ignoring what is familiar and similar to their audience's culture. Authors who write on the Latin American *pasivo/activo* model often note that there also exist a large number of "egalitarian" homosexuals in Latin America (Murray 14), yet they fail to take them into account because their existence does not foster their desire to represent Latin America as sexually exotic. Their extremely simple and essentialistic rendering of the comparison between U.S. and Latin American homosexualities avoids the complexity that the inclusion of U.S. gay top/bottom distinctions would bring out. While the differences in stigma between insertor and insertee might be real, I am partisan to the belief that they are differences of degrees and not the absolutes Joseph Carrier and his school believe. I am certain that, in mainstream heterosexual contexts, none of the *activos* in their study brag about their encounters with other men because there they would face social condemnation together with what Carrier and his school of thought consider the only object of societal opprobrium, the *pasivos*.

Nevertheless, it is interesting to note how in spite of the fact that Latino homosexualities are not solely *activo/pasivo*, some writers represent them as such in order to replicate the popular image in the United States of Latin American politically dictatorial oppression—not to speak of a perpetuation of the representations of Latin America as "simple" and the United States as more "complex." Moreover, Carrier's very possible sexual involvement with some of his young informants of considerably lower economic means points to a sexual reenactment of the relationship of neocolonialism between the dominant United States and dependent, subservient Latin America.

I believe that the most salient difference between U.S. gay and Latin American homosexual categories is not found in egalitarian and *activo/pasivo* frameworks. It lies in the issue of disclosure/secrecy, which in U.S. gay discourse has been crystallized around the image of the closet. Eve Kosofsky Sedgwick in *Epistemology of the Closet* calls the closet appropriately "a structured silence." The rupture of this silence by "coming-out" narratives enacts the birth of the gay subject in discourse while at same time, ironically, forfeiting some of the freedoms of not-being.

Many native Latin American alternative genders and sexualities do not rely on the same notion of disclosure to exist; the performance of desire is a much more defining moment than the declaration; the act is more important than the speech-act. Latin American interdictions against homosexual disclosure appear to Euro–North America as entrapment, but entrapment can occur only with the appearance of the closet. Many native Latin American homosexualities still enjoy the freedom of ignorance of the closet and thus operate sometimes with greater liberties because that which isn't part of *vox populi* is difficult for society to condemn. It becomes important to note here the correspondence between disclosure and legislation: In sharp contrast with the United States, where many states still have sodomy laws, Latin American constitutional prohibitions against homosexuality are virtually nonexistent. Whenever homosexuals are arrested in Latin America, it is usually under the charge of *indecencia pública*. In other words, what is often punished in Latin America is not the homosexual act per se, but the alleged disclosure of it in the public sphere as "public indecency." Broadly speaking, the North American closet spells liberation through disclosure and many native Latin American homosexualities operate through freedoms afforded by secrecy. The binary distinction becomes blurred with the arrival of the closet in Latin America, but if there is a binarism that must be utilized to distinguish Latin American from U.S. homosexualities, disclosure/secrecy appears to be a more pertinent one than the problematic *activo/pasivo*.

When we take a wholistic look at the representation of Latin American homosexualities, two trends become apparent. The first, produced by the political activism of gay and lesbian human rights groups based in the United States, consists of a homogenization of alternative genders and non heterosexual sexual performances through a translation of these into gay and lesbian identities taking shape within a developmental model that positions them as backwards. The second representation, found in anthropological discourse, utilizes an extreme and oppositional rhetorical strategy in order to distort Latin American homosexualities: instead of homogenization, it makes a distinction between Latin American and U.S. homosexualities by making a highly problematic distinction between an "*activo/pasivo*" system in Latin America and an "egalitarian" system in the United States—a polarized distinction that mirrors, in the sexual arena, the problematic images of tyranny and democracy that are used politically by the United States to distinguish the representation of itself from Latin America. In this way, gay discourse operates like other forms of imperialistic propaganda in which the Other is reduced to an opposite of the values desired to be represented in the imperialist self. It is different from common forms of discursive colonization in that it is concerned with the culture of an oppressed class, and not simply that of the elite.

Investigating sites within Latin American cultures that provide more genders from which to choose than are traditionally available is an important step toward the understanding and elaboration of Latin American homosexual practice and identity that would be able to overcome the historical emplotment, peripheralization, and domination by the U.S. gay and lesbian movement. The three largest syncretic cults of the Americas, Santería, Candomblé, and Vaudou, are such spaces.

Any exploration of the complex work of gender within syncretic belief systems in the Americas requires a basic understanding of the idea of syncretism as the coexistence of different ideological systems through a series of correspondences. In the history of New World slavery, the religious conversion of the slave became the single most important process for the slave's adoption of European culture. In the areas settled by Spain, France, and Portugal, slaves were required to abandon their traditional beliefs and become Catholic. In spite of this absolutist demand, slaves were able to preserve their belief systems through the phenomenon of syncretism, by which Catholic ideology was superimposed on traditional African belief systems. In Cuba, Brazil, and Haiti, the African beliefs that merged with Catholicism were essentially Yoruba beliefs, even though in Haitian Vaudou there exists a large amount of ideological material from the religion of the Fon people of Dahomey. Though Catholicism remained in a position of dominance over traditional African beliefs in these syncretic structures, the network of associations and correspondences that was created between the two systems ensured the survival of the threatened African belief system, now embedded within Catholic practice.

This ideological syncretism or merger between Catholicism and African religious beliefs is visibly evident in religious iconography. In order to indoctrinate the slaves, Catholic missionaries made use of religious images depicting important saints in Catholic theology and history. Upon seeing these images and hearing about the lives of these saints, African slaves associated them with many of their ancestral gods. Once the association between the Catholic saints and the African deities was established, Africans were able to continue worshiping their gods, now disguised as Catholic saints, without the reprimands from the church and colonial authorities.

The Yoruba god Eleggúa, for instance, is the deity of crossroads and gates. He is the messenger between the Yoruba deities, or Orishas, and the supreme God, Olodumare. In colonial Saint-Domingue, slaves associated Eleggúa, Papa Legba in

Kreyòl, with Saint Peter because of his role as gatekeeper between earth and heaven. In Cuba, slaves associated Eleggúa with the Lonely Spirit of Purgatory for his role as a messenger. Another example of this syncretism can be seen in the survival of Ogún, the Yoruba god of war, iron, and warfare. In Cuba he was associated with Saint Peter, who is represented as holding up keys made of metal. In Haiti he is called Ogou Feray and is associated with Saint James, who holds up a spade atop his white horse. Displaying the resilience of Yoruba religion in the face of migration, suppression, and technological development, Ogún, by virtue of his association with metal, also receives offering at railroad tracks and is even invoked for protection before flying on an aircraft.

Certainly here I do want to look at how the idea of syncretism in religion fosters the existence of homosexualities within its realm and how, then, the notion of syncretism might be applied to hybrid sexual formations, especially those produced at the confluence of Latin American and Euro–North American forms. Any discussion of syncretic structures will fluctuate between treating them as coherent, unified entities and treating them as composite structures with various internal elements. The fact that individuals successfully manage an integration of Latin American homosexual identities and Euro–North American models points to the importance of syncretism as a technique for cultural survival in an increasingly homogenized world. Nevertheless, the existence of forms of this ideal integration does not prejudge a discussion of these sexualities in binary terms. Syncretism, as helpful a tool in cultural survival as it is, is not always, if ever, a happy marriage between equal partners. Syncretism is fundamentally predicated by an ideological inequality that persists even after the point of coalescence. In the case of the Latino with dual allegiances to a Santería house and to participation on a Pride Parade float, the distinction between the Afro-Latino homosexuality and the North American gay identity continues to be hierarchical. This hierarchy between the two can be illustrated through the idea of linguistic translation and borrowing. To my knowledge, English has not borrowed any Spanish terms for homosexual identity. Doesn't the Spanish borrowing of "gay" point toward the hegemonic unidirectionality of cultural change between the United States and Latin America? It is this dangerous unidirectionality of borrowing of English terms into Spanish that causes me to insist on indigenous Latin American terms and categories. Because syncretic structures maintain the asymmetry of power that they themselves seek to resolve, it becomes important for me here to highlight these differences as well, even if at the risk of having the discussion take on at times a polarizing tone.

One of the foundational works in the study of syncretic cults in the Americas is Lydia Cabrera's monumental work of ethnography, *El monte*, in which she comments several times on homosexuality within Santería. She notes the presence, in Santería groups, of several homosexual men, such as Papá Colás, who "era famoso invertido y sorprendiendo la candidez de un cura, casó disfrazado de mujer, con otro invertido, motivando el escándalo que puede presumirse."[2] The purpose of her discussion appears to prove homosexuality as a long-standing and pervasive situation within Santería: "Desde muy atrás se registra el pecado nefando como algo muy frecuente en la Regla lucumí."[3] Also, Cabrera mentions a Santería legend about the goddess Yemayá having been in love with a homosexual man (56). Lydia Cabrera, who is apocryphally reputed to have had amorous affairs with other women during her lifetime, speaks of the abundance of female homosexuality in the Regla de Ocha (58). Throughout, she mentions several Yoruba names for homosexuality-practicing men: Addóddis, Obini-Toyo, Obini-Ñaña or Erón Kiba, Wassicundi or Diánkune; and for women Alácuattas or Oremi (59).

Syncretic religion is becoming an issue of great cultural and academic fascination today due to the current interest in marginalized, subaltern, silenced groups around the world. For Latin Americans, homosexual Latin Americans in particular, the interest in Santería, Vaudou, and Candomblé is tied to the greater availability of gender options within these belief systems than are found in mainstream Latin American and U.S. social contexts.

While syncretic cults are becoming a matter of much attention in academic and cultural circles in the 1990s, a fact that is attested by the relatively large number of books published on them within the last five years in Latin America and the United States, not much has been published on the role of homosexuals within these cults. Therefore, in order to supplement the few readings on this specific topic, I have had to utilize information obtained in the summer of 1997 during my one-week involvement in the Santería house "La Casa de Obatalá" in Dorchester, Massachusetts, and during a two-week visit to Haiti, where I was able to participate in Vaudou ceremonies and conduct some informal interviews on the topic of homosexuality and Vaudou.

Women occupy an important and active role in the religion. Candomblé has been led exclusively by women, the *mai de santo*, for hundreds of years in Brazil and, in spite of the recent acceptance of men as *pai de santo* of Candomblé houses, the matriarchal heritage of Candomblé is still very strong and continues to influence the continuous development of the religion. Vaudou has been historically more egalitarian with respect to the gender of its leadership. The male priest, the

Oungan, must conduct the Vaudou ceremonies with the Mambo, the Vaudou priestess. In Santería, the rule that requires that the *babalao* be male is not completely representative of the work of gender within the religion. Other than not being allowed to become *babalaos*, presumably because women's potential for maternity forbids them from killing four-legged animals, women occupy the same leadership roles in the religion as men.

The phenomenon of syncretism opens up avenues for multiple subjectivities and cross-identifications for the Orishas and for the Orisha worshipers. The identification between an Orisha and a Catholic saint need not be restricted to a strict correspondence in terms of gender. The hagiology of each saint played a much more decisive role in the association between African and Catholic figures than did gender. As a result, during the historical process of identifying the Orishas with Catholic saints, many of the gods changed gender identification. For instance, in Santería male Changó became Santa Barbara. Moreover, many Orishas are represented as androgynous, bisexual, or multiply gendered. In Santería, Olokun and Obatalá are represented sometimes as male, others as female, and often as androgynous. In Candomblé, Exu is a polysexual (Wafer 17) and genderless (Araújo 31) Orisha, Ossaim is bisexual, and Ossãe, Logunede, and Oxumare are said to be androgynous, hermaphroditic, and bisexual (Staal 228; Wafer 87).

In much the same way as the Orishas are identified with Catholic saints, so are the initiates dedicated to a particular Orisha during their initiation. This cross-identification does not need to correspond by gender any more than the syncretism between deities does, so it is not uncommon to find female initiates with a male "head" and vice versa.

Linked to this is the phenomenon of possession. This is an intensified form of the cross-identification that occurs between the initiates and their respective Orishas because through this experience the god incarnates human form. The opportunities for transgressing normative gender categories that the phenomenon of possession provides is aptly mined by homosexuals in these religions, and is probably one of the most important factors explaining the large numbers of them in Santería, Vaudou, and Candomblé. In Santería, *maricones*—male homosexuals—are particularly drawn to being initiated as children of the female Orisha Yemayá. In Vaudou, the men who inhabit the Haitian homosexual categories of *makomé* or *gwo masisi* often become *serviteurs* of Erzili Freda, the Voudou goddess of love by whom they are often possessed during religious ceremonies.

The practice of cross-gender possession has been mastered in Candomblé by the *adés*, the passive male homosexuals *filhos de santo*. As stated earlier, the participation of males in Candomblé is relatively new. Only in the 1930s and 1940s did men begin to be admitted in Candomblé circles (Landes 1947). The fact that it has been often remarked that the men who join the Candomblé religion are homosexual has been a matter of tangential discussion in many treatises on Candomblé, but a thorough study of the subject is missing from scholarship. Within the last ten years, two doctoral dissertations addressing the broader issue of gender in Candomblé have given the *adés* more critical attention: Parvati Jean-nette Staal's "Women, Food, Sex, and Survival in Candomblé: An Interpretive Analysis of an African-Brazilian religion in Bahia, Brazil" and Patrícia Birman's *Fazer estilo criando gêneros: Possessão e diferenças de gênero em terreiros de umbanda e candomblé no Rio de Janeiro*, which was published as a book in 1995.

In *Fazer estilo criando gêneros,* Patricia Birman attempts to rationalize the com-plex, gendered categories of Candomblé houses. She examines the category of the *adé*, the *mais* and *pais de santo* or mother and father of the houses, the *filhos* and *filhas de santo* or the initiates, the *ogãs* or male financial sponsors, and the *ekedes*, a category closely akin to the Western term "lesbian." The problematic that she tackles deals with the curious gender divisions in the houses of Candomblé that allow *adés* to dance in the possession ritual and not the *ogãs* and the *ekedes*, even though these last are female. Like many before her, she interprets the phenome-non of possession as a sexual metaphor of human intercourse with the divine. However, Birman concludes with the original assertion that these categories can be structurally divided around the phenomenon of possession into two groups: those who can be possessed and are therefore "feminine," the *adés* and the *filhas de santo*, and those who cannot be possessed and who are therefore masculine, the *ogãs* and the *ekedes*. Her assertion is useful in that in disengaging biological sex from gender, it arrives at an explanation as to why gender operates differently within Candomblé than in mainstream Brazilian society. Nevertheless, she curi-ously replicates a binary masculine/feminine structure around which she organ-izes the categories of a belief system that does not perceive the world in an ei-ther/or format. Instead of division and incompatibility, the episteme of syn-cretism is complementarity. Because of her unchecked Western predisposition to reduce categories to their simplest terms in order to arrive at some sort of under-lying and essential notion, I question the usefulness of her final analysis.

In spite of this, Birman manages to present an important account of the work of gender in Candomblé and to provide one of the more extended critical treat-ments of the figure of the *adé* to date. She explains that the entrance of men into Candomblé is seen by some women with suspicion. The general feeling among many women is that men should be allowed to be members of the Candomblé house and to dance in the ceremonies as long as they do not attempt to take over. Apparently some women are not so tolerant, as many *pais de santo* are currently having a difficult time recruiting *filhas de santo*. Moreover, there appear to be very sharp differences in what many of the *adés* and *filhas de santo* perceive to be the virtues of being an initiate. Birman describes how the emphasis on duty and responsibility, especially in the areas of domestic labor, has always played a crucial part of the identity of the *filhas de santo*. Many women complain that the *adés* are only interested in the spectacular and performance aspects of Candomblé. A more serious accusation involves the charge that many of the *adés* fake their possession in order to be the stars in the dancing ritual of the Candomblé ceremonies.

Birman explains how many who are members of Candomblé houses as well as many who are simply spectators in their ceremonies clearly understand that many of these possessions are not real possessions at all. For many, the realization of the fictive nature of the possession does not detract any value from them: on the other hand, it raises the Candomblé ceremony to an aesthetic level that renders homage to Afro-Brazilian religion and culture. A favorite Orisha to perform among the *adés* during the ceremonies is Iansá, the goddess of wind, storms, and lightning. In my opinion, it appears that the *adés* show a preference for Iansá because the tempestuous and temperamental femininity she represents not only offers the *adés* the possibility of experiencing femininity, but it allows them to perform a persona that, although gendered in a subaltern position to males, is nevertheless very powerful. Thus, performing Iansá is a public avowal of a desire for liberation from the constraints of gender of mainstream Brazilian society. Syncretized as Santa Barbara, Iansá has also come to be known recently for her current representation in Candomblé ceremonies as *reina dos adés*, queen of the homosexuals.

Practical Conclusions

The Latin American homosexual categories that find a niche in these syncretic cults—*maricones, makomé, bichas,* and *ekedes*—certainly do not fit into the U.S.-fabricated gay and lesbian categories. These forms of homosexuality are different from each other and from those forms of homosexuality found in the United States because they have developed within specific regional contexts. Nevertheless, we have seen how, whenever non-Western categories are given attention in the United States there is a general tendency toward presenting them as simply other versions of "gay" identities. Furthermore, the extreme polarization of Latin

American and U.S. homosexualities in certain strains of academic thought, in spite of its underscoring of differences, works together with the first homogenizing tendency in the enactment of a discursive colonization of Latin American homosexualities by research methodologies that rely on U.S. models as points of comparison.

Representation can have very real effects. Its distortion of practices and identities is able to lead to the formation of subjects who will conform to these transformed, received notions. The dissemination of knowledges of local practices and identities of homosexuality in Latin America is a necessary endeavor for the continuation of distinct Latin American gender identities. I see this present work as part of this much needed corpus of texts that is only now beginning to appear.

I would like to conclude with some notes concerning the application of the knowledge of alternative homosexual genders in Latin American syncretic cults to the mainstream gay, lesbian, queer movement in the United States and to communities of color in the United States and Latin America.

For the mainstream U.S. gay and lesbian movement, an understanding of the work of gender in syncretic cults could do the following:

1. *Denaturalize gay and lesbian identities and contextualize gender and sexual orientation identities within a specific cultural context.* This is an important point that works on alternative genders in non-Western cultures should make: an important component of homosexualities is their culturally produced condition, and therefore they do not comprise an intrinsic trait in peoples all across the world or constitute an underlying "biological" common ground that obfuscates differences of socioeconomic, racial, and geographic situation.

2. *Contribute to an awareness of a homosexual experience outside the United States.* Much of the work produced in the area of gay and lesbian studies tends to be concerned with the homosexualities in the United States. Whenever the topic extends beyond the national boundaries, it usually covers Western Europe. The rest of the world is the homosexual "terra incognita" that is being "discovered" by anthropologists who are to a great extent still trapped by the colonialist methods that have been a part of their field since its inception.

3. *Dispel the notion that "the first world" is the place that has the most freedom to offer in terms of sexual orientation.* Lesbian, gay, queer communities in the

United States need to be conscious of the way queer political struggle for political representation and cultural visibility in the United States utilizes the idea of the United States as the most tolerant, free, and accepting place in the world. This patriotic ideal is not only dangerous in its exaltation of U.S. supremacist benevolence, it is also a false portrayal, as proven by the discussion of the great acceptance homosexuals receive within syncretic cults in Latin America.

4. *Dispel the notion that people of color are homophobic.* Though initially this might appear to be a superfluous remark, it is an important one to make because it is a powerful assumption that underwrites much of the racism in gay, lesbian, and queer communities. In San Diego, the city where I live, the *Gay and Lesbian Times* has run several articles that have argued for a closer political alliance between queers and White upper-middle-class heterosexuals. This assimilationist rhetoric is coupled with putative statistical work that proves that White upper-middle-class heterosexuals are more likely to accept homosexuality as a viable option, whereas people of color are the most homophobic. This formulaic argument often ignores an analysis of how the figures might be the result of class values and are not necessarily racial. Moreover, this line of argument not only ignores the economic racialization that is at the core of inequality in the United States, but also fails to include any discussion of the dangerous loss that this assimilationist move would pose to the revolutionary potential within the gay, lesbian, queer movement.

An examination of the African religion in the Americas whose membership is largely of African descent serves to make the point that communities of color around the world have spaces in which homosexualities are comfortable.

For queer communities of color in the United States and in Latin America, an understanding of the work of gender in syncretic cults could do the following:

1. *Help to oppose total domination by the hegemonic master narrative of gay liberation in favor of more culturally pertinent form options.* As stated throughout the chapter, it becomes necessary for information on local Latin American homosexualities to be distributed in order to create histories that document the distinctiveness of these traditions. Only with such documentation can

these identities and practices survive absolute absorption by the U.S. lesbian and gay categories making inroads into Latin American society at the present time.

2. *Establish syncretic correspondences between U.S. and Latin American forms as the most practical response to homogenization.* An understanding of native homosexual subjectivities should not be followed by a total adoption of those models either. This would be presupposing that authentic, stable, and natural categories exist. Rather, the blending of the native Latin American categories with gay/lesbian categories seems ideal and is in line with the idea of the complementarity of syncretism. Authenticity is a very fragile building material. The strength inherent in the combination of materials from different sources is a better alternative to "authentic ideals" and is more in line with Latin American strategies for cultural survival and transformation.

3. *Promote useful political realignments and coalition building between queer communities of color in the hemisphere.* It becomes crucial in the era of transnational capitalism to move beyond the nation as a framework of analysis. National isolationism finds its way into the academy and expresses itself in, for instance, studies of slavery that treat it as an exclusively U.S. phenomenon. African American studies is only recently beginning an investigation of the ways its field can be enriched by the knowledge of other former slave societies in the hemisphere. In the same way as this new shift of focus provides an alternative to merely reacting to mainstream U.S. culture in order to find a communal definition and politics, so would an investigation of the possible links between queers of color in the hemisphere have potentially beneficial results.

4. *Contribute to realization that the important role syncretic cults have had in revolutionary movements elsewhere can be used to achieve the desired political goals of queer communities of color in the United States and in Latin America.* Ideology binds. Religion in general is used to achieve group cohesion, which can have significantly powerful effects. The Haitian revolution occurred as a result of the slave revolts that were organized and planned during Vaudou ceremonies. Utilizing the traditional and historical significance of these cults in orchestrating successful political changes can be an extremely helpful tool in achieving the group cohesion of queer communities of color.

Perhaps a final note should include a restating of the dangers of translating social-change agendas from economically privileged population groups to poorer population sectors. Living in the era of globalization forces us to think of the ways these differences of class are relevant on a worldwide scale and of transnational strategies that might help offset this domination. In Latin America and for lesbian and gay studies this appears to imply further thinking about the intersection of class, race, geography, and research methodologies in the cross-cultural study of gender and sexuality. A study of syncretic cults in the Americas appears to be a good point of departure for such a project.

Notes

1. For work dealing with sex between field researcher and informant, see Lewin and Leap; Kulick and Willson.
2. He "was a famous invert; surprising a gullible priest, he was married disguised as a woman to another invert, causing great scandal" (my translation).
3. "From a long time ago, the abominable sin has been something very common in the Regla Lucumí" (my translation).

Works Cited

Almaguer, Tomás. "Chicano Men: A Cartography of Homosexual Identity and Behavior." In *The Lesbian and Gay Studies Reader*, ed. Henry Abelove, Michèle Aina Barale, and David Halperin. New York: Routledge, 1993.

Altman, Dennis. "Global Gaze/Global Gays." *GLQ* 3 (1997): 417–36.

Araújo, Carlos. *ABC dos orixás*. Rio de Janeiro: Nórdica, 1993.

Birman, Patrícia. *Fazer estilo criando gêneros*. Rio de Janeiro: Dumará, 1995.

Cabrera, Lydia. *El monte*. Miami: Ediciones Universal, 1975.

Carrier, Joseph. "Miguel: Sexual Life History of a Gay Mexican American." In *Gay Culture in America: Essays from the Field*, ed. Joseph Carrier. Boston: Beacon, 1992.

Kulick, Don, and Margaret Willson, eds. *Taboo: Sex, Identity and Erotic Subjectivity in Anthropological Fieldwork*. New York: Routledge, 1995.

Lacey, E. A. "Translator's Introduction." In *My Deep Dark Pain Is Love*. San Francisco: Gay Sunshine Press, 1983.

Landes, Ruth. *The City of Women*. New York: Macmillan, 1947.

Lewin, Ellen, and William Leap, eds. *Out in the Field: Reflections of Lesbian and Gay Anthropologists*. Urbana: University of Indiana Press, 1996.

Mohanty, Chandra Talpade. "Under Western Eyes: Feminist Scholarship and Colonial Discourses." *Feminist Review*, no. 30 (autumn 1998).

Murray, Stephen O. "Homosexual Categorization in Cross-Cultural Perspective." In *Latin American Male Homosexualities*, ed. Stephen O. Murray. Albuquerque: University of New Mexico Press, 1995.

Sedgwick, Eve Kosofsky. *Epistemology of the Closet*. Berkeley: University of California Press, 1990.

Staal, Parvati Jeannette. 1961. "Woman, Food, Sex and Survival in Candomblé." Ph.D. diss., UCLA, 1992.

Wafer, James William. *The Taste of Blood: Spirit Possession in Brazilian Candomblé*. Philadelphia: University of Pennsylvania Press, 1991.

Part 4

THE NATION AS GLOBAL BORDER

11 Stealth Bombers of Desire

The Globalization of "Alterity" in Emerging Democracies

Cindy Patton

In the early 1990s, a small number of young men in Taiwan awaited their interviews with psychiatrists who would certify them as homosexual and therefore unfit for obligatory (for males) military service. Unfortunately, the highly public 1993 American debates about gays in the military had not passed unnoticed by officials in Taiwan. Although technically permitted to apply for the homosexual exclusion, those awaiting a hearing during this time were discouraged from declaring their sexuality, which was no longer considered cause of unfitness for military service. The exact reasons for this change in policy are unclear.

Taiwan was probably following the lead of emerging democracies that adopt apparently liberal stances on social issues as a means of demonstrating their modernness, or at least their distance from barbaric practices of their neighbors or their past.[1] Indeed, Taiwan may have initiated this strategy in an earlier round of publicizing liberal sexual regulations. Chao Yengning (1996) demonstrates that during martial law (1949–1989) the Kuo Ming Tang, or KMT, asserted its liberalness by claiming that, compared to mainland China, believed to imprison and execute homosexuals, Taiwan lacked draconian regulation of homosexuality.[2] It is clear, at any rate, that the present government was not responding to the demands of a minority constituency. Indeed, in 1993 there was barely a visible gay movement in

Taiwan; even today, there is nothing comparable to the visible, organized gay civil rights movement that, in the United States, demanded reconsideration of military policy.[3] Actually, it is difficult to imagine a Taiwanese gay movement demanding to serve in the military: the absolute association of the military with martial-law KMT suggests that getting out of the military is more consonant with expressing new democratic feelings.

Paradoxically, then, while seeming to promote human rights locally and adduct toward its space the global blanket of free self-expression, the 1993 policy change actually preempted identity-based liberation politics. Not speaking one's sexuality—even in the semiprivacy of the psychiatrist's interview—aligned with nationalist, progovernment (that is, pro-KMT) feeling. Far from making the state more democratic, the new policy put queerness at a further remove from emergent liberationist politics.[4] Feelings of love of men are no threat to the military (though they may cause discomfort in other quarters . . . ironically, in the new social order under way by 1995 in the briefly DDP-controlled Taipei City government!).[5] Gay men have been absorbed by the military; at least, Taiwan's homosexuals no longer benefit from an official policy that once relieved them of service. Thus, instead of the expected battery of questions about their perverse desires and deviant practices, the gay petitioners of 1993 were treated to a rant about their nationalist feelings: "You are unpatriotic! You care nothing about your country! All you are doing is trying to get out of your obligation! What is wrong with you? Don't you know the American gays *want* to serve their country?"[6]

Underneath the bleak humor of this scene lies a deeply troubling question, for sexual dissidents in emerging democracies—who are mostly not visible as a social movement—as well as for their globally visible American friends. Through what channels do discourses of sexual liberation travel—and what do they accomplish when they arrive? The fact that states can convey minoritarian "civil rights" in the absence of local actors militating for them may seem like a triumph in the globalization of human rights.[7] But isn't it a bit frightening to imagine a nation that first recognizes its gay citizens as cannon fodder? This is the fatal irony of the late modern homosexual citizen's rights: he (in some cases she) is allowed to serve in a military that does not otherwise protect his (her) sexual interests.

The use and composition of the military—sometimes all-volunteer, sometimes conscripted—have been debated in American politics since our Revolution. Many Americans believe that the post–World War II racial integration of the military paved the way for integration in other industries. See? Blacks and whites can work together! War films, television dramas, and novels of the post–World War II

decades—indeed, though less patriotic, through the Vietnam critique and reconciliation films of the 1970s and 1980s—suggested that a new sense of cross-racial
understanding emerged among men who served together. Following this logic,
and in the wake of sensational lawsuits by homosexuals discharged from the military, gay civil rights activists in the late 1980s began to argue that the military
might be a good place to "integrate" openly lesbian and gay male workers. The
class politics of this strategy was important: for many rural and poor Americans,
the military is the only way to acquire technical skills or finance postsecondary
education. Equally important was the symbolic gain that might accrue from this
arena of employment activism. For two decades, the U.S. gay movement had
fought against the state on issues like foster care, discrimination in government
employment, and allocation of welfare benefits. But at the same time, gay and lesbian Americans articulated themselves as good citizens who hoped only that
America would live up to its promise of liberty and justice for all. What better way
to emblematize this newly asserted citizen than as a patriot willing to lay down
his or her life for everyone's freedom?

Lesbians and gay men underestimated the extent to which this strategy could
backfire. The Clinton administration ended the matter with the equivocal "don't
ask, don't tell" policy (which, in those heady post–Reagan-Bush era days, included
participation by overly optimistic gay civil rights lawyers).[8] Even this problematic
solution was greeted with an antigay backlash within the military: witch hunts
against presumed homosexuals increased, and several violent incidents by
"straight" soldiers were blamed on their anger at being "forced" to serve with
queers, however silent.[9] Activists and social movement scholars learned two lessons from this episode:

1. Even if different types of oppression are experienced as "the same" by victims, the techniques of oppression arise from and are maintained through
   structurally and historically distinct mechanisms. Thus, gains by one minority do not quickly and logically translate into gains for other groups. In
   democracies, this is partly a result of the receptivity of the mainstream,
   which reacts out of apparently different "structures of feeling" to the pleas
   of the different subgroups that it oppressed differently.[10]
2. The time required by one group to achieve a particular civil goal may have
   to be repeated by subsequent groups seeking the same goal. There is no
   Teflon path to civil rights. The idea that Black civil rights are a twentieth-
   century, even post–World War II phenomenon suggests too short a time

frame for gay activism. It probably took 270 years, and not 50 years, to produce Colin Powell, a Black patriot acceptable enough to the white masses to have been courted (by both political parties!) as a vice presidential candidate.[11]

A more sanguine approach toward America's internal—"social"—politics has important implications for those who look to the U.S. social movements, and especially the gay movement, for models or lessons. In the American context, gay and lesbian civil rights efforts have been criticized by a politics glossed "queer."[12] I want to suggest here, however, that while it is exciting and potentially useful for emerging democracies to "think queer," the context of American queer politics' emergence raises questions about the extent to which it too bears false hopes about the mechanisms and possibilities of radical politics.

To some extent in the United States, civil rights strategies have afforded homosexuals very modest legitimacy in current policy debates, though there is virtually nothing to show, in the way of legal change, for the last three decades of work. For better or worse, this visibility-without-protection has solidified "rights" as the dominant mode of sexual dissidence and the last line of retreat: few are willing to abandon the quest for rights in favor of a "queer" politics that cannot guarantee its success. Open debate about any form of rights is new in Taiwan: queer activism can and is informing political strategy for sexual dissidents in Taiwan. Proposing a virtual Nation of Queerness against the Nation of Taiwan definitely has appeal! But the particular forms of Queer Nation and queer theory that emerged in the United States seem unlikely to come to grips with the territorial fragility of an island that may well be taken over (by agreement or force) by a vastly larger entity. Queer theories offer new ways of imagining novel relations among space, nation, and politics. However, two of the key elements that American queer nationalists take for granted are either marginally present or present under radically different political ideologies in Taiwan: (1) public space as a performance venue, and (2) recognizably liberationist-style identities against which to register anti-identitarian politics.

Placed in the context of Taiwan, with its current multisided debate about national identity and independence, several forms of queer theory have emerged, but as prior—rather than in reaction—to civil rights/identity politics. In addition to documenting cases of local politics that have not sought the imprimatur of other nations' insurgencies, it might be useful for local queerings to consider how they reproduce or break from the assumptions of American politics and its concepts of political space; everywhere, whether in Taiwan or Israel or South Africa, nation and identity are being queered in a special way. As a kind of friction against the hetero-state, no local queer can be authentic, but queerings can deface hetero-states, can operate as locally generative theories of bodies in orthogonal relation to nation.[13]

Jet-lagged and, having crossed the international dateline, confused even about what day it is, American-style queer theory does not know how to behave: it arrived not to harass extant, but in advance of, mainstreamed gay civil rights discourse. And however well "queer" works in Taiwan, American activists must not be self-congratulatory about the apparent globalization of their sexual politics. As avant-garde as queer politics in the United States imagines itself to be, it must stay anti-universalist. Other queers are not a local deviation from a Queer. Any queering politic must always be critical of the extent to which it hangs on to elements from the identity politics it believes it has archly opposed. Western activists find it hard to imagine politics without rights, if only as the fall guy to more radical claims. Thus, it takes Westerners some time to see that queer in Taiwan is not about quickly disposing of identity politics, but might be orthogonal to something else. (See, for example, the recent work of Ding Nai-fei and Liu Jen-peng, who argue that tolerance aligns with traditional values of Chinese courtly rhetoric.)

In the face of transnational social forces, an "emerging democracy's" adoption of rights discourse as a way to be modern may actually be politically conservative. For one thing, given the strong tendency in Western philosophy and social theory and in Western colonial practice to agglutinate the Western Enlightenment and the modern, any attempt to position a country as modern promotes the Euro-American model of the nation over and against governmentality based in religion, cultural/ethnic conventions, alternate political philosophies—like Confucianism—and alternate conceptions of modernity, for example, Sun Yat Sen's incorporation (and sinofication) of the European Enlightenment into an already articulated Chinese one, properly allowing a generation of Chinese literati to speak of their modernity as not indebted but superordinate to the later, minor European one. These "other" forces may respond—as in Singapore—by collapsing the ugly fact of Euro-American colonialism with the potentially separable idea of rights, Enlightenment style: they trump "rights" with the equally powerful discourse of authenticity, of indigenous values.

If, as I'll suggest in a moment, a vast supranational administrative apparatus now aids in the globalization of Western rights discourse, then neither the popular desire for nor the state's resistance to them can clearly be argued as Universal. For "rights" to be locally meaningful, we must interrupt the ways national and supranational bodies demand the use of rights rhetoric as a means of displaying a tie to the Euro-American–dominated "community of nations." Rights rhetoric, coin of the global realm, not only provides a modern face, but is often a prerequisite to securing funds from national and supranational monetary and development bodies. In another global flow, the corporate media use rights rhetoric to smear countries that are out of favor: when news media report only certain "human rights violations," they implicitly valorize, as points of comparison, the supposedly humane countries. For example, the United States is often the "good" country, despite its continued economic violence, even after a civil war ended slavery, against the poor and the Black, whose civil rights not to mention economic, cultural, and social viability are perpetually deferred. The model nation to which offenders are compared is highly duplicitous: which nation is it whose citizens have these fantasized rights?

Nation-Thinking

In the late 1700s the "nation," as we think of it today, was born, or rather, several different modalities of nation. The United States formed as a constitutional democracy out of a series of wealthy, and, in the current connotative register, not very oppressed colonies. France transformed itself from a monarchy into a similar, middle-class–driven democracy. Haiti had a revolution, throwing off slaveholders and forming the first postcolonial nation. More monarchies tumbled to the new professional classes, and mixed-race colonized persons threw off the nations who had colonized them. More and more territory was transformed into nation-spaces, until a few centuries and a couple of world wars later, nearly the entire globe was taken over by nations. Subject to rather different systems of imperial rule, imperial expansion, and European and American colonial domination, even the epistemologically different spaces of "Asia" were also brought into this story of Nations' Triumph. But as many scholars have argued, these various forms of nation are in fact quite different, especially those that were carved out of aboriginal peoples' land, said by Europeans to be empty.

In his seminal *Imagined Communities*, Benedict Anderson (1983) suggests several reasons why nation became the dominant—and dominating—form of geopolitical organization. First, the development of a semi-independent print capitalism allowed people who were widely dispersed to see themselves existing in a coextensive time. Placement of news articles from different regions on the same page, for example, promoted a consciousness that "what's happening over there" is not something you learn about "later" when the "news has traveled," but something that is happening now. This enabled the development of cross-regional consensus about politics among the literate middle classes and enhanced the sense that a nation was a community, even if that national identity—called "imagined community" by Anderson existed only in a hypothetical space. The reciprocal effect of this production of national simultaneity was the belief that peoples who did not live in "nations" were primitive, living in the past, or rather, languishing in mythological instead of civil time. Second, nation was contingent on the shift from theological to populist/democratic modes of legitimation, though the nontheological means varied and their break from theology and theocracy was incomplete. Finally, in two brief but powerful asides, Anderson argues that Nation was made possible by and encouraged the emergence of "political love," an affect toward the imaginary entities Nation and People strong enough to make millions of twentieth-century soldiers lay down their lives not for economic gain, but for the idea of nations and freedom.[14]

I want to augment Anderson's account. Once set in motion, the spatio-temporal logic of nations meant that there must be only nations: *becoming nation* admitted neither blank spaces nor players who want a single world order. This tendency of *becoming nation* to spawn more nations I call geophagia. This compulsion to consume—to eat—land was accomplished through performative homology: in order to break from a ragged system of theological and violent legitimation, those who sought to invent Nation had to conceive a totality of nations and, with these, conceive a judicial meta-entity like a "community of nations." In the inaugurating American case (perhaps enduring more because its charmingly powerful rhetoric is so quotable than because it is actually a good model), with no justification for refusing their king, the American colonists imagined a higher court of appeal—not a God who would shift his allegiance from the bad king to the good people, but a global community of citizens who were also residents of nations.[15] Of course, no such nations—united or not—existed at the founding of the United States, but the Declaration of Independence, emulated by political dissidents even today, argues as if there were some kind of United Nations tribunal to which it might appeal. It is because geophagia admits no other form of spatio-governmental order that we can now conceive—and only conceive—of Model Nations. Performative homologism makes it possible for a variety of nations who were once enemies to join forces in multinational peacekeeping teams. The young soldiers of this meta-national, powder blue military do not die for "political love" of their own nation, but in service of the idea of nation in general. Representing multiple, even conflicting, national interests, they can, with resort to the meta-ideal of a civil community of nations, join together to invade sovereign entities that violate the basic criterion—derived from Western Enlightenment concepts of personhood—of nation-ness.

In the recent onslaught of definitions of "globalization," it is common to see the phenomenon described as a process occurring on top of or through nations. I argue instead that Nation produces and embodies the discursive and material action(s) of what is now confusingly called globalization. I agree with those who argue that dating of "globalization," especially when conceived as a unified and undifferentiated process, is impossible. The mechanisms said to create globalization, especially those concerned with proliferation of markets, are co-temporal with the invention of the modern state and with the philosophical developments of the Enlightenment. Indeed, temporal staging is elusive; from its incarnation, the idea of nation led directly and inexorably to the self-globalization, to total proliferation of the idea of itself as the proper individual unit of government. Indeed, because nation had to break from the upwardly referential logic of theological practices of legitimation, the idea of a global community as arbitrator of valid governance is *logically prior to* or at least coincident with the idea of modern nation. Globalization *precedes* nation, since the idea of nation required such a vast spatial flow not as an independent process (i.e., *across* national borders) but as a potentiality *internal to* the very idea of nation. Thus, economic development and cultural pluralization, while they can be examined and historicized separately, are not outside the homological performative "nation." For this reason, while I consider capital expansion extremely important, and while I am cognizant of the debates surrounding the extent and interpenetration of capital and other globalizing elements (I'm most concerned with rights), I will largely bracket the role of market in my discussion of Taiwan. Despite the vastly different material conditions that capitalism has wrought, despite the capacity to use force that wealth allows, the fundamental political dispute in Taiwan relates to the propriety of nation, and policies regarding sexuality have a strange place in this discussion. Especially for nations that lack material riches or political power, seeming ultra-modern on issues of sexuality may seem like the only way for emerging democracies to compete.

What's in a Nation?

Taiwan might be considered an exceptional nation (or even, merely, a country), perpetually colonized, and ultimately (in 1949) reimagined as the locus of a government-in-exile under the watchful imperial eye of the United States. Considered territorially peripheral by nations east and west, Taiwan is a palimpsest of the political discourses that have bound and separated, colonized and liberated the East from the West, the East from itself. But in another, more significant way, Taiwan is ground zero (but not the only one!) of the complex interests that now frame and threaten to undo the very idea of nation.

In conventional terms of the making and unmaking of a nation, the history of Taiwan is the history of intrusion by nearby and later distant conquerors. Its present government, post–martial law heir to a conquering force, has only recently begun to see itself as *at home*, as not simply awaiting a triumphal return to its proper homeland. This once hyperspace government is slowly accepting itself as in possession of much less territory than it thought it ought to have. In the 1970s Taiwan was stripped of its status among the United Nations in favor of a communist China, whose politics and, especially, disregard of "human rights" practically define, by being the opposite of, the late-twentieth-century idea of a nation. Now Taiwan, newly a Model Nation (see? we even let gays in our military!) has a modern way to have face: influence is no longer as obviously tied to territory and expanse as it is to culture—Asianness, modernness—and economic timing—miniaturization, rapid relay, copying.

Because of its relation to the United States, the loudest voice in the present international debates over sexuality, Taiwan is an important case in our consideration of the fate of the nation and sexuality in the context of globalizing forces. The strange acceleration of global gay politics, in part contingent on alarm about sexuality produced through the intransigent association of AIDS with sexual deviance (or sexual colonialism), is even more extreme in Taiwan. Taiwan was under martial law during the most significant years of American and international gay politics, but its martial law era did not eradicate, merely strategically filtered the desire for things American. For complex economic and politico-affective reasons, America stands as a critical figure to Taiwan's left and right, but obviously for different reasons. The paradigmatic nation, propagator of Human Rights, inaugurator of new social movements, and centrifugal force in the globalization of hybridized European and Asian styles and intellectual tastes, America is always multiple as an object of identification.

If, as Anderson argues, America is the first nation, the first style of imagining nation, then Taiwan is one of the last. America's central problematic has always been how to establish a legitimate beginning (Warner 1990); Taiwan's is accounting for a political end despite its intensification as a postmodern economic and cultural machine. Taiwan is the vanguard, slipping quietly away from the idea that nations are best United through civility pacts, and instead operating—almost freelance—on the global market. Americans cannot directly buy stock in Taiwanese companies (for example, hot prospect Acer, competitive against both American and Japanese computer makers). But Taiwanese companies simply parcel themselves out on other stock exchanges, or sell stock through the holding funds that mediate Taiwan's official nonexistence in the all-important American financial markets. Taiwan's success—even in the 1998 "Asian flu" market and currencies crash—reveals that the nation is unraveling under a three-tiered assault:

1. The meta-capitalist network of corporate relations (globalization of markets);
2. the meta-national "community" of nations in the guise of transnational organizations like United Nations, the World Health Organization, or the nongovernmental agencies that parallel the supragovernmental bodies (globalization of human rights);
3. via bodies and ideas that leak across the official borders, under the sight line of nations' recuperative narratives (globalization of alterity).

Ironically, the globalization of human rights may be the most problematic of these for individuals in Taiwan who are developing dissenting sexual politics. Nations describe themselves through gradations of political, social, and cultural similarity and difference. Their reproductive capacity, however, is understood as a prenational force, a universal condition that everywhere demands the promotion of official heterosexuality. But almost everyone admits that the articulation of sexuality to the state is incomplete: the modes of coping with the residue of heterosexuality are the battleground for, and in some cases the criterion of, displaying national modernness. For example, global AIDS discourse has inscribed gay men within antidiscrimination/rights discourse; so too, the globalization of feminism, which, at events like the Beijing Conference, has written lesbians into the drama of human rights denied. But on the other hand, the new model nation is one that, precisely through the discourse of rights, has thoroughly medicalized sexual alterity without recognizing local queerness: to a great extent, gay men achieve visibility only at the moment they become subject to AIDS.

204

The globalization of American-style gay identity, effected through the global-ization of human rights, has in many cases been a stumbling block for au-tochthonous queers. Like the very idea of nation, the Western-style discourse of lesbian and gay liberation understands progress and assigns meaning to political dissent through a developmental theory. To call upon "identity" and "civil rights" is to invoke a prior state of lack from which one has developed a new complete-ness. With its sense of having been always and already present, its fullness of place and self, "Queer Nation" almost broke the shackles that bind radical politics to so-cial Darwinism. But in the United States, Queer Nation gained publicity against the tedium and lifelessness of lesbian and gay visibility, the representational di-mension of civil rights. However much the horses were frightened, Queer Nation was more interesting than the dull gay and lesbian neighbors whose lovely chil-dren played baseball and violins and got better grades than their heterosexually parented peers. Having weirdly dressed and pierced homos In Your Face was, though a bit scary, more stimulating than watching the election results on the in-creasing number of antigay politicians or municipal and state defense of marriage ordinances.

Whether we believe in a materialist teleology or the pendulous left-right swing of politics, one of the most commonplace self-understandings of American ac-tivists is that our movements occur in dialogic tension with a History. The stories we tell of our movements are homologous to the stories we tell of our own lives: we were once in darkness, but now are in the light, were once subject to unin-tended side-effects (the racism of feminism, the sexism of antiracism, the classism of either, the homophobia of both, the classism, racism, and sexism of gay libera-tion), but now have mechanisms for forming mutually responsible coalitions. Whether it marches ever forward, or forward only through repeated retrograde movements, these stories embed antagonistic versions of social movements in a historical dialectic. But the historico-social conditions that form the silent back-drop for producing the meaning of America's internal dissent is not separable from the very ideas of United Nations, global economic relations, and human rights developed through American and European colonialisms: the war of His-tory against local duration.

Endocolonial or colonizing, depending on where they are, American gay ac-tivists who went abroad, however important their local activism, were not free from Historicist jingoism. Their direct actions were in the context of globalizing human rights: through policy osmosis (especially in the guise of supposedly neu-tral U.S. AIDS epidemiology), American ideas about sexuality sped around the world faster than queers could fly to world congresses or fabulous vacation desti-nations. The fact that there were different registers of globalization simultane-ously had two effects: the tendency to view "native" sexualities as unproblematic until colonial regimes try to control them, and the belief that "native" sexualities are unarticulable and oppressed until liberationists arrive to help them speak. Both tropes of sexual alterity have vied for bodies in AIDS discourse: local gov-ernments have tended to invoke the former, presuming that whatever problems regarding population there may have been, AIDS, arriving in the bodies of West-ern homosexuals or sex tourists, imposed a fateful pleasure where none had been sought before. Gay groups and the transnational groups who have adopted their analysis have tended to rely on the latter, suggesting that homosexualities, in par-ticular—always present unthought, unnamed—and their liberation rely on the public statement of gay identity. But both tendencies assume some kind of lack in Other lands, a need to connect a transcendent discourse of human rights with au-tochthonous needs.

Queering Human Rights, Feminizing the State

In the United States, "rights" materialized the promise contained in the Declara-tion of Independence. The first rights were conveyed by the U.S. Constitution, but it was soon clear that this document withheld these "inalienable" capacities from specific, identifiable classes of people (indeed, the initial concept of citizenship ex-plicitly excluded slaves, freedmen, poor whites, and women). The Bill of Rights and later amendments were supposed to fix this problem, but even in the early days of the new country, economic policy and educational opportunity quite ob-viously prevented poor people and African Americans from enacting the minimal rights they supposedly possessed. Thus, in the 1950s a new discourse about racial discrimination produced the foundation for a novel legal and administrative sub-structure designed to detect and evaluate lacks and (though less well) remedy them. Once the new civil rights laws and voting acts were implemented, they served, to a great extent, as the model for claims by other excluded groups. The U.S. lesbian and gay civil rights movement also made claims as a "suspect class," but these are still working their way through the courts using a variety of differ-ent civil rights strategies.[16] Because of the emphasis on civil rights legal strategy and the intuitive sense it made to understand their group as "like a minority," les-bian and gay identity took on an ethnic-like affectivity. There were always alter-nate understandings of the source and quality of queer togetherness—including classic images of friendship, Greek democracy, or socialist camaraderie (Edward Carpenter and others saw homosexuals as the ideal citizens because they could be devoted to the nation, not the family!).

But the idea of "human rights" in Taiwan has been produced more significantly as feminist, even feminizing. At least in the early 1990s, Taiwanese gays and lesbians looked to and were aided by feminism and the emerging discourse of women's rights: the nascent gay movement is framed through gender dissent, or, indirectly, through dissent from the demand to align with family.[17] To the extent that rights are understood as a deviation from a state-building project, lesbian and gay rights are anti-masculinist; an affectivity that runs against the state is emerging as a social politics. To understand what "rights" will mean for homosexuals in Taiwan—both those who embrace them and those who opt for something more like the U.S. queer politics—we must continue to track the development of feminist politics in Taiwan.

As Shi Chyun-Fung (1995) has shown, pressing feminist claims in the new public sphere of Taiwanese electoral politics has been extremely complex. Women have always served in the Legislative Yuan as Nationalist Party members, and their antagonists in the DDP have campaigned on broad "human rights" platforms. This has produced a tacit feminization of human rights, at least in so far as it seems to be women who are in the forefront of articulating such issues to the electorate. Awkwardly enough for progressive/leftist feminists, it was a New Party feminist lawyer who managed to get the recent divorce law reforms through the Yuan. But even feminist politics has its "queer" sensibility: one candidate spatialized her politics by stepping through a hole cut in an ROC flag. She came out of, was given a violent birth in, surpassed, defaced the emblem of national identification.

We have to be careful here: feminism in Taiwan, though heavily influenced by that in Japan and the United States, has a very different trajectory, if a line can be said to exist at all. As Americans write their herstory, radical feminism of the 1970s (the period during which Taiwan was still under martial law) was an extension of and reaction against 1960s student and liberationist organizing. Understanding its roots to lie in the feminism and socialism of the late nineteenth and early to mid-twentieth centuries, the American socialist feminism of the 1970s emerged within the post–red scare sectarian movements of the 1960s. Socialist feminists hoped to return the "second wave" of feminism to a more materialist analysis. But no such historical dialectic can be narrated in Taiwan: various forms of feminism arrived almost simultaneously with little internal reference possible.

Even the global identifications of both second-wave and social feminism are

troubled in Taiwan. The nationalist impulse (e.g., the capitalist-separatist feminism of by-women/for-women-only products and events) of American radical
feminism does not haunt a transnational revolutionary socialist feminism that
seeks solidarity with men through class politics. Indeed, there is another, much
more palpable nationalism and another rather different historical relation with a
more sinister-looking socialism. Poised on the New China, with the serious question of reunification to be settled, nationalism and socialism, or better, social
democracy, are both associated with masculine state building; feminisms of the
kind seen in the United States cannot be anything but an antinationalist or at least
dangerously feminizing project. The so-called feminization of government in the
United States occurred not during a period of war, but between two wars. The social programs instituted under FDR redrew the lines between public and domestic,
reenvisioning, until the Democrats' War on Poverty and, later, the Republicans'
Contract with America, the role of government as mega-Mom. Taiwan faces this
kind of refiguration of the role of government at a time when its sovereignty, not
to mention national identity, is completely in question.

The very concept of public versus private or domestic space on which the elaboration of American sexual freedom efforts rest, and around which queer politics'
performances have centered, is radically different in Taiwan. Space is not fundamentally matrixed as male-female/public-private, as in the United States. To in-
augurate a discourse of human rights at the end of martial law is, thus, also to shift
ideas about "public space" and "privacy." Human rights, imagined by those who
want them as what Europeans or Americans exercise, are, in Western democracies,
actually divided between free speech, which relies on a "public space," and sexual
freedom, which requires "privacy." New spaces—discos, karaoke, MTV bars, marginally autonomous media, squares, like that surrounding the massive Chiang
Kai-shek memorial—attempt to accommodate both, but are not yet held in place
through social memory of *ways to be . . . here.*

The decay of social forms like the family, the inscription of conduits for circulating capitalized media, and the legitimization of liberal democracy as a governmental form—all the things that most Western political theorists either take for
granted or propose as conditions for modernity—produced the American gay liberation movement. But in Taiwan, these conditions largely don't exist, or else
have arrived simultaneously with liberationist movements. This makes it difficult
to narrate the political action of gay or AIDS politics as a break from experience of
repression in the family, movement toward a semipublic space in which community could be formed. It will be possible to write genealogies through Confucian-

ism—and Sun Yat Sen's Enlightenment revision of it—in relation to the Christianized social field and Leninist government model imposed by Chiang Kai-shek, but they will look nothing like the story of the long march from Stonewall to Queer Nation.

Queer and Where?

The recent use of computer imaging to set out the exact topography to which the new map of Bosnia would refer reveals the extent to which the old system of pointing to a piece of paper is not precise enough to settle the real-life disputes of contenders to space. The hillsides and hollows left vague on paper maps are crucial to those who live on them. As Eve Sedgwick (1990) notes, the sense of being a national is necessarily a lived relation between Nation and habitation. The exact placement of boundaries matters little to people whose government seems far away, or whose national identity is only a transient concern. The new desire for great precision in marking territory is not just an obsession with taking political space, but an attempt to include (or exclude!) the habitation of people who have thought of their home in the grammar of another national identity. But the increasing precision with which miniaturization of national space can be produced for purposes of macro-political negotiations only reveals how frantic we have become to secure nation as territory. .

We are looking in the wrong place.

The sense of space and territory that is arriving with globalized discourses of sexuality—however different from their Euro-American version they become when they touch down—exceeds concepts of nation, various though they may be. As the story of gay military avoiders suggested, timing rather than the ability to take up space is critical to sexual dissent. There may be another kind of imagined community, not one that imagines a referent territory, but one that imagines duration, defacement, poaching, postmodern occupation of space, not under, against, or even alongside the nations of the United Nations, but through, despite, as a kind of refusing-to-remember the nation as it tries to place bodies where they do not want to be.

What will be the fate of migrating discourses of sexual dissidence, in particular, gay liberation theory and queer theory, dispersed through different but related mechanisms of globalization? How are we to make any sense at all of the relation between sexualities as they are locally practiced and the discourses of sexuality as they are parlayed transnationally, say, through media hype about stylish

209

queerness or in policy discussions of AIDS? How do we understand the reciprocal relation between the global and the local, on one hand, and, on the other, the relation of both the global and local to the nations that mediate, link, or disrupt the grip of one on the other?

The drift of discourses of sexuality is more like the starship *Enterprise*'s movement through the hypothesized Worm Holes than like a locomotive on the tracks of a global capitalism. Bodies have multiple modes of taking discourses with them: they take queerness with them, to plant it where none like it was before; they move to new places and discover themselves to correspond to rules that designate them queer. Sometimes discourses arrive in places in advance of the bodies who decide to take queerness up; sometimes places hold queerness until bodies are ready to become queer. As much as the global flow of information technology, the globalization of queerness, carried by bodies, over MUD sites, like a free-riding burr stuck to the official discourses meant to halt a disease, threatens the terms in which nations have, up to this point, envisioned themselves. "Queer," if it is to have any utility, is best understood, not as a model of identity and practice that can be imitated or molded to a local setting, but as evidence of a kind of unstoppable alterity that flies, like a stealth bomber, beneath the annihilating screen of nation.

Notes

1. For example, the post-apartheid constitution of South Africa includes sexuality among the ranks of protected classes. This incorporation reflected a break from apartheid-era regulation of sexuality, recognized the activism of Black and white gay liberationists in the anti-apartheid struggle, and suggested that the new South Africa would learn from the mistakes and omissions of other democracies. Similarly, Israel dropped its antigay military regulations in an effort to stamp out homophobia within the military, which is obligatory and highly valorized, at least in many Jewish and some secularist quarters. Before the fall of the Berlin Wall, East Germany had an extremely liberal approach to homosexuality, including child support for lesbians and some civil recognition of same-sex partnerships. The unified Germany is now struggling to accommodate the differences in the evolution of attitudes toward homosexuality between the purportedly liberal democratic post–World War II West and its communist heir to the East.

2. Although most Western publishers now use the Pin Yin romanization system for

contemporary names and writings, I have preserved the system in widest use in Taiwan. However, even this system has been subject to change during the last decade.

3. All questions of beginnings are fraught: the perspective of the designator and the point of comparison to other historical phenomena might make one shy away from setting dates or time frames at all. Various writers—for example, Taiwan-based feminist scholar Chang Hsiao-hung (1998), in her account of the gay valentine episode—use the term "lesbian and gay movement" as if such a formation manifestly preexists the event recounted and analyzed. As an outsider with the American experience as a point of reference, I think it is not at all clear that a rights-oriented lesbian and gay movement exists, even yet. As I suggest here and elsewhere (1996), social movement theory has far from settled the issue of when to count a force as a movement. If we want to make the most "objectivist" comparison to the U.S., European, or Latin American models—and I don't fully endorse this institutionalist perspective as a useful way of defining the movement's beginnings—then a frank movement did not, despite the existence of various student groups and other community-based queer or lesbian/gay groups, fully emerge until the summer of 1998, when three groups—openly gay teachers, openly gay social workers, and a Marxist/queer group called "queer and class," who were active in anti-curfew and prostitute support work—joined together to rent a space that houses a hot line and drop-in center.

4. Over the past several years, activists and "ordinary gay people" in Taiwan have debated the utility of various American English-derived terms for "lesbian," "gay," "queer," and "homosexual." This nominative struggle become increasingly and publicly complex, as the media adopted some terms for some purposes, and as the Taipei city government struggled to find a term that would signal its intentions to track the development of civil rights in Western democracies (but perhaps forestall agitations like those of ACT UP or Queer Nation?). Instead of falling prey to misreadings of my own, outsider questions about the utility of such politics, I have elected to retain "queer" in its roman form. I leave for my friends in Taiwan to sort out and present the genealogy and significance of the varying locally invented, derived, and media-imposed designations for their various politics of alterity. I can't resist relating an anecdote about the fabulous porosity of phonemes as they slide across cultural and linguistic spaces. This story concerns the term *tong zhi*, which translates as a bond between same, and was used in Mao's China in place of all honorific terms. Here, it meant "comrade," and is so translated in many dictionaries. Sometime in the early 1990s, *tong zhi* came into wide usage in Hong Kong and Taiwan to mean "queer," creating a political friction with the communist usage. I like this term because it "queers" not by reclaiming a despised identity, as in the American usage of "queer," but by wryly exposing the erotic possibilities of "sameness" within nationalist identities.

So here goes: During my 1996 semester-long teaching stint in National Central University in Chung Li, I was to give a lecture series in English. My translator and I thought that *tong zhi guo* (*guo* a word that sits halfway between the Western connotations of nation and of country and could translate as either, depending on context) was a pretty decent rendering of "queer nation." Unfortunately, a recently expatriated Cantonese-speaking colleague of mine from Hong Kong conflated English homonyms in a quite amusing—but apt!—way. Unfamiliar with American sexual politics, and listening to both the English (his second language) and Mandarin (his third language) versions, he took "queer"/*tong zhi* as "peer," and rendered the whole as "peer nation." A perfectly valid translation. I was too embarrassed to correct this very senior colleague, and only a few of the best English speakers realized he was saying "peer" and not "queer," so I let the phonemic accident go. But I was also intrigued by the twist that his mishearing added to the question of cultural adoption of political ideas. From this point on, I stop searching for a Mandarin translation for what I meant to express, as an American, by "queer." Opaqueness that lies between the American and Taiwanese usage, whatever word comes to equilibrate the two, is more revealing than concealing.

5. One of the difficulties of doing research in rapidly evolving spaces is that amendment to every essay must continually occur. In late 1998, the ultra-hip DDP mayor of Taipei lost his post in an upset to a young, somewhat progressive KMT candidate. This has only complicated the scene, since the KMT, while problematic in any number of ways, is much better on prostitution and curfews than the DDP "quality of life" reforms. The losing DDP mayor had been thought a presidential contender; indeed, many believe that the mayoralty of Taipei is the stepping stone to the presidency in the next election. While many DDP supporters had grown very frustrated with the mayor and the once-illegal party, they worry about the direction of national politics if the mayor-to-president predictions hold for the new KMT mayor.

6. I learned about this episode in Taiwan's military history from several men who had either experienced or knew of others who had experienced this strange turn of events. This is, therefore, a mock quotation, but one that is probably not too far off the mark of what actually happened. Apparently, in the old system, homosexuals, depressives, and others were supposed to exhibit their patriotism by revealing their otherwise secret deficiency through which they might jeopardize their country through inept soldiering. In the new system, homosexuality has lost its link with bad soldiering, but ought not to be embraced as an identity stronger than citizen.

The government probably always knew, as several informants told me, that there is a lively homosexual subculture within the military, so much so that there are saunas (a very popular single-sex entertainment; many are elegant spas) that are renowned for the sex to be had in them. The recent Taiwanese gay film *The River* represents such a sauna. Thus, military homophobia, while real, is not the exclusive experience of homosexual men's two years' conscription. One man I talked to in the early 1990s had met his "husband" in the military, and claimed that many long-term homosexual bonds were formed in the service. The fact that these relationships mostly coexist with hetero-familial networks cannot be taken as a sign either of homophobia or of tolerance. Those who elected to go through the unpleasant, even dangerous, exemption process likely did so from commingled antipathy toward forced service to a military government they opposed politically and toward this manifestation of a society that refused to make room for the kind of open pride in difference that gay identity requires. To some extent, considering the exemption process forced individual homosexual men to connect their personal survival as queer with their political survival as dissidents.

7. Although American political science has long noted the tension between protecting the rights of minorities and aiding in the assimilation of the different into a mainstream America that conveys "majority" privileges, Eve K. Sedgwick (1990) has a particularly trenchant analysis of how this has played out in gay politics. She suggests that one approach taken by gays and lesbians has been to lay claim to a form of difference parallel to that which the law recognizes in African Americans and religious groups. Thus, a major form of civil rights activism among lesbians and gay men has been to claim protection from the tyranny of the many. This kind of activism requires that the oppressed identify themselves and quantify their oppression in order to achieve the appropriate protection or redress, a process I have examined further (1996).

This minoritizing strategy contrasts sharply, though is not entirely incompatible with, the rhetoric of human rights current among those international groups, such as Amnesty International, that pursue a globalization of human rights. Such groups invert a restrictive idea of "human"—one that was largely concerned with the capacity to act as a politico-economic unit—to instead emphasize qualities that, if limited, would render someone not human, for example, liberty of conscience and pursuit of basic needs like food and shelter. This shifts the question of rights from what makes the willing politico-economic actor to what unmakes the person, what prevents a body from fulfilling its essential being. An idea of freedom of self-expression not dissimilar to the demand to speak one's true essence as minority self à la the gay civil rights model has become globalized as a key part of the new definition of human rights. This is no coincidence, since concern about the role of sexuality and sexual repression in accelerating the HIV pandemic provided a "global health" rationale for what had once been articulated only as matters of political speech. Some countries and agencies now understand antigay repression as a legitimate claim for refugee status; however, the repression must be frank and acute. An American from a state in which sodomy is illegal would have tremendous difficulty claiming refugee status in Canada; however, a gay man from a dictator-led regime might easily make such a claim.

8. The new policy made it illegal for the military to ask about sexual orientation, but it also forbade military personnel from announcing—in act or word—that they are gay or lesbian. This complicated policy referred to a series of contradictory decisions by the Supreme Court and lower courts that attempted to distinguish identity, speaking about one's identity or acts, and engaging in acts—with or without gay identity, with or without speaking. In effect, cases that tried to establish the right to announce one's orientation under free speech laws (sexual identity here would be something like political speech); were disregarded. The disruptive outcomes that might result from such speech (or obvious acts that amounted to an announcement, therefore, speech) were considered potentially more dangerous than the limitation on free speech. In principle, a gay man or lesbian who conducted a quiet relationship that never came to light would not be in violation of the policy. Although this removed the problem of being thrown out of the military for lying about "having ever been" a homosexual, a question asked under the old policy, one could still be thrown out for announcing—or having others announce for you—that you are gay or lesbian. While this is a huge distinction in the law, in practical terms, it meant that rumors of someone's sexuality could provoke (and has provoked) the kind of public discussion of their sexuality that amounts to "telling." The phrase "don't ask, don't tell" is now widely used in American popular speech not just to refer to this absurd situation, but to indicate, more broadly, the kinds of statuses in which one can only be what one is by not acknowledging "it."

9. Arthur Dong's 1997 documentary, *Licensed to Kill*, about eight men who commit antigay murders, provides an excellent account of Sgt. Kenneth Frank, a soldier stationed at Fort Bragg, North Carolina. Shortly after the adoption of the "don't ask, don't tell" policy, Sgt. French became distraught that military discipline and national readiness would decline if lesbians and, especially, gay men were allowed in the military. One night he became extremely drunk and went to a local restaurant, chosen more for its proximity to his home than for any association with the gay community. He arrived, entered, and fired multiple rounds from his gun, yelling about President Clinton and gays in the military. He murdered four people and severely wounded seven others. None, as far as we can tell, were gay. Indeed, in his interview with Mr. Dong, Sgt. French underscores the abstractness of his target. As the interview progresses, French admits that he is still opposed to gays in the military, indeed, does not like gay

STEALTH BOMBERS OF DESIRE

people, but he realizes now that shooting up a restaurant and killing people is not a good way to exercise his political speech. Mr. Dong asks him what he would say to the gay community, who now live in fear because of his actions. In effect, Mr. Dong asks Sgt. French to understand his act as terrorism against the gay community. Sgt. French is stumped. He pauses and finally says, "I've never really thought about it that way. I guess I want them to know I'm not out to hurt them, I just wanted to make my point about the policy."

10. As will become clearer, I'm not entirely happy with Raymond Williams's elusive formulation, and wish to augment as well Benedict Anderson's oblique reformulation of it. However, the term for the moment suffices to convey the way sociopolitically constructed sentiments are deployed as micro-politics of oppression. I will show later that this affect is much more labile and more closely linked to supranational processes than Williams's own use of the term suggested.

11. Blacks served with the British against the colonies in the American Revolution, as well as serving for the colonies. Blacks also served in the Union army during the Civil War, as well as every other major war or minor skirmish in America's conquest of the New World and its later colonial possessions. It was only beginning with the American-Korean War (inheritor of America's shifting position in relation to Sino-Soviet repositioning in the 1950s) that Blacks and whites served in the same troops and, though usually in rather different jobs, on the same ships.

12. By "queer," I mean both the specific groups that have flown under the names of Queer Nation (now mostly defunct) and Grassroots Queer (an active Philadelphia group with politics much closer to early gay liberation than to terminal Queer Nation) and the anti-but-quasi-identity Queer that appears as much a style as a political statement. Both organized and nonorganized Q/queers have criticized the most publicly visible and latterly stages of the mainstream gay and lesbian civil rights movement for attempting to make "queers" normal (by insisting that we're just like you except for our small affective difference); consolidating a fixed and narrow identity that serves to regulate the limits of sexual deviancy; and creating an upscale market out of the Gay Lifestyle.

The attack on the consolidation of identity has been especially vocal and is what has been most noted by those who have watched this political dispute from the vantage point of Taiwan. While the most visually audacious queers have a very good point to make about the mainstreaming of gay politics, the battle is most polarized between young activists and the graying baby boomers who, now heads of major gay organizations, nevertheless carry the legacy of the New Left. The role of informal queer disdain for the hard work and political success of Clinton's age peers may have been as underestimated as the centrism of highly vocal gays in a few cities has been overestimated. Whatever the local alignments of gay infighting, the unfortunate similarity in rhetoric between the anti-identity movement and the smear-the-queer game of the right makes their joint attack on "identity politics" misalign the former's critique of the utility of strategic essentialism with the latter's explicitly racist, sexist, and homophobic attack on multiculturalism and tolerant pluralism. In contexts like Taiwan, where personal identities are not much promoted, it is particularly fraught to rub attacks on "identity" up against nascent claims to "civil" or "human rights." The result of these conflicts in Taiwan has been mainly to deride desire for gay identity as old-fashioned or as mimicry, while fighting for political rights that ultimately disenfranchise "queers" because they are not visible. I'll suggest at the end of this essay that this results from the structuring of sociopolitical space.

13. "Queer" ought to dispose of ideas of "natural," even though in its English version, the word itself implies an orthogonal relation to a regular or "straight" object. "Queer" in English is an old-fashioned word that was remade into a nasty taunt and then retaken as a way of being-different-in-your-face. As I understand the term's use, *tong zhi*, by playing off of the communist usage, most closely picks up this kind of friction, though perhaps with less specifically sexual—but more historically vital political—connotation.

14. Anderson mentions this early in the volume and then returns to it near the end of the original version. The second and most widely available edition adds several chapters that take the argument in a somewhat different, Foucauldian direction, obscuring the affect argument. At the time of the book's initial popularity and through this second edition, the idea of affect had largely dropped out of Continental post-Marxist theory, or been dazzlingly transformed. It was, I suspect, retained in Anderson because of the greater influence of Raymond Williams. The problem of why people are attached to their state and its "ideological" manifestations was treated through the concept of interpellation by Althusser, the elder and antagonist to many of the post-structuralist authors in vogue through the 1980s. Post-structuralists viewed feeling or sentiment to be a product of the Enlightenment project's construction of subjectivity and not a transcendent human function. Fair enough. But the problem of how individuals become willing to "lay down their lives" for an abstraction like nation still deserves to be answered, and not through psychologization. Anderson comes very close, in my view, to describing the system of tropisms that force and reinforce the nation-citizen complex. I amend him in the remainder of this section.

15. As a passing note, let me comment here that in Confucian and Daoist governmentality, the ruler always rules at the behest of a balanced order in which the imperial seat and the people have a symbiotic relationship. In the Confucian model, it is the intelligentsia, and especially students, who have the role of speaking out against imbalances of power exerted by rulers.

16. "Suspect class" is an American legal concept for a group of people who share a trait and appear to be treated unfairly under the law due to that trait.

As civil rights law has emerged in the past two decades, a number of different—and sometimes conflicting—uses have emerged: affirmative action, nondiscrimination but not active minority recruitment, compensation programs (especially in job training and housing, to redress past educational disadvantage and segregation in housing). In addition, the "right to privacy" emerged alongside it, but out of different case law. Freedom of speech has also sometimes dovetailed with more conventional civil rights legal strategies: the rights to wear "ethnic" clothes, criticize government policies regarding race, or say one is "gay" have all been asserted under First Amendment law. At present, sexuality-related cases based on the right to privacy and the freedom of speech, as well as class discrimination in employment and housing, have won at the state level in several places in the United States. However, federal Supreme Court decisions in related but not identical cases have had opposite findings. In addition, even the "victories" propose different definitions and statuses for homosexuality; see Janet Halley (1993).

17. As has been true in the United States and elsewhere, the relationship between gender and sexuality is complex, and, by extension, the capacity of queers and feminists to align is unstable. In 1998, in part due to debates about the legal status of prostitution and youth freedoms in Taipei City, a split in the women's movement between progressive feminists and state feminists was accompanied by a realignment of queers with progressive feminists, continuing more or less autonomously.

Works Cited

Anderson, Benedict. 1983. *Imagined Communities*. London: Verso.

Chang, Hsiao-hung. 1998. "Taiwan Queer Valentines." In *Trajectories: Inter-Asia Cultural Studies,* ed. Kuan-Hsing Chen, 283–98. London: Routledge.

Chang, Sung-Sheng Yvonne. 1993. "Yuan Qiongqiong and the Rage for Eileen Zhang among Taiwan's *Feminine* Writers." In *Gender Politics in Modern China: Writing and Feminism*, ed. Tani E. Barlow, 215–37. Durham: Duke University Press.

Chao Yengning. 1996. "Embodying the Invisible Body: Politics in Constructing Contemporary Taiwanese Lesbian Identities." Ph.D. diss., Cornell University.

Ding, Naifei, and Liu Jen-peng. 1998. "Reticent Politics, Queer Politics" [Wangliang Wenying: Hanxu Meixue Yu Kuer Zhenglue], *Xingbie Yanjiu* 3 (4) (October 1998).

Chengli, Taiwan: Center for the Study of Sexualities, National Central University. English version, unpublished manuscript.

Halley, Janet E. 1993. "The Construction of Heterosexuality." In *Fear of a Queer Planet: Queer Politics and Social Theory*, ed. Michael Warner. Minneapolis: University of Minnesota Press.

Harvey, David. 1998. "What's Green and Makes the Environment Go Round?" In *Cultures of Globalization*, ed. Fredric Jameson and Masao Miyoshi, 327–55. Durham: Duke University Press.

Jameson, Fredric. 1998. "Notes on Globalization as a Philosophical Issue." In *Cultures of Globalization*, ed. Fredric Jameson and Masao Miyoshi, 54–80. Durham: Duke University Press.

Kang, Liu. 1998. "Is There an Alternative to (Capitalist) Globalization? The Debate about Modernity in China." In *Cultures of Globalization*, ed. Fredric Jameson and Masao Miyoshi, 164–90. Durham: Duke University Press.

Ng, Sheung-Yuen Daisy. 1993. "Feminism in the Chinese Context: Li Ang's *The Butcher's Wife*." In *Gender Politics in Modern China: Writing and Feminism*, ed. Tani E. Barlow, 266–89. Durham: Duke University Press.

Patton, Cindy. 1996. "Queer Space/God's Space: Counting Down to the Apocalypse." *Rethinking Marxism*, 9 (2) (Summer 1996): 1–23.

Sedgwick, Eve Kosofsky. 1990. *Epistemology of the Closet*. Berkeley: University of California Press.

Shi, Chyun-Fung. 1995. "Representation of Gender in Mass Media in the Light of Bourdieu's Capital: News Coverage of Female Candidates in Political Campaigns. A Case Study of Newspaper Reporting on Legislative Campaigns in Taiwan from 1969 to 1992." Ph.D. diss., Temple University.

Sklair, Leslie. 1998. "Social Movements and Global Capitalism." In *Cultures of Globalization*, ed. Fredric Jameson and Masao Miyoshi, 291–311. Durham: Duke University Press.

Warner, Michael. 1990. *Letters of the Republic: Publication and the Public Sphere in Eighteenth-Century America*. Cambridge, MA: Harvard University Press.

———, ed., 1993. *Fear of a Queer Planet: Queer Politics and Social Theory*. Minneapolis: University of Minnesota Press.

Waters, Malcolm. 1995. *Globalization*. London: Routledge.

12 "Strangers on a Train"

Sexual Citizenship and the Politics of Public Transportation in Apartheid Cape Town

William L. Leap

Prologue: On Familiarity and Its Dangers

"Homosexuality" as we know it in today's South Africa is closely tied to the recent history of apartheid. As the following discussion will show, the technologies of apartheid—discrimination, displacement, enclosure, removal—regulated geographies and identities of male-centered, same-sex desire, just as they did for geographies and identities associated with other domains of everyday experience. At the same time, South African "homosexuality" has also been influenced by international media and other communication, by travel and tourism, and by forms of sexualized globalization discussed elsewhere in this volume. Even during the periods of greatest restriction, North Atlantic understandings of male same-sex desire and identity circulated widely within and across South African boundaries of color, race, and class, such that today's visitors to Cape Town, Durban, or Johannesburg will find much in the South African "urban gay scene" and in associated South African narratives of urban gay history that seems pleasantly familiar.

To be sure, these details of global familiarity need to be documented, and so do their basis in transnational circulations of, for example, sexual citizenship and sexual subjectivity. But reading South African "homosexuality" entirely in terms of such external influences is unwise, because it essentializes, and thereby erases, local understandings of same-sex identities and practices when it is *those* understandings—and their connections to apartheid–that need to be in the foreground of the analysis. As the discussion in the following sections will suggest, attention to local understandings is especially important when analysis explores a topic as "familiar" as public sex, and when the sites of sexual activity are as "familiar" as railway station restrooms.

Apartheid, Railway Station Restrooms, and Public Sex

Since 1996 I have been collecting life story narratives and other data to explore the differing forms of urban gay experience that have emerged in metropolitan Cape Town in recent years. Life story narratives and personalized descriptions of Cape Town's urban terrain are two of the sources of data in this project. Frequently, and in some ways prominently, gay men's life stories I have collected provide detailed descriptions of sex between men (usually the narrator and one or more "others") in railway station restrooms. The activity even has its own label in South African gay English—*cottaging*—a term that, by fusing location with forms of erotic practice, distinguishes the activity from the male-centered erotic encounters that take place at other public locations in the Cape Town metropolitan area.[1]

The railway station restrooms in question here are located inside the station's walled compound and are often adjacent to the station house (where the attendant sells tickets and answers questions about train schedules and destinations). In theory, during the apartheid years, railway stations provided separate restroom facilities for Whites, Coloureds, and Blacks. But instead of physically separate structures, many of the stations effected the segregation by erecting a wooden divider topped with barbed wire and separating what had previously been a larger facility into two smaller, racially discrete (White and non-White) domains.

There was no concierge at the doorway (as is the case for some European railway station restrooms) and because railway guards were usually more concerned with maintaining racial segregation on the railway platforms, they did not keep the restrooms under constant patrol.[2]

The absence of constant supervision, combined with the relatively confined space of the railway station and the natural alibi the comings-and-goings at any railway station provide for men who go there specifically looking to have sex, made the railway station restrooms attractive sites for cruising and, absent mutual decisions to go into the bushes surrounding the outside of the station wall or elsewhere, attractive sites for male-centered erotic exchange. Under such arrangements, White men interested in same-sex encounters could easily meet other White men with similar interests, and the same was true for men of color meeting other men of color on the other side of the partition. Moreover, if they were willing to squeeze underneath the partition, to push the barbed wire aside and climb carefully over the top, or simply to wait until the guard's back was turned and walk through the adjacent restroom door, meeting and having sex with other men could also cut across racial categories and boundaries at these sites.

Notoriety, accessibility, anonymity, opportunity—these sound like the rationales for male-centered public sex that researchers have reported from any number of locations (e.g., Coxon 1996, 118–29; Edelman 1994; Henricksson and Mansson 1995; Humphreys 1970; Leap 1996; and papers in Leap, 1998). Indeed, same-sex male sexual practices are consistent with the other expressions of "liminal" status and spatial "ambiguity" assigned to public restrooms and the eliminatory functions that take place there (Edelman 1994, 159). Viewed in both cross-cultural and psycho-structural terms, the reports from Cape Town are not necessarily unusual reports at all.

But the appearance of familiarity can be misleading, and a careful, situated exploration of similar practices is still required here. Indeed, in the case of the Cape Town cottages, the intersections of place, race, and gender that underlie these practices (and their narrative representation) are not arbitrary constructions. They reflect the oppression, privilege, and regulation of space—and of sexuality–that were central to apartheid, and must be understood in terms of that technology, its regulations, and its discontents.

Background Considerations

As a prelude to these tasks, let me make some additional remarks about the larger project, and the research strategies, with which this study is connected.[3] To begin with, my work in Cape Town parallels an ongoing study of race, class, and gay space in Washington, D.C., with which I have been involved since 1995. In both studies, I use life story narratives and map drawing tasks to explore how intersections of race, class, and gendered locations play out in gay men's lives. So far, I have collected life stories and maps or related spatialized materials from forty-five gay men in the Cape Town area–nineteen White, eighteen Coloured, and eight Xhosa or other Black.[4] Commentary on cottaging presented in those life stories and interviews provided the data base for this discussion.

Let me make clear that this essay examines cottaging practices in the Cape Town metropolitan area. Cottaging has a lengthy history in Cape Town, but the practice became particularly popular between the early 1960s and the late 1980s. This twenty-year period, which was also the period during which apartheid policies were implemented in Cape Town, is the time frame for the discussion in this essay. Moreover, even though cottaging also occurred in other South African locations during the apartheid years (see, for example, Gevisser 1994, 25ff), I am unwilling to claim, without further evidence, that the analysis presented here automatically applies to the male-centered, restroom-based sexual activities that took place at those locations.

Now some comments on language of representation: I am not happy using racialized terminology like "White," "Coloured," and "Black" in this discussion. However, the distinctions signaled by such terms also identify the boundaries regulating racial segregation under the apartheid system. In that sense, the terminology is central to the issues I am examining here, and cannot be erased.

I am also not happy using the term "gay" as a cover term for the sexual/gendered identities of the men I have interviewed. Viewed within South African contexts, "gay" signals a North Atlantic identification, a club-scene praxis, and/or an in-your-face, public sexuality that fits the gender careers of some Capetownian male-same-sex-identified men. But other men have constructed claims to male same-sex subjectivity in terms that maintain connections to South African histories, cultures, and political traditions. *Moffie*, a reference to a cross-dressing, effeminate South African man, is the most familiar of these gendered stances, though there are others.[5] Accordingly, "gay" appears in this essay to relieve the monotony of more cumbersome phrasings like "male, same-sex–centered identities and desires"; however, no categorical parallel to North Atlantic meanings should be inferred.

Finally, some comments on the usefulness of narrative-based research in the South African setting:

Recent political changes in South Africa have worked hard to eliminate the formal technology of apartheid. Consequently, the segregated facilities and associated sexual practices that are of interest to this essay are not observable at first hand, and are available only through newspaper clippings, court records, and other forms of secondary documentation—including life story narratives. It has not been difficult to find gay men in Cape Town who are willing to talk about men having sex in railroad stations. Almost every man I have interviewed, and many I have had informal conversations with, have had stories to tell about their experiences in this regard.

Using life story data for historical reconstruction may be convenient, but can be problematic. Life story narratives always contain personalized reconstructions of history, and as such they are more likely to have what Ellen Lewin calls "cultural rather than descriptive significance" (1993, 10–11). Consequently, because South African political discourse has become so publicly supportive of racial inclusion, I have become suspicious when gay men's life story narratives describe the access and acceptance extended to gay men of color in the officially "White" gay bars and other gay venues of Cape Town—including here, the railroad station cottages—during the 1950s, 1960s, and 1970s. Do these narratives accurately describe the racialized, gendered conditions from earlier times, or are these what Kleinmann (1988, 50) terms "retrospective narratizations," stories about the past retold in the present to address some "moral purpose, . . . [to] reaffirm . . . cultural values under siege, . . . [to] reintegrate social relations whose structural tensions have intensified . . . [or to] point a finger of condemnation at perceived injustice and the personal experience of oppression" (Kleinmann 1988, 50–51)?

I am reluctant to believe that the gay men I have interviewed in Cape Town are deliberately trying to whitewash South African gay history. I see no reason to question the intentionality of their narratives—that is, the narrator's sincere efforts to use the narrative moment as a site for reflecting on and making sense of the past. At the same time, given the recent changes in public discourses on race in South Africa, as well as the almost surreal conditions surrounding the "day-to-day horror of apartheid" (Ndebele 1998, 21)—conditions that made "the theme of the absurd a theme of daily living" (Moyana 1976, 95) for so many Black and other South Africans during that time, some reworking of historical details within contemporary narrative reflection seems unavoidable. Indeed, the work of the Truth and Reconciliation Commission shows how greatly the technology of apartheid encouraged and profited from other reworkings of South African history at earlier points in time.

In this sense, the Cape Town research is very much a project of "reinscription," in Prakash's usage (1995, 87, 98). As such, the research must guard against reproducing the very conditions this study seeks to expose. And as is always the case in reinscription, careful inspection of the cracks and crevices within gay men's life story narratives and attention to the fault lines, the hybrid moments, and points of erasure that those narratives contain will suggest entry points for recovering messages obscured by conventional story lines.

Reinscribing the Cottages: A Complex and Racialized Sexual Terrain

The railway station restrooms were not the only sites where men could meet men for sexual purposes before the 1990s. Hotel bars were already segregated by sex under South Africa's licensing laws, and several of these bars were known to be friendly, or at least tolerant, toward male clientele with same-sex interests. And for a time in the 1960s, so was a private club in Constantia, one of the southern (White) suburbs.

Several pubs in the City Centre also catered specifically to a male homosexual crowd—including acceptance of customers in drag and weekly drag shows. Several bars in the waterfront included homosex within the eclectic amusements they offered to their patrons. Rent-boys were also available, for a fee, along Long Street and other outside locations. House parties were also sites for meeting and mixing, and so were the gay-friendly dance bars that sprang up in sequence once disco fever hit Cape Town in the 1970s. And there was always Graaff Pool and the adjacent sites along the seawall, Cape Town's historic location for open-air cruising and furtive sexual pleasure.

Except for the bars at the waterfront (which deliberately maintained an "anything goes" ambiance), the rules and rhetoric of apartheid designated all these sites "White" public spaces. Even so, these sites were also patronized by a Coloured clientele, admittedly less so in the hotel bars, more so in the pubs and along the waterfront. There were also Coloured as well as White rent-boys, and Coloured men also cruised Graaff Pool.

To be admitted to one of the hotel bars, a Coloured man either had to be in the company of a White patron or had to be someone the doorkeeper/bouncer knew, from previous visits, to be trustworthy. Appropriate attire and demeanor were also essential—which meant that Coloured drag queens, even when wearing their finest apparel, were likely to be denied entrance into hotel bars. The pubs, particularly those with drag shows, were somewhat less restrictive about attire, and the "anything goes" atmosphere of the waterfront bars made them even less restrictive in that regard.

The Coloured drag presence was disquieting to some White gay men, who talk even today about how certain bars and pubs "went downhill" once the "drag queens" started to show up there. Much less White animosity was directed toward Coloured patrons who came closer to the White gay ideal. "We called them Persians, my dear," reported one older White gay man after assuring me that there always was "the occasional Coloured" patron at his favorite hotel bar. This phrasing—"the occasional Coloured"—shows up frequently in the narrative recollec-tions given to me by older White gay men, one of whom added, "it was an honor for a Coloured man to suck white cock." Being "accepted" in these White bars did not disrupt Coloured placement within a racialized hierarchy, and in some ways acceptance may have reproduced and revalidated it.

Importantly, Coloured gay men were not at all dependent on White venues for socializing or entertainment. Until its destruction by authorities, Cape Town's Dis-trict Six was a bustling site of male same-sex opportunities, with "gay"-friendly bars and pubs, house parties, business establishments, and—particularly for the drag queens—visible public identities. Whites were welcome at these locations, and some White men preferred them to the more conservative sites in the City Centre.

Coloured residents began to be forcefully removed from the City Centre in the 1960s, when the provincial government began implementing the requirements of the Group Areas Act. Removal meant relocation from in-town neighborhoods into new residential communities on the Cape Flats. Male same-sex components of Coloured in-town culture were undamaged by relocation. "Gay"-friendly bars, pubs, and other businesses reopened, public identities reemerged, and so did White interests in these facilities and opportunities. Indeed, by the late 1970s, one "Coloured" disco in the Flats had become one of the Cape Town area's hottest "gay venues," and White men from the City Centre could always be found among the clientele.

Coloured interests in the City Centre's male same-sex opportunities also sur-vived enforced relocation. But access to the City Centre was now quite difficult, because of the distance separating the City Centre and the Cape Flats. Travel to the City Centre was now dependent on having a car, knowing someone who had a car, or a willingness to negotiate the politics of Cape Town's system of public transportation.

The life stories I have collected from White and Coloured men do not say very much about Black same-sex–identified men, or about their connections to the male-centered locations, identities, and practices within the City Centre, District Six, or the Cape Flats Coloured communities. This narrative erasure of Black pres-ence is understandable, given the racialized politics of apartheid, but it is also in some ways surprising.

As was true for other persons of color under this system, Black access to the City Centre was sharply curtailed during daytime hours, and controlled even more rig-orously after sunset. And except for instances where residence in white areas was

225

a condition of employment (e.g., domestic workers, gardeners), Blacks lived in the township areas at a distance from the City Centre (further away than the new Cape Flats Coloured communities) and worked in facilities located near their homes. Accordingly, distance ensured that Black men would be less likely to be part of the "gay scene" in the City Centre during this time period.

At the same time, the townships were uncomfortable and crowded spaces, and the prying eyes of relatives, neighbors, and police informers were everywhere. While there are traditions of township-based, male-centered same-sex practices, identities, and long-term relationships, township residents were likely to be subjected to teasing, ridicule, and other negative sanction if their associations with these practices, relationships, and identities became public knowledge. Far better for them to explore male same-sex interests outside the township setting.

Race, Regulation, and the Politics of Public Transportation

And this brings the discussion back to the politics of public transportation in apartheid Cape Town.

To reach the City Centre, or any other "in-town" location, residents of the Cape Flats and the townships who did not have access to an automobile were at the mercy of the routings and schedules of the minibus taxis (which began providing services to Cape Town–area townships in the mid-1980s), the public buses, and the trains.

Important to remember, minibus taxis, buses, and trains operated during daylight hours, but ceased operations shortly after sundown. Cape Flats and township residents who took public transportation into the City Centre and missed the "last" taxi, bus, or train to their home communities were certainly inconvenienced. But they were also likely to be subjected to police harassment, interrogation, and even arrest for (literally) being in the wrong place (that is, a *White* place) at the wrong time.

Once they began operation, minibus taxis were the least expensive form of public transportation. The drivers and assistants were Coloured or Black, the customers were almost entirely Coloured or Black, and their fees were within the price range of low-income Cape Flats and township dwellers.

The buses were more expensive than the taxis and ran much less frequently, and their services were less reliable in other ways. And because so many bus routes ran between the Cape Flats/township communities and the suburbs rather than directly from the Flats into the City Centre, patrons who traveled by bus usually had to change buses one or more times before they reached their intended location downtown.

The trains were also expensive, measured against a township dweller's income, but were certainly efficient. The trains ran according to carefully maintained, predictable schedules. Unlike the taxis and the buses, trains were not affected by highway traffic, and moved passengers quickly between township locations and the City Centre.[6]

White ridership was rare in the minibus taxis and on many of the public bus lines, and this kept the taxis and buses closely identified with peoples of color. Even today, less progressive White residents of Cape Town referred to the minibus taxis with the derogatory phrase "Kaffir buses."[7] In contrast, riding the trains was not stigmatized because of its association with a single population. But the trains were racialized spaces, all the same. Trains carried White, Coloured, and Black patrons, but in segregated locations on each train. White patrons paid a higher premium than Coloured or Black patrons, and rode in the "first-class cars" reserved exclusively for their use. Coloured and Black patrons paid almost half the first-class fare, but rode in the less comfortable, more crowded third-class cars.

But while the trains reproduced racial distinctions, the trains also subverted those distinctions in particular ways. In addition to providing direct linkages between the Coloured communities, Black townships, and the City Centre, train routes also connected the City Centre with suburban White communities to the south and northeast, with the beach resorts at Simonstown, and with other locations of regional interest to White travelers. Since Cape Flats and township residents rode the same trains as Whites, riding the trains enabled movement between racially proclaimed spaces, and provided access to those spaces, in a sense not available to them when they traveled on foot, in their own automobile, or by taxi or public bus.[8]

And even if Coloured and Black riders were prohibited from leaving the railway station at some "White" locations, they could still catch glimpses of the people, houses, buildings, and activities these "White" locations contained, while the train slowed to enter the station, while White passengers boarded or disembarked, and while the train began its movement to the next station on the line.

Of course, the movement between segregated spaces, the access to White locations, and the glimpses into White experience that riding the train allowed— all of this "subversion" of apartheid created through train travel was temporary. It had no long-lasting effects on regulations or technology. The truth of this point was driven home most directly when the Coloured or Black passenger reached his terminal point. He left the train and walked to the exit—the *uitgang*, the "way out," as it is marked by the sign attached to the walled enclosure. Leaving the train station, persons of color walked away from the conveyance that momentarily relaxed the racialized restrictedness of movement and the regulation of place and space in daily life, and returned to sites and contexts of restriction and regulation. In that sense, the "way out" was also, and unavoidably, the way "back in."

How Cottaging Articulates with Apartheid

How Is a Cottage Like a Train?

It is not a coincidence at all that the cottages were a visible feature of the landscape leading to the "way out" of the train station and train riding and the "way [back] in" to the harsher realities of apartheid. At both sites, the racially transgressive opportunities and activities were momentary, and did not create any real disruption in apartheid's regulatory authority. But just as the train ride offered opportunities for movement and glimpses of an otherwise inaccessible lifestyle, cottaging offered opportunities for movement and glimpses of an alternate politics of racialized (male) sexuality. Moreover, cottaging allowed persons of color to position themselves as primary actors in the construction of that alternative—even if (as on the train) the alternative construction lasts but a moment.[9]

Did Cottaging Heighten Anti-Apartheid Sentiment?

Ross Higgins (1998) has suggested that outdoor cruising in Montreal during the 1950s and 1960s provided homosexual men with a basis for networking, community building, and other Stonewall-like changes in urban experiences. I can't make equivalent connections between cottaging and gay liberation for Cape Town, but I do think it is worth wondering whether the opportunities for sex across racial boundaries that the cottages enabled helped to mobilize a male, same-sex–based, anti-apartheid consciousness on the part of frequent participants. If so, some of the race-positive sexual narratives given to me by Capetownian White gay men may not be as artificially reflective as I first thought.

Just How Unique Were the Cottages?

Still, read in terms of location, the cottages are very different from Cape Town's other cruising areas and other sites where racialized boundaries get momentarily disrupted. Almost all those sites were within the City Centre, adjacent to it, or otherwise dominated by White presence, and whatever male-centered, same-sex encounters occur (or are initiated) at those sites become filtered through the claims to privilege that whiteness conveys. Accordingly, while a person of color might have been welcome at such a site, that person was still very much "out of place." Remember, when the "occasional Coloured" entered the officially White bar, "we call them Persians, my dear." And when Coloured men and White men had sex under the seawall at Graaff Pool, "it was an honor for a Coloured man to suck a white cock."

A person of color may also have been "out of place" in a railway station rest-room, but he was not "out of place" in quite the same way. The hotel bars and Graaff Pool were "White spaces"; their association with the City Centre made that clear. But the railway stations were multiracial locations, not "White space" ex-clusively. A person of color may have been "out of place" by crossing the partition that separates "White" from "non-White" facilities, and could have been arrested for violating the laws mandating the racial segregation of public facilities, just as would have happened if he were caught violating restrictions on racialized space in other locations. If, however, a person of color and a White man were caught having sex in the White-only restroom, they would not have been arrested for vi-olating the racial segregation demanded by the Group Areas Act or the Immoral-ity Act. No, they were arrested for public lewdness, vagrancy, or the violation of South Africa's prohibitions against (male) sodomy—that is, arrested for commit-ting a sexualized, but not a racialized crime.[10]

Where Are the Black Gay Men?

Peoples of color is a convenient phrasing, but it is also somewhat misleading, par-ticularly when applied to discussions of male-centered public sex in railway sta-tion restrooms. Indeed, while I have collected life story discussions about cottag-ing from White, Coloured, and Black narrators, Coloured men figure much more prominently in those discussions than Black men, regardless of the narrator's racial background—and do so, I think, for good reasons.

Cottaging, in the sense described here, spoke directly to Coloured men with male-centered, same-sex interests and desires. For example, cottages provided a public space that was "White" but not entirely "White"-dominated. The sexual ac-tivities that took place there created alternative forms of sexual citizenship that transgressed racial divisions, if only momentarily. And being adjacent to the "way out" of the railway station (and the "way [back] in[to]" racially restricted urban spaces), cottaging was also convenient for Coloured men who were not interested in going to the City Centre's "White" bars, or would be unlikely to be admitted to those bars, if they tried.

Cottaging conveyed somewhat different messages to Black men with male-identified, same-sex interests. I have already mentioned the vulnerability imposed on township residents under the apartheid system, and the barriers that low income, limited mobility, and constant community surveillance imposed on the Black construction of male-centered experiences. Unlike the case in some of the Coloured communities, the Black townships did not generally support claims to public subjectivity based on male-centered same-sex desires or cross-dressing practices. For those reasons, townships became locations to get away from, and the City Centre, while certainly a bastion of White-centered privilege and non-White oppression, became a site where township residents could escape the surveillance and intolerance of their neighbors.

If escape was prompting a township resident to ride the train to the City Centre, the purpose of travel would have been to get to the City Centre as quickly as possible. Any glimpses into suburban White space that occurred on the way would be of secondary importance to that end, and so would sexual encounters within one of the cottages.

Of Course, White Men See All This Differently

Viewed through the lens of apartheid, the interests of White men who pursued male same-sex experience at the cottages were very much unlike the interests of persons of color whom they met at these locations.

For one thing, remember that White men who lived within or adjacent to the City Centre did not need to depend on train travel to navigate the apartheid city or to gain access to its locations of whiteness. For them, train travel was an elective mode of transportation, and riding the train was more a matter of personal interests than pragmatic concerns or necessities.

White men who tell stories about visiting the cottages did not always equate these sites, or their situated sexual practices, with racial, sexual, or political transgressions. Instead, White narratives describe the cottages in terms of "coming out" experiences or other key points in their gender career, or as sites where narrators enjoyed particularly memorable moments of sexual triumph.

Consistent with this stance are the comments White narrators make about the railway system itself. Trains don't "go anywhere" in these life story narratives, and railway stations are described independently of any references to railway movement. Instead, railway lines and train stations are static locations, which are waiting to become sites for the narrator's sexual convenience. Understandably, narrators make few references to railway passengers; the persons inside the cottages were the ones who really matter to these stories, not the persons who are actually riding the trains.

Of course, "White gay men" and "White narrators" are not unified categories. There were some White men who lived in more distant suburban communities, particularly the Afrikaner communities that line the eastern roadways linking the City Centre and Stellenbosch. For men from these communities, and in a sense very similar to that for men from the Black townships, train travel provided alternatives to the restricted settings found within their home communities. For these men—and in a sense very different from Coloured men—the "way out" actually became a "way in[to]" new gendered sites and opportunities. The commonality of interests linking Afrikaner and Black men, and separating both groups from Coloured men, underscores the complex interweavings of race, class, gender, and space that apartheid technologies created and on which those technologies so greatly depended.

Rethinking the Presence of Globalization

I argued in the opening section of this essay in favor of studying the local significance of seemingly familiar practices like cottaging, and my discussion of cottaging has shown how much can be learned when the "familiar" is examined in terms of its local meanings and local histories. But globalized meanings have influenced the social reality under discussion here, and while I do not want a transnational focus to dominate this conversation, certain broader themes now need to be brought into the "local" analysis.

For one thing, the recent transfer of political power from the Nationalist Party to the African National Congress has given rise to claims that apartheid has come to an end, and that South Africa is now living in a post-apartheid moment. Reflexes of these claims show up in scholarly writing, political commentary, news reports, and other forms of everyday discourse. Personal narratives from today's South Africa, especially those given by persons of Coloured and Black backgrounds, speak to these issues somewhat differently. Certain administrative and oppressive structures may be dissolved, but legacies of apartheid-based inequality and restricted opportunity endure. The startling rates of HIV incidence in South Africa—as many as 25 percent of the Cape Town metropolitan area's adult population may be HIV-positive, some sources estimate—speak powerfully to this issue, as do ever-increasing unemployment rates, absence of job creation initiatives, and the declining value of the rand against the U.S. dollar and other North Atlantic currencies.

Saying that South Africa is "post-apartheid" makes it safe (and politically correct!) for outsiders to establish connections with South African businesses and resources, and push for a restoration of broader ties with transnational capitalism. Framing those discussions in "post-apartheid" terms also makes it easy to overlook the enduring presence of social/racial inequalities, or to assume that such conditions, while serious, will soon make a transition into better times.

White gay men's stories about "gay" life in Cape Town during the apartheid years—and the stories about cottaging reviewed in this essay fall into this category—are often framed as "post-apartheid" narratives. That is, the stories describe how bad conditions were under apartheid, but then suggest that those conditions are beginning to show signs of improvement. In a second version of this "post-apartheid" theme, these stories suggest that post-apartheid–like changes had begun to be attested in gay bars and other venues long before they began to appear in other (for example, heterosexually dominant) social domains. For example, some stories discuss the presence of persons of color in gay venues frequented by White gay men, and the efforts by White patrons and bar owners to prevent the transracial presence from being discovered during police raids. Other stories (like those reviewed here) suggest the frequency of interracial sexual experiences, and also of gay dating and long-term gay relationships that crossed the color barrier, during the apartheid years.

My point here is not to question the real-life occurrence of the events and/or relationships, but to note how such remarks figure prominently in gay White men's recollections of homosexuality during the apartheid years.[11] And by doing so, these stories present gay culture under apartheid as actively transgressive of apartheid's severe racial/social restrictions, and imply that, as a group, gay men in Cape Town were actually forerunners in the struggles against apartheid.

This inference can certainly be drawn from many of the cottaging stories reviewed in this essay. And by drawing such inferences, Capetownian gay men situate themselves, and their histories, within the broader traditions of activism, social protest, and efforts toward social changes associated with Stonewall-related *gay* identities in North Atlantic and other settings worldwide. In that sense, gay men's narrative-based transgressions of apartheid, highly meaningful within a South African context in their own right, provide powerful support for their claims to a transnational, gay-centered sexual citizenship.

Notes

This essay was prepared for presentation at the Center for Lesbian and Gay Studies conference on "Queer Globalization: Citizenship, Sexuality, and the Afterlife of Colonialism" (CUNY Graduate Center, New York, April 23–25, 1998). The research described here was supported, in part, by a summer research grant (1998) from the Dean of Faculty, American University, Washington, DC; my thanks to the Senate Research Committee and to the Dean of Faculty for this award. While in Cape Town, I have been a visiting fellow at the Centre for Rhetoric Studies, University Cape Town, and a visiting faculty member in UCT's Theory of Literature Programme; I am grateful to Phillipe Salazar and John Noyes, respectively, for organizing these appointments, and their benefits, on my behalf. My thanks to the men whose life story narratives have helped me understand the railways and the cottages, and to Eileen Findlay (Department of History, American University) and Wolfram Hartmann (Department of History, University of Namibia), who gave thoughtful critique to earlier drafts of this essay.

1. This is very much unlike gay American English *cruising the toilets*, which distinguishes sexual *pursuit* from the particulars of *context*. The fusion of activity and location displayed in the South African phrasing anticipates the argument developed in the remainder of this essay.
2. In the late 1960s and the late 1980s, provincial and local governments mounted campaigns to minimize the public visibility and social effects of homosexual practice. Railway station restrooms were prime targets in both campaigns—restroom doors were locked early in the evening, and railway guards and police increased their surveillance while the restrooms were open and increased the number of arrests for public indecency. In both time periods, once these efforts resulted in a sharp decline in the frequency of same-sex erotic activities conducted at these sites, the intensive surveillance came to an end, and railway guards returned to their less rigorous policing policy.
3. Also worth noting is the fact that I grew up in North Florida in the 1950s and early 1960s, during the days of segregated schools, churches, lunch counters, and other public facilities, and during the first years of mobilization against desegregation. Memories of these days shaped my expectations about apartheid and my interpretations, and in some instances misinterpretations, of daily life under that system.
4. Eight of these interviews, three White, three Coloured, and two Black, have been collected by students who have taken my "gay space" seminar at UCT and are also working with me on this project.
5. Chetty explains (1994, 115), "Moffie, coined in the coloured communities of the Western Cape, has become the South African equivalent of 'queer', 'faggot' or 'flikker',

with extremely derisive connotations. Nevertheless, particularly among coloured gay [*sic*] men themselves, it has been reappropriated, with some pride, as a term of self-identity." Often "moffie" is associated with cross-dressing Coloured men who claim a gender-crossing stance in public settings through other means.

6. All train routes converged on the system's main terminus in the City Centre; there are cross-town minibus taxis and buses, but there are no cross-town trains.

7. *Kaffir* is a derogatory term for persons of color that dates to the earliest years of British colonial rule in India, southern and eastern Africa, and other locations.

8. Taxis and buses did not provide similar visual access because they traveled along the major highways, which ran between, rather than within, these residential communities.

9. Coloured men's discussions of the cottages speak directly to this point. To cite only one example here: South African gay activist Zackie Achmed's overview of his childhood in the Salt River Coloured community (Achmed 1994) is filled with instances where Zackie uses personal charm and/or sexual practices to upstage moments of White domination and control. In this sense, cottaging played a critical role in this dimension of his gender career and (I argue further) in the formation of his commitments to political/sexual activism. Not accidentally, I think, the title of Zackie's essay underscores the inversions of familiar authority that the events in his life story were intended to convey; he called the essay "My Childhood as an Adult-Molester."

10. Think of it: It was a violation of apartheid law if a person of color put his foot inside a White man's bathroom, but not a violation of apartheid law if a person of color put his cock inside a White man's mouth.

11. Indeed, out of almost eighty men interviewed for this project to date, only one respondent has dismissed these accounts of transracial gay experience. All others have referred to such experiences, sometimes in great detail, in their storytelling.

References

Achmed, Zackie. 1994. "My Childhood as an Adult-Molester: A Salt River Moffie." In *Defiant Desire: Gay and Lesbian Lives in South Africa*, ed. Mark Gevisser and Edwin Cameron, 325–41. Johannesburg: Raven Press.

Chetty, Dhiannaraj. 1994. "A Drag at Madame Costello's: Cape Moiffie Life and the Popular Press in the 1950's and 1960's." In *Defiant Desire: Gay and Lesbian Lives in South Africa*, ed. Mark Gevisser and Edwin Cameron, 115–27. Johannesburg: Raven Press.

Coxon, Anthony P. M. 1996. "Different Scenes: Public and Power Sex." In *Between the Sheets: Sexual Diaries and Gay Men's Sex in the Era of AIDS*. London: Cassell.

Edelman, Lee. 1994. "Tearooms and Sympathy, or The Epistemology of the Water-closet." In *Homographesis: Essays in Gay Literary and Cultural Theory*, 148–70. New York: Routledge.

Gevisser, Mark. 1994. "A Different Fight for Freedom: A History of South African Lesbian and Gay Organizations—the 1950s to the 1990s." In *Defiant Desires: Gay and Lesbian Lives in South Africa*, ed. Mark Gevisser and Edwin Cameron, 14–87. London: Routledge.

Henricksson, Benny, and Sven Axel Mansson. 1995. "Sexual Negotiations: An Ethnographic Study of Men Who Have Sex with Men." In *Culture and Sexual Risk: Anthropological Perspectives on AIDS*, ed. Han ten Brummelhuis and Gilbert Herdt, 157–82. Newark: Gordon and Breach.

Higgins, Ross. 1998. "Baths, Bushes and Belonging: Public Sex and Gay Community." In *Public Sex/Gay Space*, ed. William L. Leap, 187–202. New York: Columbia University Press.

Humphreys, Laud. 1970. *Tearoom Trade*. Chicago: Aldine.

Kleinmann, Arthur. 1988. *The Illness Narratives: Suffering, Healing and the Human Condition*. Cambridge: Harvard University Press.

Leap, William. 1996. "Language Risk and Space in a Health Club Locker Room." In *Word's Out: Gay Men's English*, 109–24. Minneapolis: University of Minnesota Press.

———, 1998. *Public Sex/Gay Space*. New York: Columbia University Press.

Lewin, Ellen. 1993. *Lesbian Motherhood: Accounts of Gender in American Culture*. Ithaca: Cornell University Press.

Moyana, T. 1976. "Problems of a Creative Writer in South Africa." In *Aspects of South African Literature*, ed. C. Heywood, 92–121. London: Heinemann.

Ndebele, Mjabulo. 1998. "Truth, Memory and Narrative." In *Negotiating the Past: The Making of Memory in South Africa*, ed. Sarah Nuttall and Carli Coetzee, 19–28. London: Oxford University Press.

Prakash, Gyan. 1995. "Postcolonial Criticism and Indian Historiography." In *Social Postmodernism: Beyond Identity Politics*, ed. Linda Nicholson and Steven Seidman, 87–100. London: Cambridge University Press.

13 Like Blood for Chocolate, Like Queers for Vampires

Border and Global Consumption in Rodríguez, Tarantino, Arau, Esquivel, and Troyano (Notes on Baroque, Camp, Kitsch, and Hybridization)

Joseba Gabilondo

The Queer Refashioning of Global Masculinity

Since the release of *The Crying Game* (1992), the 1990s have shown a global taste for "queer" films. Most of these films were originally released outside Hollywood (*Farewell My Concubine*, 1993; *The Adventures of Priscilla Queen of the Desert*, 1994; *Fresa y Chocolate*, 1994; *Madame Butterfly*, 1995).[1] However, Hollywood caught on very quickly and duplicated the original foreign fascination with the queer (*Philadelphia*, 1993; *Interview with the Vampire*, 1994; *Stargate*, 1994; *Ed Wood*, 1994; *To Wong Foo*, 1995; *Birdcage*, 1996; *In and Out*, 1997). Furthermore, Hollywood managed to expand it onto a new realm: the "straight and queer" melodrama or comedy (*Threesome*, 1994: *The Opposite of Sex*, 1997; *Chasing Amy*, 1997; *My Best Friend's Wedding*, 1997; *The Object of My Affection*, 1998). Although the fascination with queer films has been globally sanctioned by Hollywood, these queer films respond to very different foreign national agendas and sociopolitical situations, which do not share much in common except perhaps the end of the Cold War and capitalism's globalization.

Nevertheless, and at the risk of metanarrativizing the specific negotiations taking place between different national situations and globalization, I believe that these films use the same discursive strategy of mobilizing a desiring male queer character in order to relegitimize and articulate a new global hegemony around the different national masculinities and hegemonies set in crisis by globalization. This maneuver is not different from the general capitalist strategy of globalization whereby hegemony is articulated through the mobilization of local and subaltern identities. As Stuart Hall claims, "I think of the global as something having more to do with the hegemonic sweep at which a certain configuration of local particularities try to dominate the whole scene, to mobilize the technology and to incorporate, in subaltern positions, a variety of more localized identities to construct the next historical project" ("Old and New" 67). In this respect, the above films are queer only at a subaltern level, and their main political agenda of global hegemony remains very much hetero-masculinist. The globally relegitimized hetero-masculinist position is what Hall calls the "dominant particular" ("Old and New" 67). The reason these films do not relegitimize their respective national masculinities as global from within a national heterosexual framework of desire is global too. In the past, the task of legitimizing hetero-masculinity had been assigned to the national heterosexual woman through the technology of the modern novel. Nowadays, however, because the risk to national masculinity is perceived as coming from without, from another ghostly global masculinity, the global relegitimation of national masculinities is carried out within a masculinist discourse. The mobilization and representation of a desiring male queer subjectivity, as the subaltern position, is simply a lesser evil in the attempt to articulate what could tentatively be called "new global hetero-masculinity."[2] In other words, the male queer position represented by these films is a historical by-product or noise generated by a hegemonic global hetero-masculinity. In short, these "queer" films are simply part of a larger group of different sexual technologies mobilized worldwide for the purpose of articulating such a global hegemony.

However, the most recent wave of global fascination with masculinity, as represented by *The Full Monty* (and mirrored domestically in the United States by *Boogie Nights*, both 1997), no longer requires a desiring queer position in order to establish and legitimize itself as desirable (although queer characters are present). In *The Full Monty* we witness the emergence of a new and very "queer" heterosexual masculinity that has learned to perform from its counterparts, the drag queens and heterosexual women. Now masculinity can perform the phallus—although it has not yet dawned on this new masculinity that "the performance of the phallus as performance" is rather a queer thing to do, for heterosexuality must perform the phallus as the signifier of the law, the (patriarchal) law of the Other (Lacan 693–94).[3] Thus this new move ultimately points to the fact that hetero-masculinity was all along the hegemonic position at stake in the "global queer films."

These films will not be studied here as "the quilting point" (Lacan 805) through which some global phallus and its queerly refashioned new hetero-masculine symbolic order can be isolated. Nor is the goal of this essay to denounce the new ways a globally refashioned homophobia and misogyny are being enforced by a putative global hetero-masculinity. Here I will rather opt for the opposite strategy of concentrating on a specific location. Thus I will center on a group of representations taking place at a precise location. I believe that "situating" (Haraway), "mapping" (Jameson), and "localizing" (Hall, "The Local")[4] are some of the most effective strategies of avoiding the fetishistic and very Lacanian effect of legitimizing masculinity by way of problematizing and queering it beyond its specific and local formations. Creating a *critical queer desire* toward global hetero-masculinity ultimately helps in the articulation of a global hegemony carried out in the first place by the "global queer films" of the 1990s.

This essay will map out several cultural representations of the border, the U.S.-Mexican border, in order to isolate the specific ways the queer and the global are determining each other in such a location. Following José D. Saldívar's own genealogy of Chicano cultural writing, I judge crucial to emphasize that "U.S.-Mexico border writing entails a new intercultural theory making sensitive to both local processes and global forces, such as Euro-imperialism, colonialism, patriarchy, and economic and political hegemonies" (35). Thus, following this project, I will first analyze two films that "border" each other in unsuspected ways: *Like Water for Chocolate* (1992, Alfonso Arau) and *From Dusk till Dawn* (1996, Robert Rodríguez). Then, once the global is locally isolated through the analysis and mapping of these two films, I will proceed to pinpoint the sexual and queer articulations by which the global locates itself at the border.

In order to isolate this global/queer intersection of the border, I will then analyze another two texts that would be considered "peripheral" to border culture because of their "Cuban" component. However, and because of their peripherality, they will help to underscore the queer "gobality" of the border. My selection also aims at emphasizing the centrality of "border" discourse in any Latino representation. The first text, or body of texts, is constituted by the journalistic accounts of the serial crimes committed by a drug-trafficking sect led by a Cuban American homosexual at the border Mexican town of Matamoros in 1989. The second text is a video performance by the lesbian Cuban artist Ela Troyano entitled *Carmelita Tropicana: Your Kunst Is Your Waffen* (1992), which relocates the globalization of the "border" in Latino New York. In this respect the selection of these two texts wants to continue the collaborative precedent established by Mexican and Cuban performing artists Guillermo Gómez-Peña and Coco Fusco in their *Couple in the Cage* and *English Is Broken Here,* on the one hand, and Chicano and Cuban film critics Chon Noriega and Ana M. López in *The Ethnic Eye: Latino Media Arts,* on the other.

Finally, and taking the sexual articulations effected by the two above "peripheral and queer texts" as standpoint, I will then reread "central" border culture. This rereading will ultimately permit me to discuss the specific and local articulations taking place between border, globalization, and queerness, while avoiding at the same time the risk of critically legitimizing the new, queerly refashioned, global hetero-masculinity to which I referred at the beginning. As a result of this localization, other issues will come to the fore: camp, kitsch, baroque, hybridity, abjection, consumption, and AIDS.

Imagining Border Consumption: Like Blood for Chocolate

I believe my perception of *Like Water for Chocolate* radically and irrevocably changed after I saw the generic film extravaganza entitled *From Dusk till Dawn,* written by Quentin Tarantino and filmed by border film director Robert Rodríguez.

Since the latter film has not known the widespread success of the former, let me advance its plot "in thirty words or less." *From Dusk till Dawn* is about two brothers (Tarantino and George Clooney) who, after robbing a bank in the United States and taking hostage a family along the way (Harvey Keitel, Juliette Lewis, Ernest Liu), cross the border in order to meet a Mexican contact (Cheech Marin). This contact is supposed to provide the two brothers with a new identity and life that will allow them to enjoy the bounty of their bank robbery. In other words, the two brothers cross the border in order to purchase a new identity. The meeting with the contact is scheduled to take place in a Mexican bar the morning after their arrival. The two brothers decide to spend the night at the bar with the hostages but, when the sun sets, they realize that the bar is a vampire nest in which border clients are devoured for dinner. Tarantino, Keitel, and others are devoured by Mexican vampires; only Clooney and Lewis survive. At the end of the film, as Clooney rides away alone, the audience is allowed to see the back of the bar on the edge of what seems to be a precipice but turns out to be a buried Mayan (?) pyramid. The bar is the top of the buried pyramid.

After seeing Tarantino's hybrid of "buddy film" with bank robbery, border-crossing, and vampires, I began to realize that the cultural exchanges taking place across the border are being represented as consumption, but more precisely of the digestive type: be it food or human beings, be it chocolate or blood.[5] It is about abject consumption. It is not a coincidence if *Like Water for Chocolate* became the largest box-office grossing foreign film in Hollywood to that date while Tarantino and Rodríguez were acclaimed as the wonder boys of (central, border) "independent" Hollywood with the release of *Pulp Fiction* (1994) and *El Mariachi* (1992), respectively. Furthermore, when this connection is established between consumption and border, other films such as *Cronos* (1992, Guillermo del Toro) come to mind. At the same time, other cases of filmic U.S. consumption of Latin American magic realist literature and culture, such as *The House of Spirits* (1993) or *Evita* (1996), might appear under a very different light. Finally, films like *Independence Day* (1996) end up revealing their specific geopolitical location, for it is about aliens dropping by to consume a globalized United States.

By examining these two representations, *Like Water for Chocolate* and *From Dusk till Dawn*, this essay aims at underscoring a new imagination forming across the border in which different forms of economic, cultural, and sexual consumption are being represented as digestion. This geopolitically coded abject imagination is already pointing to a new desire, which, unlike any previous codification, is definitively consumerist in nature. Thus if such border desire exists, one must analyze the formation of a new imagined community of consumption, an imagined NAFTA community of sorts, represented so far by the articulation of two subject positions: the vampire and the shopper. In the above two films, shoppers are vampirized, vampires bought, and all of them consumed as exchange subjects of an imaginary NAFTA economy.

If one asked whether this "digestion" is part of the border culture theorized by Gloria Anzaldúa, I would suggest that it rather represents the latter's commodified version. This commodification is part of the mechanism of expansion deployed by global capitalism. As Hall argues,

in order to maintain its global position, capital has had to negotiate and by negotiate I mean it had to incorporate and partly reflect the differences it was trying to overcome. It had to try to get hold of, and neutralize, to some degree, the differences. It is trying to constitute a world in which things are different. And that is the pleasure of it but the differences do not matter. ("The Local" 32–33)

I believe that these films show the specific differences and identities being consumed by capitalism and resisted by the local border subjects. But the resulting NAFTA culture expands beyond the boundaries of the historical border and encompasses both nations—the Mexican and the U.S.—as becoming extensions of the same divide, a global divide, and as I will show later, also a very queer divide indeed. More generally speaking, I would like to assert that North American culture is rethinking and "consuming" the border condition of global culture by mobilizing its subaltern, local border: the Mexican–North American border and all the cultural identities that are hybridized at this border (Latino, Latin American, and Spanish). What interests us here is how this local border is queered as global border in order to create the hegemonic articulation of "global heteromasculinity."

Kitsch, Camp, Baroque, Hybridity

If the style or code of the abject exchange taking place between the two films is analyzed, kitsch and camp come to the fore. All the filmic images of consumption are linked and determined by their camp and kitsch style. Although I will later define precisely both kitsch and camp, it is important to emphasize first that camp and kitsch cannot be easily separated in these border filmic representations, opposite the Anglo-Saxon Hollywood tradition. In these two films, camp and kitsch are stretched as a historical continuum of referents. The reason kitsch and camp can no longer be differentiated within this continuum is geocultural: both belong to the same tradition in Hispanic cultures, the baroque and the hybrid.[6] Camp and kitsch, in their Hispanic baroque and hybrid excessive continuity, allow for the fusion of elements that in U.S. white culture need to be dealt with in different discourses, codes, and formations. In Rodríguez's film, for example, the main act at the vampire bar is a Salomé-like dance performed by actress Salma Hayek. As she dances with a white boa wrapped around her body, she walks down a platform toward Tarantino. Completely seduced and intoxicated, he then proceeds to drink from her toe as she pours liquor down her leg. This scene is a hybrid condensation of referents deriving from Mexican popular representations of Aztec iconography, American film noir, European romantic painting, biblical discourse, cabaret, and so on. This hybrid excessiveness able to condense kitsch and camp is not tolerated in traditional Hollywood films.

As David Bergman reminds us in the introduction to his *Camp Grounds*, the novelist Christopher Isherwood already had established in his novel *The World in the Evening* a distinction between high and low camp, thus stressing the hierarchical and aristocratic origin of camp. According to Isherwood, low camp would be "a swishy little boy with peroxide hair, dressed in a picture hat and a feather boa, pretending to be Marlene Dietrich" (4). In contrast, high camp would be "the whole emotional basis of the ballet, for example, and of course of baroque art. You see, true High Camp always has an underlying seriousness" (4). Indeed, camp, in Anglo-Saxon countries, is born at the height of the modernist consecration of the divide between high and low cultures, as sanctioned and canonized by its high priest, Oscar Wilde. In Victorian societies, camp represents a historical memory of a bygone aristocracy that the camp artist reclaims in order to differentiate himself from the rise of bourgeois Victorian culture. Thus if camp becomes a male-gay-centered cultural practice in the Anglo-Saxon world, indeed it is because the gay man comes to occupy the privileged position from which to look down on bourgeois art and its supporting institution, the nuclear heterosexual family. In the Anglo-Saxon world kitsch, unlike camp, is popular and low-class; it can be heterosexual and can also be reappropriated by everybody but the middle class. The highly commodified culture revolving around Elvis is probably the outmost exponent of kitsch culture in the United States. The essentialist dehistorization of camp as queer effected by later critics such as Susan Sontag and Moe Meyer effaces camp's specific historical and class formation.

Camp has also a very definitive geopolitical dimension. Although Andrew Ross hints at it within the Anglo-American context in his "Uses of Camp," he does not deem it fundamental when elaborating a theory of camp (140). However, and as Sylvia Molloy argues, this geopolitical component is very much at the core of gay camp and can be best captured, in the Hispanic-Anglo-American context, through the analysis of a historical encounter, that of José Martí and Oscar Wilde. When Martí, the foundational figure of modern Cuba, observes Wilde at a lecture given by the latter in New York, he rapidly identifies the baroque excessive attire, the extravagance, of the English dandy (Molloy 37). Wilde's appearance, interestingly enough, reminds Martí of his own cultural and aesthetic project for Latin America. However, the geopolitical and sexual coding of these queer baroque looks makes Martí react quickly in a critical fashion and, surprisingly enough, adopt an unprecedented neoclassical stand that contradicts his representational and cultural politics. As Molloy concludes, "Martí needs to fall back on classic criteria of temporal harmony, at odds with his habitual ideology of art, in order to critique Wilde's unresolvable, unsettling difference" (38). In other words, the Martí-Wilde encounter registers, on the one hand, the complementary gay-ification of baroque into camp and "vulgarization" of kitsch into working-class taste in the Anglo-Saxon world and, on the other, the persistence of its political and cultural history in the Hispanic world.

Thus, I would suggest that the encounter between *Like Water for Chocolate* and *From Dusk till Dawn* in this other turn of the century, our century, somehow reflects and continues this genealogy of cultural encounters. In these films the Anglo-Saxon camp-kitsch and the Hispanic baroque meet again. However, this time the encounter takes place the other way around: the U.S. viewer of *Like Water for Chocolate* and Tarantino (the writer of *From Dusk till Dawn*) want to meet this rather camp, queer, and excessive world of the Hispanic baroque, one that exceeds both Anglo-American kitsch and camp.

Before I focus on the films, it is important to attempt a genealogy of the baroque in order to justify its incorporation to this discussion. As Marsha Kinder explains, following Román Gubern, baroque culture helped to organize the European Catholic monarchies against Protestantism:

While Luther and his followers used the vernacular to interpellate faithful spectators into religious dogma as individuals, the Catholic clergy turned to a pictorial language of violent sensuality, spectacle, theatricality, and excess, so that they could continue to interpellate the faithful as members of a mass audience. . . . The church authorized a system of representation to be promulgated both by its missionaries and its artists—a visual and theatrical iconography that could be read by people across vast differences in language and culture. (141–42)

In other words, the formation of the Protestant subject and its ethics, which gave rise to capitalism in Northern Europe, was culturally counteracted by the Counter-Reformation in Southern Europe and its Latin American and African colonies. Consequently Catholicism deployed the baroque culture of excess and hybridity in order to articulate an ethics of masochism and resignation among the masses. As no bourgeois revolution achieved success in Southern Europe and Latin America, the baroque aesthetics continued to mark and shape later cultural formations throughout the nineteenth century up to our days.

In the Hispanic world, the lack of a hegemonic middle class allowed the persistence of a baroque culture marked by its lack of modernity and its ability to contain the excess of older cultural formations such as pre-Columbian and premodern cultures. Furthermore, and since romanticism, this baroque culture fed the stereotypical and othering imagination deployed by Northern European empires when visiting their southern outskirts. To the gaze of the Northern European capitalist tourist, the baroque continuity in the Hispanic world represented a classless cultural utopia where camp and kitsch, low and high, coexisted. *Carmen* and the bullfight became respectively the stereotypical body and spectacle representing this coexistence. In the case of Latin America, Néstor García Canclini summarizes the debate about modernity by saying that "we have had an exuberant modernism with a deficient modernization" (41). He elaborates the cultural results of this exuberant deficiency by introducing his theory of hybridity:

Latin American countries are currently the result of the sedimentation, juxtaposition, and interweaving of indigenous traditions (above all in Mesoamerican and Andean areas), of Catholic colonial hispanism, and of modern political, educational, and communicational actions. Despite attempts to give elite culture a modern profile, isolating the indigenous and the colonial in the popular sectors, an interclass mixing has generated hybrid formations in all social strata. (46)

The lack of any reference to the distinction between camp and kitsch in García Canclini's own discourse is not a deficiency but the consequence of the pervasiveness of a hybrid and excessive baroque legacy. Precisely this legacy is the one that yields an "exuberant modernism" in modernity while maintaining its native and colonial origins. As García Canclini himself argues, these different historical layers coexist simultaneously in Latin America, thus defying lineal chronology: "the whole crisis of modernity, traditions, and their historical combination leads to a postmodern problematic (*not a phase*) in the sense that the modern explodes and is mixed with what is not modern; it is affirmed and debated at the same time" (266, my emphasis). Thus in the following, I will use the terms "baroque" and "hybrid" interchangeably, in their postmodern nonsynchronicity, in order to emphasize respectively excess (baroque) or nonreducible identity (hybrid).[7] The tension between both terms will allow us to incorporate the discourse of camp and kitsch in the Hispanic tradition while emphasizing their nonmodern irreducibility. In turn, the triad camp-kitsch-baroque will permit us to introduce sexuality in the formation of these cultural representations in a way that the institutional and sociological analysis of García Canclini does not.

The Imperialist Subject and Symbolic Surplus Value

Based on this genealogy of the Hispanic baroque and its contemporary persistence in postmodern hybridity, one could tentatively conclude that Hispanic baroque appears as a desirable alternative for contemporary U.S. globalization. At this point the United States is searching for a new cultural logic capable of surmounting the limitations of European modernity and its political-cultural formation, the nation-state. In other words, contemporary U.S. imperialism is seeking cultural

codes capable of enabling the articulation of a nonnationalist imperialist hegemony, one that will be acceptable and desirable to a world-scale consumerist mass.
U.S. imperialism is looking for the logic that would legitimize the hegemony of a
"global melting pot." At this point, the logic of baroque imperialist cultures from
the past, with their high tolerance for hybridity and excess, turns out to be more
appealing to U.S. imperialism than Northern European national cultures.[8] The
baroque, in its excessiveness and hybridity, allows for the deployment of discourses that exceed a national framework and spread over the imperialist one. The
baroque represents for U.S. imperialist culture a way to transcend Protestant indi-
viduality and consequently regain a subjective excessiveness, hybridity, and
power suitable for global expansion—even if this "reaching out of the individual
Protestant self" lingers in destruction and masochism.

The historical and excessive hybridity of *From Dusk till Dawn* and its appropriation of the baroque responds to this imperialist move of expansion and exploitation vis-à-vis new postcolonial cultural resources: the baroque tradition. In
the film, there is a trade and reappropriation of surplus carried out in very traditional imperialist ways. Within this new imperialist appropriation of the baroque,
Rodríguez-Tarantino's film mobilizes every conceivable Mexican stereotype in its
historical hybrid excessiveness in order to pour in the traumatic U.S. national history of interventionism throughout the world and obtain in return a new global
cultural logic and subject, in short, a global hegemony. The vampire bar across
the border is a symbolic "baroque maquiladora" for the processing of U.S. national individualist culture and its conversion into global baroque subjectivity
and discourse.[9]

From Dusk till Dawn is full of allusions to Vietnam, Korea, the civil rights movements, and so forth, as is any previous Tarantino film. His films are always a collection of historical and cultural references filtered and fetishized through filmic
references. The use of a black exploitation film star, Fred Williamson, alongside
the use of Latinos Cheech Marin and the rock band La Bamba, makes room for the
negotiation of all sorts of domestic problems. In the film, the U.S. shopper
Clooney comes to the border to buy a new identity. However, in the transaction,
he smuggles U.S. domestic problems: the crisis in the United States' intervention-
ist economic policy toward its neighbors—from Mexico to Vietnam—and its con-
sequent inability to continue an imperialist expansion. Then Clooney lets the
Mexican laborers-vampires consume and reprocess his identity, if not economically, at least symbolically: they consume and get rid of Tarantino and the rest of
the people embodying U.S. imperialist problems. Only a baroque subject such as

245

the vampire is able to consume and reprocess this imperialist subjectivity. Once the reprocessing work is done, Clooney refuses to pay for the Mexican vampire labor and liquidates them. The exchange stops and he keeps the symbolic surplus value in the form of global hegemonic value.

Furthermore, Clooney fights the Mexican vampires with the commodities left behind in the bar by previously killed truckers: water guns, condoms, construction tools, and so forth. The commodity becomes the weapon against the vampire. Commodities give Clooney the advantage and legitimation in a trade in which vampires can only exchange their bodies and labor, their baroque and hybrid symbolic labor. Vampire labor becomes "natural, biological, or animal-like." Consequently, and after the reprocessing of U.S. national subjectivity into global NAFTA subjectivity is finished, the vampires are terminated and so their labor's full value—not only its surplus value—is retained by the U.S. imperialist subject. Vampires are the cheapest and most productive form of labor. When Clooney walks out of the bar the following morning, he is the owner of all the symbolic labor carried out by the Mexican vampires inside the bar: he is now the new global NAFTA subject ready to pursue U.S. expansion further south.

Once the transaction is completed the baroque moment reoccurs: the vampire-laborers are identified as imperial. The final shot establishes the historical excessiveness and hybridity of the filmic representation and its imperialist lineage. The U.S. subjects are acquiring the Mayan (Aztec) and Spanish empires' baroque cultural logic of excess and hybridity—as cultural surplus value—not simply the labor of a national working class across the border. "This is not imperialism; it is simply the accidental encounter between empires." Imperial credentials are important when establishing global orders. This U.S. eagerness to become the Other, and yet to dominate the Other as postcolonial subject, prompts precisely the vampire logic of the film. Once the imperial genealogy of the parties involved is identified, the film ends. Clooney walks away as the new NAFTA consumer ready to adopt his new identity: the NAFTA global *comprador*.

The National Woman and Kitsch

However, it is important to understand the sexual and gender dynamics brought about by the redeployment of the Hispanic baroque as North American imperialist (global) culture. Although the discussion of *From Dusk till Dawn* reveals that the consumption *by* the Other is being coded as masculine, global, and baroque, the consumption *of* the Other is still carried out within a feminized, heterosexual, national, kitsch logic, as the analysis of *Like Water for Chocolate* reveals. It is choco-late against blood. In other words, the film *Like Water for Chocolate* effaces the baroque and hybrid excess of the original novel when it comes to consuming the Other.

Nation-states in the situation of Mexico are striving to join global commercial ventures such as NAFTA by presenting themselves as desirable nations for foreign investment and consumption—ultimately regulated by the U.S. economy. Con-versely, the U.S. imagination wants to consume kitsch representations of national Others in the specific form of feminine, low-class, heterosexual, and desirable im-ages and objects. Here the heterosexual and feminine containment of kitsch amounts to reification and control.[10] Thus, in this context, it is not surprising if the filmic jewel of this cultural exchange, *Like Water for Chocolate*, has been turned into national Mexican kitsch for U.S. domestic consumption. The filters applied to the film's images render lighting homogeneous and continuous so that the his-torical complexity of the narrative text on which the film is based is taken away. Furthermore, by collapsing domestic and national spaces—the 1911 revolution—around the consumption of food, in a fashion reminiscent of TV cooking shows and commercials, the film becomes a kitsch representation. The racial erasure that the film effects further emphasizes the national kitschification of Mexico as white-criollo and non-mestizo. The final shot representing a recipe book threat-ens to become an allegorical rendering of a commercial ad for the promotion of national kitsch: buy the book, consume Mexico (some Caribbean islands already promote themselves in this way). At the center of this other Mexican national kitsch, masculinity is vacated, and hence the new foreign national product is ready to be consumed along heterosexual lines of desire: Mexico is a desirable ob-ject for U.S. domestic consumption. Mexico becomes available at the local mall as cookbook, film, ethnic restaurant, and so forth.

However, it is important to notice that the strand of magic realism regulating the novel betrays the filmic attempts to reduce the narrative to national kitsch. In other words, there is an inherent historical heterogeneity in the book, which pre-vents the narrative from becoming national. The impossibility of actually cooking the recipes of the novel functions as the book's allegorical resistance to consump-tion. The book cannot be "eaten." Ultimately, the U.S. film viewer ends up buying a baroque simulacrum of Mexican national kitsch. The hybrid continuity between kitsch and camp in Hispanic cultures allows for this excessive and baroque simu-lacrum of national kitsch.

Once the relation between kitsch and national consumption is established, opposite the global hybrid, other films such as *Cronos* and *El Mariachi* can be analyzed from this vantage point. At the beginning of *Cronos*, the camera presents the Spanish imperial lineage of the product to sell: the Cronos device. This device is an alchemic, organic machine that allows its users to achieve eternity by making them vampires. As does *Like Water for Chocolate*, *Cronos* represents an allegorical object, the Cronos device, which in anachronistic representation as baroque technology is denied to the U.S. buyer. Rather than giving the baroque device away, Federico Lupi, the grandfather and hero in the film, prefers to smash it, and thus allegorically signify the end of the baroque logic in Mexico. Lupi destroys that very same logic that would ensure "global eternity" to the U.S. imperialist subject. However, it is too late; the refusal to embrace the border economy of U.S. expansion relocates the filmic subject in the vampire position: Lupi has become a vampire and we are back to *From Dusk till Dawn*.[11]

The film *El Mariachi* could also be read as the kitschification or "de-baroquization" of Mexican masculinity. The mix-up between guitars and guns serves as a narrative ploy to introduce a normal man in the position of superhero and thus defy the conventions of the warrior adventure genre. However, the counter-genre introduction of a normal man is not simply a discursive strategy to criticize Mexican machismo or Hollywood masculinity (Ramírez-Berg 121–22). It also represents a vacated masculinity that is turned once again into national kitsch: the mariachi. The film shows us, if not an absent masculinity as in *Like Water for Chocolate*, at least a kitschified and very consumable masculinity void of agency. The film presents masculinity as an agency-less commodity, a consumable object; hence its desirability to U.S. audiences.[12] The remake of *El Mariachi*, *Desperado* (1995), and the new presence of Spanish actor Antonio Banderas reintroduce the hybrid and excessive historicity of the Hispanic baroque: what in *Cronos* was the colonial origin of the baroque (the Cronos device) in *Desperado* becomes its global masculine representation.

The Global Vampire and Baroque

The above mainstream films present cases of successful imperialist consumption: the Other is successfully exploited (*From Dusk till Dawn*) or consumed (*Like Water for Chocolate*). However, when the Other cannot be reduced to either economic position, the Other's ensuing resistance to consumption is registered as endowed with both agency and sexuality. In other words, the irreducible hybrid excessiveness of baroque culture is registered as both subjective and sexual. Furthermore, when the Other cannot be consumed, its sexuality comes to the fore and is represented in its irreducible excessiveness: the Other is queer. Precisely what is registered as queer is this simultaneous economic and sexual excessiveness. As the analysis of the Matamoros sect reveals, when the Other is on *the other* side of the border it becomes a *vampire*. However, when the Other is on *this* side of the border, as in the case of *Carmelita Tropicana*, it becomes *homosexual*. Thus the Other's irreducible excess marks it as queer while its geopolitical location makes it either vampire or homosexual. Ultimately the queer subject's Otherness, its Hispanic hybrid baroque excessiveness, points to the fact that the Other no longer can be contained as either foreign (vampire) or domestic (homosexual), for ultimately the Other is global and queer, and hence irreducible.

As the analysis of *From Dusk till Dawn* shows, when the U.S. shopper crosses the border and ventures into the global arena, this shopper wants to consume and exploit the Other but is afraid to be consumed by the latter. The Other is baroque, hybrid, imperial, and masculine, precisely what the U.S. subject desires to become. If *From Dusk till Dawn* shows the heterosexual fantasies of successfully consuming and exploiting the Other without being queered by it, the Matamoros sect's crimes show the opposite, that is, the fears and nightmares unleashed by the Other's consumption in their utterly queer and sexual nature.

The 1989 incident at Matamoros, Mexico, involves a sect of drug traffickers practicing a form of magic with connections to Santería—Palo Mayombe. If the Matamoros incident is a "famous" page in U.S. history, it is not because of its cultist character; there are plenty of cultist sects in the United States. Its sensationalism is directly connected to the fact that the cult is practiced by the Other across the border.[13] As the *Houston Post* claimed in sensationalist headlines, "Slayings Rival Worst Cases of Mass Murder in America: The Satanic Ritual Murders of Mark Kilroy and Eleven Others in Matamoros Mexico Rival the Worst Mass Killings in USA History." What is at stake is the fact that the Other can rival the North American subject and consume it. In this sense Edward Humes captures the historical character of this border imagination when he claims in his account of the crime that "Not since the disappearance and murder of DEA agent Enrique 'Kiki' Camarena four years before had a crime against an American in Mexico drawn such unprecedented attention" (240).

This incident captures the outermost fear of the imperialist U.S. subject: that the Other can consume it, and unlike in *From Dusk till Dawn*, the Other might retain not only the surplus value, but the entire labor embodied by the U.S. subject itself.[14] The U.S. media further emphasized this excessive consumption. First the media implied that the sect had fashioned itself mirroring the worst fears of U.S. mass culture as portrayed by horror film. Once the mirroring effect was assured, the other became the Other: a global vampire able to fulfill every fantasy and fear defining the U.S. subject. Cannibalism or Satanism had nothing to do with the sect, except the fact that the U.S. media expected them from a perfect global Other. As Humes points out, "the gang was accused falsely of practicing cannibalism, satanism, and of basing their religion on a horror movie about Santeria called *The Believers*. . . . the self-appointed [U.S.] spokesmen in the case could not seem to stop themselves. Oprah and Geraldo were on the phone, and they were only too happy to oblige" (260).

Although the sect had carried out several human sacrifices within the drug-dealing circles of Matamoros without being detected, the ritual killing of a U.S. subject triggered the police investigation and the media attention following the arrests. However, the sacrifice of a U.S. subject—Mark Kilroy, a white, blonde college student—was part of the logic dictated by the drug traffic. Since the drugs were part of a border economy, the magic had to be too. As the sect leader claimed, "The spirit of a gringo college student would make their magic supreme in the United States, as it already was in Mexico" (228).

Here also economic (drugs) and cultural (Palo Mayombe) consumption is simultaneously practiced. As a result, the Mexican media coined a single name to denominate the double nature of this consumption: *narcosatánicos* (Humes 281). Humes notes the point at which the entire group of drug traffickers started to believe firmly in the cult and thus the drug traffic also became a "cultural trade." The group stole drugs from another rival gang. As retaliation, the gang kidnapped one of the members of the group (Ovidio). The leader of the group, Constanzo, instead of negotiating with the rival gang, decided to make a human sacrifice to solve the problem. They kidnapped and killed a hitchhiker: "Constanzo had performed the ceremony and said Ovidio would be freed. Then it happened, just as he said it would. . . . The drugs had been resold in Houston for another $800,000, all profit. All it had cost was some hitchhiker's life—a bargain by . . . [the] new system of accounting" (Humes 204). In other words, a human sacrifice generated a net profit of $800,000. Eventually Constanzo, the leader, theorized the single economy consisting of drugs and human rituals in the following way:

Their magic . . . was like some huge engine that used blood for fuel. When the motor was idling, only a little fuel was needed, a sacrifice every month or so. But now, with drugs and money pouring in and traffickers being knocked off, the need for protection was never greater. The engine was racing, and the blood had to keep pace with the money. *(Humes 218, my emphasis)*

At the core of this double economy, there is hybrid excess of both agency and sexuality. All the drug traffickers as well as the victims are men. This is a masculine economy and hence queer masculinity, because it is sexually excessive, gains hold over the excessive economy and becomes central. As Humes explains, the leader of the sect, Adolfo de Jesús Constanzo—a Cuban American from Florida relocated in Mexico—was "gay." Moreover, Constanzo's homosexuality granted him leadership because the heterosexual members of the sect could not match "the pleasure" he experienced in the ritual killings. He was the member of the sect who obtained the greatest surplus value from this economy and thus was entitled to the leadership. Furthermore, the other drug traffickers' heterosexuality made them vulnerable to the excessive logic of the cult. As Humes explains,

With each offering of blood and flesh tossed into the cauldron, Constanzo pleaded to the gods and the dead for protection and invulnerability. . . . [During a specific ritual] Constanzo sent the pale and nauseous Elio [assistant] from the shed and slammed the door shut on the makeshift temple. In a moment of obscene privacy, the priest of Palo Mayombe ripped his victim's clothes off and began a ritual rape of the man.

Later, Constanzo told his followers that the mutilation of victims before killing conditioned their spirits to serve in the afterlife, inside the nganga [cauldron]. Evil death breeds evil deeds, Constanzo said. Torture was essential. "They must die screaming," he told them.

But there was no denying another, simpler reason for the torture: Constanzo enjoyed it. None of the followers missed it. Seeing that fierce joy on el Padrino's [Constanzo's] face at another's pain was the most fearful thing of all, worse than the killing itself.

More than anything else, that murderous look made all of them try their best to please the dark Cuban sorcerer [Constanzo]. Anything short of total obedience, they knew, might put one of them behind the closed door of Constanzo's temple on the border. *(201–2, my emphasis)*

This excessive economy of drugs and ritual is queer at its center because of its bordering and masculinist logic. The ultimate vampire, the ultimate Other, is queer. Robert Tracy and Ken Gelder point out respectively that, at the turn of the nineteenth century, the new woman (Tracy 46) and the colonial subject (Gelder 12–13) needed to be contained through the representation of the vampire. Similarly, at the turn of the twentieth century, the homosexual man and

251

the non-U.S. subject need to be contained through the very same representation of the vampire.[15]

Commenting on the film *Falling Down*, Richard Dyer hypothesizes that whiteness, the mark of the imperialist (global) subject, and homosexuality are intertwined because of their connection with death: "a trope of white culture equates whiteness, homosexuality, and sex *tout court*. . . . white sex is queer sex. This is a triple source of anxiety: it is inherently perverse; it is a bringer of death (in the form of AIDS); and, above all, because so much at the heart of all white anxieties, it is non-reproductive" (220). Although Dyer refers to "non-reproductive" only in its biological dimension, I would also like to emphasize its economic implications. The white imperialist subject is one that consumes without re-producing bodies or capital and hence is condemned to die unless he keeps preying on all other subjects (women, colonial subjects, etc.).

Moreover, the analysis of the above incident points rather to a more complex picture: whiteness might ultimately be about local, male homosexuality, but nonwhiteness is about globality and male queerness. The global vampire can be both nonheterosexual and (non)reproductive: biologically nonreproductive, culturally reproductive. This position coded in the figure of the global vampire, a baroque hybrid vampire, is one that U.S. imperialism fears but, at the same time, needs. The global vampire, unlike the white imperialist subject, can also prey on the white imperialist subject and bring death to the latter while enjoying it. If the imperialist subject is homosexual, the global vampire is queer, and thus exceeds homosexuality.

Curiously enough, this construction does not permit the non-U.S. subject to become homosexual; this subject can only be excessively queer. The global vampire is not allowed to desire its own kind. The global queer subject is required to desire the imperialist white subject and become the latter's perfect, yet excessive, mirror. The representation of the global vampire is about creating global homophobia and global misogyny, but in this specific way: the global vampire is always masculine and is forced to desire only the imperialist white subject. Female gender, regardless of whether it is heterosexual or lesbian, is relegated to the national, domestic sphere.[16]

The final irony, however, comes from the fact that the global vampire, Adolfo de Jesús Constanzo, was a U.S. citizen. His Cuban ancestry and his knowledge of Spanish, his baroque past, allowed him nevertheless to relocate to Mexico, another Hispanic country where his knowledge of Palo Mayombe, although of Cuban-African origin, mixed well with the Mexicans' own rituals and magic.

Baroque culture once again enables a vampire's global and free-floating excessiveness and hybridity. Even a U.S. subject can become the Other, the global vampire, because of his baroque hybrid heritage. The Hispanic baroque is global even at the border. The aliens of *Independence Day* come from Matamoros.

The Local Queer and Camp

If the global vampire as queer subject signifies the crisis of U.S. imperialism across the border, the Latino queer, on this side of the border, brings about another imperialist failure in its specific queer and Hispanic coding of consumerism. As the analysis of Troyano's *Carmelita Tropicana* suggests, the Other exceeds consumerism in its locality and reveals the global and queer nature of its excessiveness.

As Frances Negrón-Muntaner argues, Latino queer cultural productions in the U.S. occupy an "inexistent" position for the white homosexual community (59) and, I would add, the Latino heterosexual community as well. She also points out the tendency to conflate Latino and African American queer culture under the latter and thus homogenize racial and ethnic differences as a single, homogeneous difference (59). Thus, Latino queer productions are always forced to become "homosexual with an ethnic touch" or Latino and hence "nonhomosexual," or even a "subgroup" of queer African American culture. I would like to add a geopolitical component to Negrón-Muntaner's explanation: Latino queer productions stress the fact that the global border is not simply a border between nations, between first and third worlds, but between sexualities. Latino queer culture emphasizes that the global border is also constituted as an inner, "domestic" border. The border is not simply a geopolitical, economic, and racial divide, but also sexual. The "consumption" taking place across this other inner border is also marked by the desires and anxieties unleashed by the acts of consuming and being consumed. Here consumption not only means the joys of baroque hybrid consumption in mainstream Latino, Latin American, and Spanish cultures, but also the anxieties derived from poverty, lack of political power, ignorance, and AIDS. This consumption, although fully queer and Latino, is also global and cannot be understood within the limited national confines of either the United States, Mexico, Latin America, or Spain. Furthermore, because of its global location, queer Latino consumption points directly to the economic and social repercussions of being left "outside" consumption.

The global location of the Latino queer becomes underscored in Ela Troyano's

Carmelita Tropicana: Your Kunst Is Your Waffen (1992) in ways that are pertinent to my discussion of consumption and baroque hybridity. As José E. Muñoz points out, *Carmelita Tropicana* mixes all forms of Latino, Latin American, and Spanish elements: "Troyano employs this mixing across time and cultures to achieve a radical camp effect that reveals, in exaggerated terms, the *mestizaje* of contemporary U.S.-Latino culture and politics" (136). The mixing of iconography, music, and mise-en-scène from traditional Latin American, Latino, and Spanish cultures is clearly located in the Loisada of New York, where the action of the film takes place. But at the same time, this shift underscores the fact that the specific location is simultaneously a condition of the globalization of Hispanic cultures, not just Cuban, Mexican, Latino, or Spanish national cultures. In other words, the specific locality of her cultural production is simultaneously a condition of global culture. When discussing the appropriation of the bolero as means of melodrama in queer films such as *Carmelita Tropicana*, Negrón-Muntaner points out that this musical use renders their Hispanic condition a location, not an identity: "the bolero is never free of contradictions and excess; it resists normalizing discourses such as those of marriage and family . . . the use of the bolero is a strategy for symbolic integration—not marginalization—into the body social of an imagined Latino/pan–Latin American community" (71–72).

When the cultural hybridity of *Carmelita Tropicana* is analyzed from the Anglo-Saxon perspective of kitsch and camp, both appear in a continuum that cannot be broken up. The film reappropriates the entire social spectrum of cultural registers and referents of Hispanic and non-Hispanic U.S. cultures. From 1950s leather jackets à la Brando, military uniforms, and Spanish flamenco costumes to business executive outfits, New York high-platform shoes, 1960s Jetson-looking outfits, "Carmen Miranda" looks, and glamorous diva-like performing spaces, the entire spectrum of kitsch and camp is present in *Carmelita Tropicana*.

In this respect, Troyano's queer reappropriation of Hispanic and U.S. cultures is similar to the global vampire, the queer Other: she threatens to reappropriate and consume any cultural item whatsoever without respect for national and social borders. She threatens to "eat up" U.S. culture. Just like mainstream baroque Hispanic culture, her queer cultural appropriations are excessive and hybrid as both kitsch and camp. The only difference lies in the fact that her appropriation is not commodified consumption but sexual, queer consumption. This form of consumption defies mainstream Hispanic culture not in its hybridity and excessiveness (either kitsch or camp) but in the way it is carried out: outside the norms sanctioned by the commodity market. The sexual location from which excessive consumption is carried out is different from mainstream Hispanic baroque. In queer Hispanic consumption, position, not identity, is at stake.

However, and unlike the case of the global vampire, the excessive, hybrid, and sexual consumption of Hispanic culture carried out by Troyano does not step outside Hispanic culture: it is inscribed within. This is the meaning of her self-aware performativity. She is performing and marking her performance of queer consumption of Hispanic/U.S. cultures so that the audience is incorporated within her performance instead of being alienated by the distance of an alien queer representation, the queer Other. Here Troyano stops being the Other, the queer, the vampire, and becomes a Hispanic baroque performer. Unlike in the Anglo-Saxon world, drag performance has a specific place among nonqueer audiences in the Hispanic world. Hispanic heterosexual couples go to watch drag performances as a normal venue of entertainment. The central performance of the film, the singing of a ranchera song in jail, is not either melodramatic or camp, but both melodramatic and camp. The final repetition of the ranchera performance by Carmelita at the end of the film—in which she pays homage to her compañera Di, who by then has died of AIDS—is also inscribed within the old tradition of singing for the lost love. Consequently the final performance of the ranchera can be interpreted as both a political act of homage to a fallen comrade and an implicit acknowledgment of a lost love. It is not the logic of "either or" but the excessive hybrid logic of "both x and y" that incorporates the audience into the performance.

At the same time, Troyano's performance is also highly conscious of consumerism and social class. The film tells among other stories that of Di, a homeless, drug-addicted, white lesbian who becomes the CEO of her own company. Di's is a story of economic success and happiness tinted with sorrow and chagrin as she falls victim to AIDS. In other words, and unlike any of the previous narratives of consumption (*Like Water for Chocolate, From Dusk till Dawn,* Matamoros), *Carmelita Tropicana* makes the audience aware of the real costs and implications of consumerism. Consumerism is not simply about desire but also power; its lack creates situations that lead to risk and death, a very global and queer death. In this way when Carmelita and her friends meet Di, the encounter takes place across a global border, albeit very local in its global condition. This encounter mirrors that other of Mark Kilroy, a white man, with the drug-trafficking sect in Matamoros. In both cases, consumption leads their white protagonists to death. Hence consumption is not about whiteness, but about the global encounter of whiteness and Hispanic ethnicities. In the Matamoros case, the class privilege of a U.S. white college student vacationing across the border leads him to death, as he encounters the Other who eats everything: drugs and souls. In *Carmelita Tropicana*, the homeless white woman encounters help and acknowledgment in the Hispanic queer community. Carmelita, instead of "eating" the white subject, exceeds her "death" by representing and validating the consequences of Di's life. Carmelita becomes the vindicator, teller, and performer of the deadly encounter across the border between unprivileged queer subjects.[17]

bell hooks takes an anti-consumerist stand when discussing whiteness's racial encounters with and desire for the Other in her "Eating the Other" (21–39) and "Is Paris Burning?" (145–56). hooks's position is structured by her concern toward the ways global whiteness consumes its Other and, more specifically, African American otherness. Thus, she concludes that consumption can only become the consumption of the Other. However, from a Hispanic location in which consumerism, as a form of excess, does not conflict directly with politics, Troyano takes a very different stand: there is no place outside consumerism in global culture. Troyano implies that consumerism must be turned into a form of political activity and empowerment, because otherwise consumerism others the subject, the queer subject, as "vampire."

In this respect, Troyano helps us to reread films such as *Paris Is Burning* (1990, Jennie Livingston). This film is not simply a performance of sexual and racial identities but also an act of consumption of culture and identity. Most young poor people involved in voguing portrayed by the film do not simply perform an identity void of consumerism, as bell hooks's analysis implies. They perform identity as consumerism; hence the sophisticated fetishistic culture they develop around "wearing the commodity." Voguing is about being able to acquire the right brand-name dress, in contrast to the homemade dresses of the older generation of drag queens. It is this consumerism that unites the poor young people in queer houses/families and gives them the location from which to perform their queer identities, marked as global at their core—hence the Atlantic title of the film. *Paris Is Burning* also illustrates that the failure to successfully perform a consumerist, queer identity has tragic consequences: violence, drug addiction, prostitution, AIDS, and death. Hence in *Paris Is Burning*, the queer subjects develop a very sophisticated form of politics based on the simulation of consumption, which symbolically compensates for their lack of capital. Their bodies become the location in which the commodity, as brand-name dress, is simulated in order to gain a queer access to empowerment and consumption.

In this respect I would agree with Muñoz when he defines Troyano's performance as camp (139–40), although I would rather confine the term "camp" to

Anglo-Saxon culture.[18] However, "Hispanic camp," unlike its Anglo-Saxon counterpart, is not defined by its hierarchical opposition to kitsch and mass culture. "Hispanic camp" is not about high-culture resistance to consumerism. Rather the opposite; "Hispanic camp" is about exceeding consumerism, is about consuming consumerism, without denying it. "Hispanic camp" is the excess of consumerism. "Camp" is as baroque and hybrid as kitsch, but at the same time is queer. Queerness, in the Hispanic world, does not represent an interior closet, but an excessive sexuality that nevertheless is interior to Hispanic culture. It is not hidden in the closet but located outside consumerism and within the baroque. "Hispanic camp" is about the queer body that exceeds the heterosexual familial body and, by consuming it, places itself in interior excess. In this respect too, the reduction of Hispanic queer culture to homosexuality, as a formation consistent with the heterosexual nuclear family, is an imperialist maneuver. Hispanic queer culture is global in its excessiveness; it cannot be reduced to any national homosexuality, be it North American, Latin American, Latino, or Spanish.

The mapping of the four texts analyzed above yields a situated map in which the global and the local become queered in their tensions to consume and be consumed as U.S. economic and cultural imperialism expands globally by mobilizing the subaltern Hispanic culture of its border. This discourse derives from my own location within a queer Hispanic world. As a Spanish Basque, I am the whitest of the Hispanics and the most Hispanic of the whites. I am the most "cristiano viejo"; this was the current category used among Hispanics when whiteness was not yet an operative imperialist formation. At the same time, I belong to that part of Europe that will never be "modern" or postmodern, and hence fully white. I cannot but locate myself within this global and dividing border, as both the shopper and the vampire, the white and the Hispanic. I must be aware that, at least for the time being, it is my political responsibility to capture the global and sexual duality of any representation *tout court*. A failure to do so would reduce me to either position and hence I would have to consume my Other, or be consumed by my Other.

Notes

I would like to thank Hank Okazaki and José Muñoz for their contribution to this essay.

1. I believe that Hispanic and Latin American films such as *La muerte de Mikel* (1983) and *The Kiss of the Spider Woman* (1985) are forerunners of this trend due to the political situation of the respective countries of production.

2. In *Imperial Leather* Anne McClintock makes a good case for the inherent heterosexuality and misogyny of modern imperialism in its cognitive and representational deployment of woman as liminal figure of conquest. Whether this new "queer" phase discussed here is simply transitional or a new departure from modern imperialism remains to be seen.

3. However, the failure of decidedly hetero-masculinist films without performative awareness, such as *Striptease* (1996), in which women remain the visual object and support of the male gaze, might point to the fact that "good old hetero-masculinity" is in crisis.

4. Hall only uses the nominal form, not the verbal. The latter is my own derivation.

5. McClintock points out that the imperialist representations of the colonial other as capable of consuming the Western subject through cannibalism are as old as the colonization of Latin America itself (27).

6. Here "Hispanic" must be understood as encompassing Latino, Latin American, and Spanish cultures.

7. I follow García Canclini when he favors the term "hybrid" over "mestizaje" or "sincretismo": "I prefer this last term [hybridization] because it includes diverse intercultural mixtures—not only the racial ones to which *mestizaje* tends to be limited—and because it permits the inclusion of the modern forms of hybridization better than does 'syncretism,' a term that almost always refers to religious fusions or traditional symbolic movements" (11 n.1).

8. Interestingly enough, this logic is already present in U.S. music. Its African American base seems capable, for other reasons, of embodying this excessive and global logic. Thus the new fascination with the neighboring Hispanic baroque could be interpreted as a movement from domestic resources (musical) to new foreign and neighboring ones (visual) in an expanded imperialist cultural move that began at home.

9. In this respect *From Dusk till Dawn* is not different from other Tarantino films. In *Pulp Fiction*, the scene at the basement of the pawnshop in which one of the protagonists is raped by a man helps to reorganize and legitimize the heterosexual structure of the film, whereas in *True Romance* Mexico reincarnates the traditional heaven of Hollywood outlaws. In other words, spaces of differences (queer, national, or ethnic) help to structure and solve the narrative crisis present in Tarantino's films.

10. The new series of U.S. TV commercials, popularized in the 1990s, in which different national or ethnic segments from all over the world are mobilized around a U.S. business in order to legitimize the latter's globalization (most famously ATT) are very important in this context. They are one of the privileged sites in which the U.S.

kitschification of the rest of the world has experienced the most systematic and refined elaboration.

11. Interestingly enough, in *Cronos* the parental figures are absent and substituted by the grandparents in what could be read as the vacation of the nuclear family and its institutions, sexual and national. Thus the vacation of traditional national culture does not lend itself to kitschification. I don't think that introduction of the grandmother as teaching tango lessons in Mexico is a coincidence: Argentine culture is present in a Mexican film in order to signify hybridity and excess in clear defiance of national kitsch. At the same time, tango can be easily identified as part of Argentinean national kitsch. Thus we have a "baroque excess of national kitsch." In turn, the North American pursuer of the Cronos device adopts all the queer mannerisms of camp (classical music, aristocratic walking stick, knowledge of European history and languages, no explicit sexuality, decadence, etc.). In other words, this film becomes national kitsch—simulated through allegory and baroque excess—for the camp consumption of the North American viewer.

12. Ramírez-Berg concludes that *El Mariachi* "calls into question . . . dominant notions of masculinity, heroism, the U.S.-Mexico border, and, finally, cinema. You can hardly be more provocative or more subversive than that" (126). I would agree with him in this assessment of the textual and ideological potential of the film. However, this does not preclude the overdetermination or counterdetermination of a kitsch reception. Although Ramírez-Berg does analyze the dynamics of film-genre politics, he does not address the issue of border cultural reception through national kitsch. At the same time, I believe that genre film does actually allow for the coexistence of opposite and potential receptions. Only a combined sociological, anthropological, and political analysis of reception can determine the cultural status of a film—an ever-changing status.

13. Complementarily, a quick sampling of news from that moment points to the fact that violence is prevalent around the drug traffic but never becomes national headlines in the United States. The *Houston Post* reported the following news on the same dates: "The discovery of twelve mutilated bodies in Matamoros is the second incident in two weeks involving mass murders and drug trafficking in Mexican border towns. Twelve bodies were found previously near Agua Prieta in Sonora state" ("Grisly Findings"). Drug traffic–related violence extends even to prisons: "Anti-terrorist troops and riot police officers surrounded a state prison in Matamoros Mexico on May 18, 1991 after a battle between rival drug gangs in which officials said 18 people were killed and five wounded" ("18 Reported"). These news items never become popular in the U.S. media because of their lack of a cultist component.

14. As Peter Applebome reported in the *New York Times*, "Following the arrest of five people of a drug ring in Matamoros Mexico who are charged with the occult killings of at least 13 people, the increasing violence and murder associated with drug smuggling along the U.S.-Mexican border is featured." In other words, even the *New York Times* becomes attentive to the border situation once the new economy of drugs becomes a bodily economy involving U.S. subjects.

15. Humes incorporates different statistics in his book in order to enhance the vampire dynamic across the border: "The authorities in Mexico City already knew that. In the previous two years, there had been sixty ritual killings of adults in Mexico City. Two of them occurred after Constanzo was killed. Fourteen babies were found sacrificed during the same period" (371–72); "A study by the Texas Department of Public Safety revealed that, from 1985 through April 1989, 226 cases of ritual crime were reported, mostly in South Texas near the border. Again, most of the crimes involved drugs, and most were related to Afro-Caribbean black magic, not satanism" (373). However, Humes does not include similar statistics about the United States and thus others the vampire as a border or Mexican figure.

16. The only woman involved in the drug trafficking ring of Matamoros, la Flaca, was chosen by Constanzo as his lover and priestess. However, Constanzo hardly engaged in sex with la Flaca and she did not take direct part in the drug trafficking. Thus one can conclude that Constanzo was aware that any queer subjectivity also needed to perform "heterosexuality" in order to be legitimate and exceed traditional heterosexual masculinity: la Flaca was simply kept as a figure of Constanzo's "queer and excessive" heterosexuality.

17. Finally, another possible encounter, just as important, must be postponed for lack of space: that of Carmelita watching *Like Water for Chocolate* and *From Dusk till Dawn*. At that point female gender and its global-domestic location, a double location, should be underscored.

Troyano's latest film, *Latin Boys Go to Hell*, further problematizes the influence of consumerist culture as represented by TV soap operas and dramas and the way queer subjects need to learn to "consume consumption" at the risk of dying in the attempt. **18.** Obviously this creates a terminological problem. However, terms such as *pluma* and *loca*, I think, could be a better departure.

Cited Works

Anzaldúa, Gloria. *Borderlands: The New Mestiza: La Frontera*. San Francisco: Aunt Lute, 1987.

Applebome, Peter. "Torrent of Violence by the Rio Grande." *New York Times*, 17 Apr. 1989, A14. Online. Nexis, 7 Aug. 1998.

Arau, Alfonso, dir. *Like Water for Chocolate.* Arau Films International, 1992.

Babuscio, Jack. "Camp and the Gay Sensibility." In *Gays and Film,* ed. Richard Dyer, 40–57. New York: Zoetrope, 1984.

Bergman, David, ed. Introduction to *Camp Grounds: Style and Homosexuality*, 3–16. Amherst: University of Massachusetts Press, 1993.

Del Toro, Guillermo, dir. *Cronos.* Venta Films et al., 1992.

Dyer, Richard. *White.* New York: Routledge, 1997.

"18 Reported Slain in Gang Strife at Mexican Prison." *New York Times*, 19 May 1991, sec. 1:7. Online. Nexis, 7 Aug. 1998.

Fusco, Coco. *English Is Broken Here: Notes on Cultural Fusion in the Americas.* New York: New Press, 1995.

Fusco, Coco, and Paula Heredia, dir. and prod. *The Couple in the Cage: A Guatinaui Odyssey.* Authentic Documentary Productions, 1993.

García Canclini, Néstor. *Hybrid Cultures: Strategies for Entering and Leaving Modernity.* Minneapolis: University of Minnesota Press, 1995.

Gelder, Ken. *Reading the Vampire.* New York: Routledge, 1994.

"Grisly Finding 2nd in Weeks in Mexico." *Houston Post*, 12 Apr. 1989, A14. Online. Nexis, 7 Aug. 1998.

Hall, Stuart. "The Local and the Global: Globalization and Ethnicity." In *Culture, Globalization, and the World-System*, ed. Anthony D. King, 19–39. Minneapolis: University of Minnesota Press, 1998.

———. "Old and New Identities, Old and New Ethnicities." In *Culture, Globalization, and the World-System*, ed. Anthony D. King, 41–68. Minneapolis: University of Minnesota Press, 1998.

Haraway, Donna J. "Situated Knowledges: The Science Question in Feminism and the Privilege of Partial Perspective." In *Simians, Cyborgs, and Women: The Reinvention of Nature.* New York: Routledge, 1991.

hooks, bell. *Black Looks: Race and Representation.* Boston: South End Press, 1992.

Humes, Edward. *Buried Secrets: A True Story of Serial Murder, Black Magic, and Drug-Running on the U.S. Border.* New York: Dutton, 1991.

Jameson, Fredric. "Cognitive Mapping." In *Marxism and the Interpretation of Culture,* ed. Cary Nelson and Lawrence Grossberg, 347–57. Urbana: University of Illinois Press, 1991.

Kinder, Marsha. *Blood Cinema: The Reconstruction of National Identity in Spain.* Berkeley: University of California Press, 1993.

King, Anthony D., ed. *Culture, Globalization, and the World-System: Contemporary Conditions for the Representation of Identity.* Minneapolis: University of Minnesota Press, 1998.

Lacan, Jacques. *Écrits.* Paris: Seuil, 1966.

Livingston, Jennie, dir. *Paris is Burning.* Prestige and Off White Productions, 1990.

McClintock, Anne. *Imperial Leather: Race, Gender and Sexuality in the Colonial Context.* New York: Routledge, 1995.

Meyer, Moe. "Introduction: Reclaiming the Discourse of Camp." In *The Politics and Poetics of Camp*, ed. Moe Meyer, 1–22. New York: Routledge, 1994.

Molloy, Sylvia. "Too Wilde for Comfort: Desire and Ideology in Fin-de-Siecle Latin America." In *Negotiating Lesbian and Gay Subjects*, ed. Monica Dorenkamp and Richard Henke, 35–52. New York: Routledge, 1995.

Muñoz, José E. "Flaming Latinas: Ela Troyano's *Carmelita Tropicana: Your Kunst is Your Waffen* (1993)." In *The Ethnic Eye*, ed. Chon Noriega and Ana M. López, 129–42. Minneapolis: University of Minnesota Press, 1996.

Negrón-Muntaner, Frances. "Drama Queens: Latino Gay and Lesbian Independent Film/Video." In *The Ethnic Eye*, ed. Chon Noriega and Ana M. López, 59–78. Minneapolis: University of Minnesota Press, 1996.

Noriega, Chon, and Ana M. López, eds. *The Ethnic Eye: Latino Media Arts.* Minneapolis: University of Minnesota Press, 1996.

Ramírez-Berg, Charles. "Ethnic Ingenuity and Mainstream Cinema: Robert Rodríguez's *Bedhead* (1990) and *El Mariachi* (1993)." In *The Ethnic Eye*, ed. Chon Noriega and Ana M. López, 107–28. Minneapolis: University of Minnesota Press, 1996.

Rodríguez, Robert, dir. and pro. *Desperado.* Columbia Pictures Co. and Los Hollogans, 1995.

———. *El Mariachi.* Columbia Pictures Co. and Los Hooligans, 1993.

———. *From Dusk till Dawn.* Dimension Films et al., 1996.

Ross, Andrew. "Uses of Camp." In *No Respect: Intellectuals and Popular Culture*, 135–70. New York: Routledge, 1989.

Saldívar, José D. *Border Matters: Remapping American Cultural Studies.* Berkeley: University of California Press, 1997.

"Slayings Rival Worst Cases of Mass Murder in America: The Satanic Ritual Murders of Mark Kilroy and Eleven Others in Matamoros Mexico Rival the Worst Mass Killings in USA History." *Houston Post*, 12 Apr. 1989, A14. Online. Nexis, 7 Aug. 1998.

Sontag, Susan. "Notes on 'Camp.'" In *Against Interpretation*, 275–92. New York: Farrar, Straus, and Giroux, 1986.

Tarantino, Quentin, dir. *Pulp Fiction*. Miramax Films, A Band Apart, and Jersey Films, 1994.

Tracy, Robert. "Loving You All Ways: Vamps, Vampires, Necrophiles and Necrofilles in Nineteenth-Century Fiction." In *Sex and Death in Victorian Literature*, ed. Regina Barreca, 32–59. Bloomington: Indiana University Press, 1990.

Troyano, Ela, dir. *Carmelita Tropicana: Your Kunst Is Your Waffen*. First Run and Icarus Films, 1992.

———. *Latin Boys Go to Hell*. Strand Releasing, 1997.

About the Contributors

Joseba Gabilondo is an assistant professor at the Center for Basque Studies at the University of Nevada, Reno. He is finishing two books on ethnic minorities and postnationalism in Spain and Europe, which focus on the Basque case. He has published several articles on Hollywood cinema, Basque culture, and queer theory. He is also editing a monographic issue for the *Arizona Journal of Hispanic Cultural Studies* on the Hispanic Atlantic.

Gayatri Gopinath is an assistant professor of women and gender studies at the University of California at Davis. Her work on gender, sexuality, and South Asian diasporic culture has appeared in the journals *GLQ, Positions,* and *Diaspora,* as well as in the anthologies *Burning Down the House: Recycling Domesticity* (ed. Rosemary George) and *Asian American Sexualities* (ed. Russell Leong).

Janet R. Jakobsen is the director of the Center for Research on Women. Before coming to Barnard she was an associate professor of women's studies and religious studies at the University of Arizona. She is the author of *Working Alliances and the Politics of Difference: Diversity and Feminist Ethics;* coauthor (with Ann Pellegrini) of *Love the Sin: Sexual Regulation and the Limits of Religious Tolerance;* and coeditor (also with Ann Pellegrini) of "World Secularisms at the Millennium," a special issue of *Social Text.* Her essay is part of her current book project, *The Value of Freedom: Religion, Sex, and America in a Global Economy.*

Miranda Joseph is an associate professor of women's studies at the University of Arizona. She is also the coordinator of the Committee on Lesbian, Gay, Bisexual and Transgender Studies and the director of the Sex, Race and Globalization Project. She was a Rockefeller Fellow at the Center for Lesbian and Gay Studies (1997–98) and a Bunting Fellow at Radcliffe College (1999–2000).

Katie King is an associate professor of women's studies at the University of Maryland, College Park. She is currently working on a book to be entitled *Methodologies across Fields of Power: Feminisms, Writing Technologies, and Global Gay Formations.* She has been involved in U.S. women's movements and lesbian and gay activism and curriculum since the early 1970s. She teaches such courses as Lesbianisms in

Multinational Reception, Feminism and Writing Technologies, and Nationalities, Sexualities, and Global TV.

Lawrence M. La Fountain-Stokes is a Puerto Rican academic, writer, and gay activist. He received his Ph.D. from Columbia University in 1999. The title of his dissertation is "Culture, Representation, and the Puerto Rican Queer Diaspora." He is an assistant professor in the Departments of Puerto Rican and Hispanic Caribbean Studies and of Spanish and Portuguese at Rutgers, the State University of New Jersey (New Brunswick).

William L. Leap is a professor of anthropology at American University, where he works hard to keep lgbtq studies in the university curriculum. He is the author of *Word's Out: Gay Men's English*, and editor of *Public Sex/Gay Space* and (with Ellen Lewin) *Out in the Field*.

Bill Maurer is an associate professor of anthropology at the University of California at Irvine. He is currently conducting research on alternative financial forms and globalizations. His most recent publications on the cultural logics of finance and money appear in *American Ethnologist* and *Public Culture*.

Cindy Patton is Winship Distinguished Research Professor and associate professor of interdisciplinary studies at the Graduate Institute of the Liberal Arts, Emory University. She is the author of several books on AIDS and on sexuality, most recently *Queer Diasporas*, coedited with Benigno Sánchez-Eppler, and *Global AIDS/Local Context*.

Ann Pellegrini is an associate professor of drama at the University of California at Irvine. She is the author of *Performance Anxieties: Staging Psychoanalysis, Staging Race* and coauthor, with Janet Jakobsen, of *Love the Sin: Sexual Regulation and the Limits of Religious Tolerance*. She and Jakobsen have also coedited a forthcoming volume of essays on "World Secularisms at the Millennium," a shorter version of which was published as a special issue of *Social Text* (fall 2000). She is coeditor of another forthcoming collection, *Queer Theory and the Jewish Question*, and is currently completing a new solo project on performance, excess, and belonging, entitled *Shameless*.

Chela Sandoval is an associate professor of critical and cultural theory for the Department of Chicano Studies at the University of California at Santa Barbara. She is the author of *Methodology of the Oppressed* as well as numerous articles that range in topic from CyberCinema to feminist global studies. Her forthcoming work includes an edited volume of articles from Aztlán and a foreword to the second edition of *This Bridge Called My Back*. Her current research is on the subject of cyberspace, cinema, and the digital divide.

Silviano Santiago is the author of *Stella Manhattan*; *Histórias de família*; *Keith Jarrett no Blue Note*; and *Viagem ao México*. A collection of his essays, *The Space in Between: Essays on Latin American Culture*, is forthcoming.

Roberto Strongman received his Ph.D. from the Literature Department at the University of California, San Diego. His primary area of focus is comparative Caribbean cultural studies and literature. His current work concentrates on Caribbean allegorical narratives of personal and political development from 1950 to the present.

About the Editors

Arnaldo Cruz-Malavé is an associate professor of Spanish and comparative literature at Fordham University in New York. He is the author of a study on the intersections of nationalism and sexuality in the prose fiction of the Cuban author José Lezama Lima, *El primitivo implorante*. He has published numerous essays on Hispanic Caribbean and U.S. Latino literatures and cultures. His essays have appeared in anthologies such as *Entiendes? Queer Readings/Hispanic Writings*; *Sex and Sexuality in Latin America*; and *Queer Representations*.

Martin F. Manalansan IV is an assistant professor of anthropology and of criticism and interpretive theory at the University of Illinois, Urbana-Champaign. He is also a member of the Asian American studies faculty. He has published essays in *GLQ: A Journal of Lesbian and Gay Studies, positions: east asian cultures critique*, and *Amerasia*. He is the editor of *Cultural Compass: Ethnographic Explorations of Asian America*. His book *Global Divas: Filipino Gay Men in the Diaspora* is forthcoming.

Gay *(continued)*
  movement, 195, 197; rights, 138. *See also*
  Gay and lesbian consumers; Gay and les-
  bian identities
Gay and lesbian consumers, 139
Gay and lesbian identities, 181
Gender, 231
Gibson-Graham, J. K., 74
Global capitalism, 71, 73, 210, 240
Global gay formations, 40
Global hegemonic heteronormativity, 5, 8
Global hybrid, 248
Global modernity, 9
Global queer films, 238
Globalization, 2, 4, 5, 8, 72, 74, 79, 101, 102,
  151, 199, 202–205, 209, 231, 236–239
Global/localization, 74, 75, 78, 80, 84, 92
Gordon, Avery, 72
Grant, Duncan, 106–107, 112
Guillory, John, 53

Hall, Stuart, 86, 237, 240
Haraway, Donna, 141
Harris, David, 142
Harvey, David, 53–55, 84, 87
Heteronormativity, 102, 139
Heterosexual, 135–137, 138, 237, 242, 247,
  251, 257
Hindu nationalism, 156
Hollywood, 241
Hollywood masculinity, 248
Homoerotic desire, 155
Homophobia, 205, 238
Homosexual citizen, 196
Homosexuality, 61, 89, 134, 135, 139,
  141–142, 180, 182, 188, 195, 219, 224,
  228, 232, 238, 249, 251, 252
hooks, bell, 256
Human rights, 207
Hybrid, 249
Hybridity, 243–245, 253

IGLHRC, 2, 34

ILGA, 2
Interracial sexual experience, 232

Kasanjian, David, 84
Keynes, John Maynard, 72, 101–102,
  104–105, 108, 110, 112–119, 123, 125;
  aesthetics, 104, 106, 113; enterprise, 114;
  liquidity, 114–116; probability, 109, 111,
  113; speculation, 114
Kinder, Marsha, 243
Kinship, 85
Kitsch, 241, 244, 246–248

Laclau, Ernesto, and Chantal Mouffe, 80
Lee, Ang, 151
Lesbian, 134, 142, 150, 154
Lesbian desire, 156
Lesbian feminism, 38
Lesbian identity, 39, 136
Lesbian sexuality, 143, 155
Lesbianism, 41, 43, 143, 153
Liberal pluralism, 80
Local, 231
Local homosexuality, 40
Localization, 75
Lorde, Audre, 23
Low trust societies, 77
Lowe, Donald M., 140–142
Lowe, Lisa, and David Lloyd, 73

Male homosexuality, 142
Male queer subjectivity, 237
Market-reformed Protestantism, 63–64
Marx, Karl, 86–88
Medicine, Bea, 20–21
Middle America, 56
Minority identity, 134
Modernity, 152–153, 199, 208, 244
Modernization, 78
Mohanty, Chandra Talpade, 38, 178–179
Molloy, Sylvia, 242
Moore, G. E., 104–105
Munoz, Jose, 256–257